A Lot to be Thankful For

By Mary Haakenson Perry

To Lela,

Best wishes!

Mary Perry

A Lot to be Thankful For
Copyright © 2013 by Mary Haakenson Perry
ISBN 978-1-890692-24-4

Any errors of fact or omissions are purely accidental and
unintentional. The author apologizes in advance for any
misspellings of names herein.

Wizard Works
PO Box 1125
Homer AK 99603
wizardworksak@gmail.com

Table of Contents

Dedication

This book is dedicated to the memory of my mother, Esther Haakenson, who passed away on March 12, 2013. Her example of perseverance through adversity inspired me to write this book. I hope her story will bring a smile to your face as you read, and an appreciation for the gallant spirit and unshakeable faith that sustained her throughout her life.

Foreword

This book is based on stories my mother told me. I have no axes to grind, and only wish to tell the story of her life to the best of my ability. I have given myself license to change names or leave off surnames when Mom's stories were less than complimentary, or when she couldn't remember the real ones. I've told the stories as accurately as I could, but as in any memoir, Mom's perspective no doubt will differ somewhat from others' accounts of the same events. When Mom gave direct quotes I incorporated them; at other times I created dialogue, based on what I knew or what she'd told me about the characters and how they might speak, to help move the story along.

I want to thank the people who have helped with this project. My brothers Tim, Robert, John, Ken and Ron contributed memories and helped to pinpoint events in time. Thanks go to Tim, his wife Melody, John and Ken for their editing suggestions. Melody's mother, Rita, lent some of her journal pages from that era to help jog memories of what was happening at the time. My cousins Travis, Alice and Ruth contributed pictures and helped with historical accuracy. My editor, Jan O'Meara, led me through the publishing process to bring the whole thing to fruition.

Esther's First Year -1920

Laura awoke from a fitful sleep, unrelenting pain searing her abdomen. The sweat drenching her body could not be blamed solely on the heat of the late June morning. "Alice!" she called weakly to her five-year-old daughter. "Take Leonard over to Aunt Helen's and tell her I need help."

Alice picked up her 16-month-old brother and hurried to the nearby home of Laura's sister. Helen arrived within minutes.

"I told you to go to the doctor when you first started getting sick," Helen scolded. "You've got that baby to think about, y'know." She stooped down and laid her hand on her sister's damp forehead. "Ach! You have a high fever. I'm gonna call Franz." Helen hurried out of the small hut in search of her husband.

Laura closed her eyes and watched the black mists swirl inside her eyelids. Her last thought before losing consciousness was a prayer: "Please, God, don't let me lose this baby."

Nearly a week later, she opened her eyes, feeling weak and disoriented, but blessedly free from pain. "Am I in the hospital?" she wondered, taking in the sparse and sterile-looking furnishings. As if in answer, a woman in a nurse's uniform appeared in the doorway. "Oh, good; you're awake. We were worried about you."

"What's going on?" asked Laura, still struggling to make sense of her surroundings.

"You're at the hospital in International Falls," the nurse told her. "You've been unconscious for the last six days. You had a terrible infection, but luckily you responded to treatment." She paused, then said softly, "I'm sorry, but you lost your baby."

"When was it born?" Laura asked.

"This morning—July first. A little girl."

"I wasn't due till late August. She was over six weeks early." Laura lay in bed, grieving for the little one she would never hold, then she heard a faint sound, like an infant gasping for breath. "Is that my baby?" she asked the nurse.

"Yes, but she's not going to live," the nurse said, not unkindly. "If you hold her now it will only be harder on you when she's gone. It's better that you think of her as dead already. She's only four pounds—she's not going to survive."

"Could you just put her over here beside me?" Laura asked.

"Really, Mrs. Larson, it would be better…"

"Just for a little while?" Laura coaxed.

As the nurse still resisted, Laura's maternal instinct reared up. She snapped, "She's not dead yet, so don't act like she is. I want to see my baby!"

Reluctantly, more to calm her patient than for any other reason, the nurse brought the tiny, gasping infant and placed her in Laura's arms. "Hi, Baby, I'm your Mama." Laura snuggled the cold little body close to hers. The watching nurse shook her head, feeling that this poor woman was just prolonging the inevitable parting from her critically ill child. In 1920, babies born several months early rarely survived, even when the mother was healthy. What chance did this one have?

Laura ignored the skeptical onlooker and concentrated on her baby. Slowly the warmth from her body transferred to the little one in her arms. The two dozed; whenever Laura awoke, she checked to be sure the baby was still breathing. Softly she sang lullabies and hymns in English and Swedish to her tiny daughter. Hours passed; finally the labored breathing calmed. The baby stirred and gave a weak cry.

"I'll bet you're hungry," Laura said. She unfastened her gown, and offered her daughter her first taste of nourishment. After a few minutes of trial and error, the baby got the idea, and nursed enthusiastically.

Laura leaned against the pillows and thought back on the events that had brought her to this point. She recalled growing up in Red Wing, Minnesota, the youngest daughter of Swedish immigrants Pete and Sarah Swanson. "Then my childhood ended," she said to herself, remembering that awful day in 1909 when her mother died. Adding to this shock, her father, Pete, who had worked as a potter in Red Wing, promptly moved with Laura and her 10-year-old brother, Edwin, to the far western reaches of North Dakota and attempted to become a farmer. Having no experience, he wasn't good at it. Laura was forced to drop out of school to work with her father, keeping house for him, raising her younger brother, and cooking for a procession of hired hands.

Her mind flinched away from the thought of one particular hired man, but the memories forced their way in. She pictured her 17-year-old self—lonely and naïve—and how Ralph had appeared to be the answer to all her prayers. He smiled at her and spoke flattering words, and she allowed herself to hope that he might want to marry her. Her dreams collapsed one day in the fall of 1914. She had gone out to gather firewood for the cook stove. Timber was scarce in that area and she had to walk some distance from the house. Out there, with no one around to hear her cries for help, Ralph accosted and raped her. "Never again," she'd promised herself, "I'll never trust a man again."

When Ralph moved on with his threshing crew, Laura attempted to put the episode behind her. A few weeks later, she realized things weren't going to be that simple. She was pregnant. When she could no longer avoid it, Laura gathered her courage and told her father what had happened. That conversation still caused pain years later. Pete reacted much as she feared he would. "So now you're gonna have a baby and ya don't have a husband. Well, ya can't stay here."

"What am I supposed to do?" she'd cried.

"I dunno, go stay with your sister in St. Paul or somethin'." Pete turned his back on his devastated daughter, making it clear he wasn't about to share the dishonor she'd brought on the family.

Seeing no alternative, Laura moved to St. Paul and remained there until her daughter, Alice, was born in July of 1915. After Alice's birth, Laura relocated to Saskatchewan. There she met Fred Larson, a young Norwegian who worked on a threshing crew. Though she'd vowed never to trust a man again, she felt she might make an exception in this instance. She told him about Ralph and was surprised by his response: "Ralph! I know him. He's a no-good if I ever saw one. He'd better not cross my path or he'll sure get what's comin' to him."

Laura and Fred married and, in January of 1919, welcomed a son, Leonard. A year later, they decided the family should move back to the United States. Fred would remain in Canada temporarily, joining them in Minnesota as soon as work permitted. In May of 1920, Laura and the children arrived in Ranier, Minnesota, where Laura's sister lived, and moved into a small shack near Helen's home. They were barely settled when Laura had fallen ill. Now she looked down at the infant in her arms. She'd never seen such a tiny person. "You're tough, though, aren't you?" she addressed the child. "You're gonna make it. We'll show them." The baby stared back at her mother, then gave a contented belch and closed her eyes. Laura cuddled her close and felt her own eyes growing heavy. The two sank into sweet, healing sleep.

Laura and her newborn spent several weeks in the hospital, together gaining health and strength. The baby, whom Laura named Esther Lucille, weighed only 4 pounds at birth, and the doctor wanted her to weigh at least 5 pounds before releasing her. Finally, though, Laura's strong will prevailed; she convinced the doctor that she knew enough about babies to care for Esther at home. Her sister Helen and husband arrived to take them home.

The distinctive smell of International Falls met Laura as she stepped out of the hospital. The Falls, as the town was known locally, had been built around the paper industry. The mills provided employment for much of the population of the area, while others, like Helen's husband, Franz, worked in the logging industry, supplying wood for the mills.

Helen helped Laura to the car and got her and the baby settled in the back seat. Laura relaxed as Franz drove east out of International Falls. Out the right window she watched a forest of spruce and tamarack trees, interspersed with a few houses, slide past. On the left lay Rainy Lake. About four miles out of the Falls they drove through the small town of Ranier. Several miles beyond Ranier, Franz pulled the car into the yard of the home where he and Helen lived with their large and ever-growing family. Like Laura, Helen had married an immigrant whose father's name was Lars. While Laura's Norwegian husband, Fred, spelled his name "Larson," Franz, being Danish, spelled his surname "Larsen." This distinction was called upon often throughout Esther's childhood, as the Larson/Larsen cousins explained to anyone who asked that, while related, they were not all siblings.

As soon as the car stopped, the Larsen offspring came pouring out of the house to greet them: Richard Franz, whom the family called Boy, Arvid, Robert, Helen, Grace, Florence, Vern and Earl. (Lila, Kenny, Iris and Larry came along in later years, bringing the number of children to an even dozen.) Laura's two children—Alice and Leonard— emerged from the crowd of cousins and ran to greet their mother and baby sister. Alice was charmed by the tiny baby, while Leonard was just happy to see his mother again.

Laura immediately set about doing what she could to keep her preemie alive. She knew Esther shouldn't waste her precious reserves of strength in keeping her body warm. Even though it was summer, the baby needed an incubator. Laura started with her boiler—a metal, oval-shaped tub normally used for rinsing clothes. She set canning jars filled with hot water around the edge of the boiler and laid Esther, well-wrapped in blankets, in their midst. As they cooled, she replaced them with hot jars. At times when she'd been baking, she would let the oven cool to the right temperature, then set the baby inside. Unconventional as this practice was, it worked, because Esther grew and flourished, tripling her weight from 4 pounds to 12 pounds in the first year, just as the experts said she should.

Fred finally met his little daughter in January of 1921 when he finished his job in Canada and joined his family. With winter temperatures that often hovered at -20 degrees or colder, Fred quickly saw the need for a larger, more solidly built home to replace the tumbledown shed in which Laura and the kids had been living. He located one—which they always referred to as "the yellow house"—down near the shore of Rainy Lake, in an area known

Esther at 4 months old, with Leonard and Alice.

as Crystal Beach. The family moved in as soon as they could, no doubt glad to leave the ramshackle hut behind.

Several months before her first birthday, Esther showed that being small in stature does not indicate a lack of spirit.

"Look Mama, Esther's almost walking." Grasping the baby's tiny hands, six-year-old Alice guided Esther over to where Laura was readying bread for the oven. Though only 8 months old and less than two feet tall, Esther was ready to try her legs.

Laura crouched down and held out her arms. "Come here, Esther," she coaxed. Alice let go, and Esther staggered a step and tumbled into her mother's arms. The bread temporarily forgotten, Laura and Alice took turns helping Esther practice her new skill.

That evening when Fred got home from work, he joined the others in expressing amazement and amusement at the sight. "She looks like a walking doll," Fred declared.

Although the family had very little of anything to spare, Laura was always on the lookout for neighbors who might need a helping hand. She had an especially soft spot for the local bachelors whom she was convinced would never eat a decent meal without a woman to cook it. Hence, rarely a meal went by at the Larson home without one or two extra place settings.

She had a few rules which she enforced with everyone, including her husband. For one, no smoking was allowed in the house. This was unusual in a day when smoking was nearly synonymous with adulthood. Men who didn't smoke, chewed. Most of them called their chewing tobacco by its Swedish name, *snus* (pronounced "snoose"). The kids were aware that Papa, after eating his ritual spoonful of sugar at the end of a meal, went outside for a chew of *snus*. Laura had to train him, as well as the bachelors who came by for meals, that the kitchen stove was not the place to spit their *snus*. Anyone who removed the stove lid and looked like he was about to deposit a wad of spit into her fire would hear about it from Laura. The men respected Laura and were happy to follow her rules, as her cooking more than offset the inconvenience of stepping outside for a smoke or a chew.

Meals and visits always began and ended with the offer of a cup of coffee. Coffee in the 1920s was brewed by boiling water, then adding a generous amount of ground coffee. After several minutes of boiling together, the mixture was removed to a cooler part of the stove where it was allowed to sit until the grounds settled to the bottom of the pot. This elixir was then poured into cups and served. Naturally, some of the grounds remained floating freely in the liquid, so each cup retained rather more roughage than is seen in most of today's brews. When the meal was over, each cup had a tablespoon or more (depending on how carefully the coffee had been poured) of grounds remaining in the bottom.

Esther, still only the size of a hefty newborn, provided entertainment to the adults during meals as she roamed around the room, even walking under the table without having to duck to keep from bumping her head. What most of the diners didn't realize was that she had an ulterior motive for loitering near the table. Laura soon learned if she turned her back while clearing the table, her tiny daughter quickly clambered up onto a chair, reached out and grabbed a used cup with its puddle of coffee grounds, swigged down the liquid and crunched happily on the grounds. No one knows how Esther developed such an early love of coffee, but it remained her favorite drink all through her life.

Early Years

Just weeks after Esther started walking she suffered an injury which put an end to her coffee-stealing shenanigans, at least for a while. As Laura worked around the kitchen one evening, she carried Esther in the crook of her arm. Leonard, firmly entrenched in the terrible twos, threw himself, screaming, against Laura's leg, demanding his share of attention. Laura reached down with her free hand to deal with Leonard, and as she did so Esther lurched backward, slipping out of her mother's grasp. Laura instinctively tightened her arm against her side to keep Esther from falling. Unfortunately, all she retained hold of was one leg. Although she broke the baby's fall, the damage was done. Esther's upper left leg fractured where it had twisted in Laura's grasp. During her 6 weeks in a cast, Esther was forced to creep, but shortly after the cast came off she was back on her feet, filching coffee grounds as boldly as ever.

When Esther was about 19 months old, her parents presented her with a baby sister, Gladys. Gladys entered the world as a full-term baby, weighing only a few pounds less than Esther did at the time, and quickly made up the difference. This new little one became not only a sister, but best friend and confidante, in a bond that lasted throughout their lives. As the girls grew, people who didn't know them assumed they were twins. Less than 2 years after Gladys arrived, their youngest brother, Laurence, was born. He turned out to be the terror of the family, as Fred, or Papa as the kids called their dad, favored and spoiled his youngest son.

The family lived in the yellow house for several years while Fred worked on a log home which would be large enough to accommodate everyone comfortably. This house, located about 2½ miles east of Ranier, was the first home

Esther remembered, as she was about four years old when the family moved in. The house sat on a side road in an area known as Clark's Colony. To the left and right were neighbors' houses. Behind stood a thick growth of pine, tamarack and spruce trees, offering a ready supply of firewood for anyone handy with a saw or axe.

The simple log house with its tarpaper roof wasn't spacious, but provided more room to the growing family than the two-room house in which they had been living. The dining table and chairs were to the left of the door. The kitchen filled the rest of the left side and was dominated by a large wood-burning cook stove. In the middle of the house, back to back with the kitchen stove, a free-standing potbellied wood heater provided warmth to the living room during the winter months. A stairway started along the living room wall, then turned and followed the rear wall up to the bedrooms. Heat from the potbellied stove was supposed to travel up these stairs to the bedrooms, but usually seemed to lose its way. The kitchen stove contributed a minimal amount of heat to the upstairs by means of a hole Fred had cut into the ceiling above it. Because this vent and the open stairway in the living room were not efficient conductors of heat to the bedrooms, it was not unusual to see frost on the floor upon arising on winter mornings.

Laura put the area under the stairs to good use by setting up a small pantry there. Along the pantry wall facing the living room sat a large pump organ that Laura often played.

The Larson home in Clark's Colony.

For several years, all of the family slept upstairs. Fred and Laura's bed and a crib for baby Laurence occupied the room above the kitchen. The room over the living area contained sleeping arrangements for the other four children. Furniture was scarce, and what they had was old or homemade. Fred built a small cot for Leonard along one wall of the bedroom. Against the opposite wall, the three girls shared a couch that folded down into a double bed.

This couch was an extremely distant cousin of today's sleeper sofa. The whole thing folded down more or less flat, but rocked like a teeter totter if the two sides were not evenly weighted. Alice, being five years older than Esther and a good bit heavier than either of her younger sisters, learned she had to plan ahead in order to keep the bed on an even keel. If both Esther and Gladys were in bed when Alice got in, she could safely lie down on her side. But if one of the other girls got up during the night for an outhouse run, Alice's weight caused the bed to collapse, sending whichever smaller girl was left flying out of bed, and spoiling the night's rest for everyone.

A dependable water source soon became an issue for the family. Fred dug a well in the front yard and installed a hand pump. Extracting water involved at least two family members. As soon as they were big enough to reach the handle, Esther and Gladys were expected to help with this chore. Esther would begin by energetically pumping the large handle up and down, up and down, while Gladys peered hopefully into the spout, searching for a trace of liquid. By the time the first gurgle emerged from the pump's throat, Esther was exhausted.

"You take over," she told Gladys. Quickly switching places, Esther held a bucket to the lip of the pump while Gladys took her turn vigorously attacking the handle. With luck, a trickle of water would emerge from the spout before Gladys also got too pooped to pump. In times of little or no rain, the well dried up completely.

Such an inconsistent supply of this vital necessity compelled the Larsons to rely on their nearby friends, whose wells tapped into more bountiful water tables. Anytime the kids went down the road to play with neighbors, their mother made sure they carried some sort of container in which they could bring back water. It might be a bucketful or only a cup, but every bit was utilized to the fullest extent. Some went into a bucket on the countertop which was used for drinking and cooking; the rest was poured into the large boiler on the back of the cook stove, to be collected until laundry time.

A well-worn path from the back door led to the family's privy. Indoor toilets were unheard of for most of the area's residents. When Fred built it, Laura specified he build it with two seats—one of regular height for adults, and a lower one for the children. Laura also made sure it had sturdy walls and a solid, locking door. Many outhouses were thrown together as a sort of afterthought and had gaping holes in the sides or a blanket for a door. Laura insisted that the Larson outhouse provide more privacy. And while many people recycled their Sears and Roebuck catalogs for toilet paper, the Larsons used real toilet paper. For a family in their circumstances, this was a precious commodity, so their mother impressed upon each child during potty training: "You use two squares. Only two." (The modern mind shrinks from the mental pictures conjured up by this economy.)

The outhouse became a bone of contention for Esther and Gladys when they reached the age of helping out with household chores. Often, as soon as the dish water was heated, Gladys would say, "I have to go to the outhouse."

"Here we go again," thought Esther from her station at the dishpan. The minutes ticked by as she swabbed, rinsed, and set the dishes on a towel to drain. Finished with washing, she wiped down the countertop and started on the table before Gladys reappeared. "You sure timed that just right," Esther snapped.

"I can't help it; I had to *go*," Gladys protested. "Honest, I got back as quick as I could."

Esther threw a dish towel at her sister. "Well, I saved the drying for you. You can finish up yourself. I'm done!"

This show of pique was only partly because Gladys had once again ducked out on her chores. Esther genuinely missed the fun the two girls had when they worked together. Gladys had a quick wit and a knack for telling stories. Added to that, her ability to mimic an unsuspecting target's speech and actions often had both the girls doubled over, screaming with laughter. Any task seems to get over more quickly when you can laugh your way through it.

Not long after the family settled into the house in Clark's Colony, Leonard went exploring. At 6 years old, he was a fearless and gregarious youngster. He returned bursting with news. "Mama, there's a real old man named Knut across the road. He can't talk too good. He takes care of a whole bunch of rabbits, but he's so old, he can't hardly work. He's real shaky."

Laura, whose heart was always touched by those in need, set out to learn more about Knut. She walked across the road to meet the man for herself. The first thing she saw as she entered the yard was a double row of twenty or so cages, each containing one or more rabbits. "What on earth does he need with all these rabbits?" she thought.

Approaching the house, she noted that, though simple, it seemed to be well built. She knocked on the door, which was opened by Knut. Laura found that Leonard's report had been accurate.

Fred with children, Back row: Alice and Fred. Front row (l-r): Gladys, Laurence, Esther and Leonard. (ca 1926)

Knut spoke very little English. Drawing on her mother tongue, learned from her Swedish parents, and some Norwegian picked up from her husband, Laura determined that the old man was a hired caretaker for the owners, who lived in the Falls and rarely came out to the farm. She observed Knut's constant tremors, which made any movement difficult to control. His gait was slow, and aided by whatever object was near for him to grab. He gladly accepted Laura's offer of Leonard's help with feeding and watering the rabbits. As the years went by, she often sent food to the old man, and even taught Leonard the correct way to butcher rabbits, when Knut asked him to assist with that chore.

Several bachelors shared homes on either side of the rabbit farm; these men often found their way to the Larson home at mealtimes and were never turned away. One of these was Pete Johnson, a tall, thin man known to all by the moniker Long Pete. Pete's land was rich, black soil — the kind that grew all the plants the Larsons' land would not. He also kept a flock of chickens.

Long Pete became a fixture around the Larson home and a dependable friend, as well. He worked in the Falls, so was gone for many hours each day. He had no interest in raising a garden, but didn't mind sharing in the bounty of one grown by someone else. Since the Larson property had such poor soil, Laura and Pete worked out a deal in which she and the children tilled Pete's land into a garden, and Pete

Long Pete Johnson and Leonard.

14

ate meals with the family whenever he wanted (which was nearly every day).

There were other mutually advantageous deals between Pete and the Larsons. He paid Alice a few pennies to clean house for him, and the younger children worked the garden and took care of his chickens. In winter, Alice also stoked the stove so Pete returned home from work to a warm house.

One experience Alice and her sisters had at Long Pete's gave them an insight into perhaps one of the reasons the man was still a bachelor. Alice entered Pete's house to do her weekly cleaning and since her sisters were with her, she put them to work. She was running late, and knew it was going to be difficult to get finished before Pete got home.

While Esther did the dishes and Gladys swept the floor, Alice cleared the countertops. "Eewww!" she exclaimed. She gingerly picked up a fuzzy bluish-green object. "Pete's bread is completely covered with mold!"

The idea of tossing out the entire loaf never occurred to her, but neither did she consider leaving it as it was. She picked up a knife and carefully trimmed off every trace of mold. Just as she finished, the door opened and in walked Pete.

"Oh hi, girls," he said. "Thanks for cleaning up for me."

"Your bread was moldy," Alice informed him. "But I trimmed it off."

"What? Why did you do that?" Pete demanded. "You're wasting perfectly good food!"

He strode to the cupboard and carefully collected all the moldy scraps into a pile. As the girls watched, aghast, he picked up the pieces one by one and ate them.

Behind him, Gladys turned toward Esther, her face twisted in a grimace of revulsion. "I-i-i-ish," she whispered. Barely controlling her snickers, she fled from the house with Alice and Esther on her heels. The three raced down the path toward home, giving vent to their disgust in a torrent of giggles. Pete never looked up from his moldy feast.

Though a stand of trees obscured Clark's Colony from the main road, the walk up to the road was only a matter of a half-mile or so. The area around International Falls and Ranier was a popular spot for "city folks" from Minneapolis and St. Paul to come for summer vacations. The Larsons used these tourists as a source of income. When Pete's garden produced sufficient radishes, carrots and peas, the kids piled some of their bounty into a little wagon, pulled it down to Crystal Beach, and sold vegetables to the summer people.

Visitors from other parts of the area were rare, but occasionally some of the relatives came to visit. Laura's sister Julia and her husband lived in St. Paul for most of the year, but they joined the flock of tourists who descended on the Rainy Lakes region in the summer. They owned a small cabin up near the Franz Larsen farm, and when they came to town they often stopped at the Fred Larson home. The sight of Aunt Julia's car pulling up in front of the house always sent Laurence running across the back yard as fast as his legs would move. He tore down the small path through the woods till he felt he'd gone far enough so no one would follow. If he heard voices calling his name, he chose to ignore them. What caused this spurt of anti-social behavior? Kisses. Aunt Julia always greeted each nephew and niece with a big hug and kiss. Since the Larsons were not a demonstrative family, Laurence would avoid the visit entirely rather than submit to a smooch from Aunt Julia.

Franz and Helen usually left the children at home when they came into town. The couple often stopped in for a cup of coffee with Laura and Fred. Franz and Helen loved to sing and a visit from them usually ended up as an impromptu jam session. Laura pulled out her violin and mouth organ (as they called the harmonica) and the Larsens sang duets. The kids listened if they weren't busy with chores, but knew this musicale was for the adults. Children of that era were to be seen and not heard unless specifically invited by the adults.

The arrival of the Larsen cousins was always a special event. On those rare occasions when the children accompanied their parents, the Larson/Larsen kids made full use of every minute. The woods behind the house provided a backdrop for any game the kids could think up. When they got older, sometimes the crew walked over to Rainy Lake to play in the sand or take a dip.

School in Ranier

Two months after her sixth birthday, Esther started first grade. In preparation for the big day, her father gave her a haircut. Fred had a reputation as a competent barber among the local youngsters and bachelors who came to him when they needed a trim. The males all received the same basic cut—tapered short on the sides, with a little more length on top. Alice, Gladys and Esther were Fred's only female clients, with good reason. No consideration was given as to hair type or flattering style. He cut their fine, blonde hair starting directly below one ear, straight around the back to the other ear. A quick snip across the forehead gave them bangs. Done. The style was quick to cut and easy to comb, but far from attractive. The girls wore this same hairdo for years, until they discovered the joys of perms and pin curls in their late teens.

Esther's school dress also was fashioned at home. Her mother saved the cloth sacks that flour came in, and turned them into shirts for the boys and dresses for the girls. She usually made Esther and Gladys matching clothes, since they were much the same size. Most flour sacks were plain white. To enliven the dresses, Laura often bought a cake of dye and colored the cloth before sewing it. She used a worn-out but still fairly well-fitting article of clothing as a pattern for the new garment. The dresses were simple button-front or pullover styles; a sash around the waist provided fit. Laura always made a matching pair of underpants—what they called "bloomers." The bloomers had a small pocket in which the wearer could tuck a hanky, a few pennies or some other treasure.

Now, sporting a fresh haircut, new dress and bloomers, Esther set off with Alice and Leonard for her first day of school. They walked out the Clark's Colony road to the bus stop on the main road, where they would catch the bus for the 2 ½ -mile ride to Ranier.

At the school, Alice helped Esther find the combined 1st and 2nd-grade classroom. She introduced her to her teacher and promised, "I'll be right upstairs in my class." Leonard, an old hand at school, marched off to the 3rd-4th-grade room. The teacher, Miss Jensen, helped Esther find a seat at one of the small desks made for the youngest of schoolchildren. Esther wriggled herself up onto the seat and sat with her legs dangling. She was by far the smallest child in the class.

She scanned the room, relieved to see a few cousins and playmates among the blur of faces around her. It was nice to know that she'd have some ready-made friends, since her constant companion, Gladys, was still at home, too young for school. The teacher began with introductions, and then moved on to a lesson. She picked up a piece of chalk and wrote something on the blackboard. At least, she must have written something, as she began to ask children what they saw. Esther, horrified, realized she saw nothing up there but a black blur where the board hung. She huddled in her chair, hoping the teacher would not call on her.

The moment she dreaded arrived. "Esther, what is this?" Miss Jensen asked, pointing toward that dark fuzzy spot.

"I don't know," mumbled Esther, embarrassed and confused. Why couldn't she see what the other kids saw? She squinted her eyes, but nothing got clearer. The teacher moved on to another student, leaving Esther hot and ashamed of her failure. She had to find out what was up there. Though kids weren't allowed to leave their seats, she finally slipped out of her chair and walked up to the black board. Oh! Those were letters and numbers the teacher had written. She knew those. She had listened and learned from Alice and Leonard. She felt the teacher's eyes on her, and scuttled back to her seat.

Later Miss Jensen took her aside. "Can't you see the board?" she asked.

"I can if I get close enough," Esther replied.

"Let's move your desk closer then."

Together they positioned her desk directly beside Miss Jensen's, where it would be the closest seat to the front of the classroom. The move accomplished, Esther found herself much better able to participate in class work. In later years, when whole sentences or questions were written on the board, she would have to walk up, memorize as many lines as she could, and quickly go back to her seat and write her answers. Then she'd go back and repeat the process. She'd had poor eyesight for as long as she could remember, so it never occurred to her to mention the fact to her parents. She figured what she saw was what everybody saw.

Esther loved school, but unfortunately her stamina was not up to the physical challenges. One morning just days after school started, she arose with a sore throat, feeling weak and sluggish. Her mother, who suffered from frequent bouts of poor health, recognized the signs. "Are you sick?" she asked. She felt Esther's forehead. "You have a fever," she continued. "You'd better stay home today."

Esther couldn't summon up the strength to argue, and obediently went to bed. The day at home stretched into a week, then a month, then longer. Occasionally she felt well enough to attempt to go to school, but found she didn't have the strength to walk the half-mile to the bus stop, so back to bed she went.

There was no money for doctors, so Esther remained confined to her bed, running various grades of fever and feeling weak and ill for the rest of that school year. Laura eventually moved a bed into the living room where the kids could climb up and visit when Esther felt strong enough. She loved books, and spent hours quietly looking at the pictures and sounding out what words she could.

Occasionally, a woman doctor who lived a mile or so away down the main road came by to check on the family. This lady, Dr. Mary, knew from her visits that Esther needed her tonsils removed in order to end her ongoing illnesses. She urged Laura to consider it, but every conversation ended the same. There was no money for an expensive medical procedure. Rest and salt-water gargle would have to suffice.

The following year was nearly a carbon copy of the first. Esther started back to first grade, since she hadn't completed enough of the curriculum to move on. Within a short time, the sore throat, fever and aches returned, forcing her back to bed, where she remained again for most of the school year. Gladys was still at home, as she would not turn six until winter, so the two girls spent time together on the bed whenever Esther was able. An Edison crank phonograph sat near the bed. At times, Esther could insert the cylinders and turn the crank to play it. At other times, Gladys operated the machine, as Esther felt too weak to do even that much.

The summer Esther turned eight her mother met with the teachers, and they all agreed that, because of Esther's age and the capacity for learning she had shown during her brief school experiences, she should enter second grade in the fall. Esther felt relief, not wanting to enter first grade yet again, especially now that Gladys was also starting school. After all, regardless of her size, Esther *was* the big sister.

On the first day of school Esther and Gladys entered the classroom together, glad they would be in the same room, even though not in the same grade. Then the teacher broke the bad news: word had just come down from the head office in International Falls that no students would be allowed to skip a grade if they had not completed the work. For the third year, Esther took her seat among the first grade students. Even at the age of eight, she was still the smallest child in the class.

Esther's health stabilized somewhat over the next year. She still had bouts of illness and fever which necessitated days at a time of being home, but she managed to spend enough time in class to pass the tests at the end of the year and move legitimately to the second grade. This became the pattern over the next few years. She was sick often enough that the bed remained in the living room. Gladys, who was not a fan of schoolwork, would crawl up beside Esther and hand her a book, "Esther, read this to me."

Sore throat and fever weren't the only physical ailments Esther had to endure in her early years. Nearly every night she sought out her mother. "Mama, I have a toothache," she whimpered as she cradled her cheek in her hand. The term, "toothache" was actually an understatement. Pain coursed through her upper jaw from so many different points that it was hard to show her mother exactly where it hurt the worst.

"Open up," said Laura, "let me see." She surveyed her daughter's teeth. Though Esther was still in grade school, cavities were eating away at nearly every one of the upper teeth. No wonder she was in pain. Laura got out the clove oil, soaked one of the tiny cotton balls, and carefully pressed it into the cavity that Esther indicated was causing the worst pain that night.

Oral hygiene was not a high priority in the family, but Esther's teeth seemed to be in worse shape than the other kids'. Maybe being a preemie had something to do with it. Maybe she was less regular with brushing than the others. The reason didn't really matter, though; there was no money for dental care, even if there had been a dentist close by.

At school one day, Esther came out of the outhouse, looking around to find Gladys, with whom she usually spent recess. A commotion near the back of the school building caught her attention. Curious, Esther moved closer. As she neared the group, she was horrified to hear some of the bigger boys taunting a small child huddled against the wall, crying. She recognized the little boy as Arne, who was from one of the poorest families in the community. His clothes had holes, his nose dripped as he wept, his uncovered ears stood out large and red.

Anger surged through Esther, giving her a strength she didn't know she had. Charging the group of tormentors, she kicked, slugged and fought her way through till she stood protectively in front of Arne. She glared at the one bully who'd withstood her attack. "Mind your own business, Broomstick," he sneered.

Broomstick! Of all the names he might call her, he'd picked the one she hated most. She swung her fist and felt it connect solidly with that mocking face. Not knowing whether to be glad she'd deflected attention from Arne or concerned for her own skin, she turned and raced to the fence in the corner of the schoolyard. She braced her hands against the fence and started kicking her leg out behind her. If the guy tried to get close enough to harm her, she intended to do a little damage to him, as well.

All this commotion attracted the attention of everyone on the playground, including the teacher. "Esther! Come inside this instant!" commanded Mr. Grant. The teacher marched her into the school building, ready to mete out a fit punishment for the crime of fighting at school. He was curious to know, though, what had caused the normally quiet Esther to become such a tigress.

"Now, tell me what that was all about."

Esther stuck out her chin. Trouble or not, she wasn't going down without letting the truth be known. At least the part that pertained to Arne. "Those kids were pickin' on Arne just because he doesn't have nice clothes and 'cause he's slow. I had to stick up for him. And I'd do it again," she added defiantly.

The teacher was quiet for a moment, then said, "You did right to protect Arne. I'll deal with those boys. But you still need to be punished for fighting. I'm going to suspend you from school for the rest of the day. Get your things and go home."

Adrenalin still pumping, Esther gathered her lunch bucket, hat and coat and prepared to leave. As she headed for the door, Gladys caught up with her. "Esther, what happened? I saw you fighting with those boys, then Mr. Grant hauled you off. Where are you going?"

Esther summarized the situation. Gladys's eyes grew big in her solemn face, as the two contemplated Esther's fate. They both were thinking about what was going to happen when she got home. Their parents had often told them, "If you get in trouble at school, you'll be in more trouble at home."

"I'm coming with you," Gladys declared. She grabbed her own coat and lunch bucket. The sisters made the three-mile walk mostly in silence. As her anger cooled, Esther appreciated Gladys's show of support, though she knew it wouldn't protect her from Laura's wrath. The Larson kids were expected to behave in school, and they knew the consequences of not living up to that expectation.

Arriving at the house, Esther crept inside and found her mother. "Mama, I got sent home from school."

Laura turned around and saw both daughters standing with resolute looks on their faces. Esther decided she'd better get the story out immediately or she might not have the chance. She rushed into speech. "Some big kids were bullying Arne, and it made me mad. I had to fight to make them stop."

Laura hesitated. She couldn't in all good conscience punish Esther for doing exactly what she would have done in the same situation. "Tell me the whole story," she invited.

Thus encouraged, Esther poured out all the details and ended, as she had with Mr. Grant, by saying, "And I'd do it again!"

"It sounds like Arne needed your help," Laura concluded. "But maybe next time you should find a teacher and not try to fix it all by yourself. Well, now that you're home, you might as well help me get supper ready."

The sisters glanced at each other with looks of surprise mingled with relief. Fortunately for them, their mother's demands of good behavior took a back seat to her sense of fairness.

Laura's innate generosity and desire to help others made a big impact on Esther even during those early years. The Larsons had little money to spare, but Laura tried to help when she knew of someone who had even less. Occasionally she'd hand Esther a coin twisted into a handkerchief.

"Esther, here's a penny," she'd say. "I know Benny's mother can't afford a pencil, so you get one for him."

Esther accepted the hanky and tucked it into her bloomer pocket. At school, she'd figure out how to get the pencil to Benny without anyone else noticing. Even at her young age she realized dignity was about the only thing some of her neighbors had. To give to someone in need was not done for praise, but simply because it was the right thing to do.

Teachers seemed to recognize a quality in Esther that caused them to seek her out for special jobs. One year a little boy enrolled in school who would now be considered developmentally delayed. Jack needed extra assistance with all aspects of his day, including lunch time. Shortly after the boy started school, Esther's teacher came to her.

"Esther, I want you to sit with Jack during lunch and help him."

Every day Esther sat with the boy, grabbing bites of her own lunch while supervising Jack. She made sure he ate his food with a minimum of mess, cleaned him up afterwards, and fended off the taunts of those who would have teased him because he was different. Though she didn't know why she was chosen to assist him, she performed the task without complaint, knowing she'd want the same to be done for her, had their positions been reversed.

"Esther, come up here." Esther heard her mother's weak voice calling from the bedroom. She climbed the stairs and entered her parents' room. The family's poodle/terrier mix, Toodles, danced through the door in front of her and leaped up on the bed.

Laura's face was drawn and pale from another of her frequent bouts of illness, but she chuckled at her pet. "Did you come up to be a sick lady with me? Oooh, Toodles is a sick lady."

Hearing those words, the dog flopped onto her back beside her mistress, lay her head on the pillow and closed her eyes. Toodles tolerated the rest of the family, but her heart belonged to Laura. Given the choice of running outside with the kids or staying with their mother whether she was laid up from illness or at work around the house, Toodles always chose Laura.

Laura turned her attention back to Esther. "Get that basket of stockings over in the corner. I want you and Gladys to unravel them so I can use the yarn again.

"Okay," Esther retrieved the basket and headed down the stairs, leaving the two "sick ladies" to keep each other company. She found Gladys and informed her, "Mama wants us to get this yarn rolled up for her."

Eventually the woolen stockings that protected their legs from the winter cold got worn to the point that Laura could no longer darn them. When this happened, she had the girls unravel the yarn and wind it neatly, then she recycled it by knitting it into new stockings for the next winter.

Now on a warm summer day the girls sat on the front steps, pulling out stitches and rolling up the yarn. Suddenly Gladys looked up and said, "What's Leonard got?"

Esther squinted down the road in the direction Gladys indicated, but all she could see was a blurry shape that she knew must be her brother, because Gladys said it was. She strained and blinked, willing the image to get clearer, though from past experience she knew it wouldn't.

Gladys kept a running commentary as Leonard approached. "He's got a big black thing with him. What is it? Oh—it's a huge tire. Wonder where he found it. What's he gonna do with it?"

Leonard rolled his prize up to the steps and said, "Look what I found out on the main road. It musta fallen off a big ol' truck."

The yarn forgotten, the girls inspected the tire, which stood almost as high as Esther's chin. "What're you gonna do with it?" asked Esther.

"I'm gonna roll it," answered Leonard, with a look that clearly said only a girl could come up with such a dumb question. He immediately acted on this statement, giving the tire a shove. It rolled a couple of turns, then Leonard leapt into action to keep it upright. He headed jerkily down the dusty road, jumping from side to side to control the tire's forward motion. The girls and Laurence joined him, pushing on the tire when it came their way, laughing when it escaped their control and crashed to the ground.

"Okay, get outta the way," Leonard commanded once he felt he'd mastered the technique. He gave the tire a push to get it rolling and stood back to get a run at it. Rushing the tire, he grabbed it, leapt up and astride, riding over the top and coming down in front of it.

"Let me try!" demanded Gladys, but, try as she might, she was a little too small to make the leap up and over the tire.

"Get inside it," suggested Leonard. "I'll give you a ride."

Gladys stuck one foot through the hole and curled up into the space. She looked uncomfortable, with her knees nearly in her mouth and elbows sticking out at the sides. "Don't you drop me," she commanded.

Leonard carefully started the tire, and rolled it down the road. "Lemme out!" yelled Gladys, "I'm gettin' dizzy."

She unfurled herself from the hole and scooted away from it. "I don't like that," she stated.

Esther stepped forward. "I wanna try." Her smaller frame fit nicely into the tire's hole. She grasped the thick rubber outside edge of the hole, and pulled her arms in close to her body. "Ready," she said.

Once again, Leonard started the tire with a shove. Down the road it bowled, its drivers racing behind and its passenger whirling in the midst. Reaching the end of Clark's Colony road, the kids turned the tire around and headed back, since Esther showed no sign of wanting to get out. At the top of a small rise, the tire picked up speed and careened on ahead, with Leonard in hot pursuit.

Inside the tire, Esther gripped the rubber rim. She could feel the air rushing by as she spun faster and faster down the hill. Oddly enough, she felt no fear. Her feet braced against the sturdiness of the tire, she reveled in the speed and freedom. The rate of speed slowed, and she knew she was past the hill. Leonard's footsteps sounded loud as he pelted toward her, doing his best to catch up. She felt a slight jiggle as he regained control of the tire and brought it to a halt.

"Whee!" Exhilarated, Esther tumbled out of the hole. "That was fun!"

Laurence gave it a try next, but was a trifle too small and young to keep his position in the hole. Gladys refused to get back in, so the seat of honor belonged exclusively to Esther. Throughout the summer, when lacking other forms of entertainment, Esther would climb into the tire and Leonard would take her for a spin.

Another favorite summer activity was going to the lake. Just out Clark's Colony road and across the main highway lay Rainy Lake, with its sandy beach and calm waters. Often, once their chores were finished, the youngsters would implore their mother, "Can we go swimming?"

Clear summer days brought searing hot sun. A dip in water was one of the few ways to escape the smothering heat. The Larson kids stripped down as far as the modesty of the era allowed. The boys went shirtless and barefoot, wearing only rolled up trousers. Gladys wore a sleeveless blouse. Alice owned a real swimsuit, as it was required for swimming class at school in the Falls. Esther, whose skin was extra-sensitive, always wore a top with sleeves that covered her shoulders. Still, the sun burned and blistered her skin right through the cloth. Both she and Gladys wore short light skirts with the matching homemade bloomers.

When Laura gave permission, the kids raced down the road to the beach. Esther ran straight to the lake and plunged in. She savored the coolness of the water which offset the unrelenting heat of the day.

Laurence, who viewed the lake more as a place of prey than of play, roamed off with his fishing pole to a quiet spot. He might catch a couple of pickerel, which would supplement the family's dinner table.

Alice demonstrated the skills she'd learned in school by climbing up the ladder and diving gracefully off the high board. Esther practiced jumping off the lower board. Gladys waded in as far as her skirt length would allow, but refused to entrust the water with her body. Leonard, pants rolled up to mid-calf, dashed through the shallows, never letting the water depth creep past his ankles.

"C'mon in, Leonard," called Esther. "It feels so good." She treaded water as she coaxed her big brother.

"Huh-*uh*!" replied Leonard.

Esther didn't see how just wading in the water could be any fun at all. She paddled over to Gladys. "Just try it. Look how easy it is to float." She lay back in the water, feeling light as a leaf.

Gladys shook her head decisively. "No thanks, I'm fine right where I am."

The lake wasn't the only body of water in which Esther enjoyed a swim. Several years earlier, Alice had gone berry picking with some of her friends, and discovered a large gravel pit down a path through the woods off Clark's Colony road. Though the gravel pit was no longer in operation, it had been a major producer of gravel for the local roads. Several tracks had been built, where railroad cars were driven in and filled with gravel. The holes left when the steam shovels scooped out gravel had filled with water, making beautiful swimming pools of various lengths and depths. The first one they called "the shallow pond" for obvious reasons. This is where Leonard and Gladys usually chose to stay. Esther wanted more depth to her experience, though, so she scrambled up the rocky bank and walked along the railroad track to the next pool. This one ran along the track for nearly a quarter of a mile, and had some great areas for diving. Having swum across this pool, Esther climbed up and over the track to still another pond.

Meanwhile, back at the shallow pond, Leonard ran off with some neighbor kids, leaving Gladys to her own devices. She didn't want to go home, but she began to get nervous about being alone with all that water. "I'd better find Esther," she told herself.

She waded the rest of the way across the shallow pond, climbed the embankment to the railroad track, and picked her way down the other side. There was no sign of Esther, but she was now at the larger pool, long but not terribly wide. Picking the narrowest point, she gingerly stuck her foot in the water. Hmmm — not bad. Slowly, feeling her way with her toes, she waded into the pond. The water crept up around her knees, then her thighs. Now her skirt was floating. Nervous, but determined to be brave, she fixed her eyes on the far bank — another gravel slope leading up to the tracks. Just a few more steps and she'd be on dry land again.

With the next step the bottom dipped and Gladys found herself in water up to her chest. Afraid to back up onto the shallower area, and even more afraid to step into the unknown territory ahead, Gladys did the only thing she could think to do—yell for her sister. "Esther!" she screamed. "Help me!"

One pond over, Esther heard the panicked calls. She immediately turned and called back, "Where are you? I'm coming!" She plunged into the water and stroked quickly across, to a constant chorus of howls from Gladys. Scrabbling her way up the gravel slope, she ran along the tracks toward the source of the ruckus. The sight of Gladys standing in water any deeper than her knees was enough to make her pause and exclaim, "How on earth did you get there?"

She slid down the bank and extended her hand. "Here, grab my hand and I'll help you over. You're only a step from the shore."

"No!" screeched Gladys, "It's gonna be too deep! Get me outta here!"

"Well, I can't get you out if you don't take my hand." Esther stepped into the water next to the shore. "See, it's no deeper than where you are, and you're already wet so…"

By this time Gladys was in full hysteria mode. "Take me back the other way," she pleaded.

"Okay." Still keeping hold of her sister's hand, Esther clumsily side-stroked past Gladys and stood where Gladys had been just before the bottom fell out from under her. "Turn around and step up and you'll be fine."

Gladys complied, and felt the water recede from her upper body. The girls stood in the middle of the pond, still clutching hands. "Are you okay now?" asked Esther. "All you have to do is walk back to the track and climb out."

"You come with me," Gladys commanded, tightening her grip.

Torn between impatience and sympathy, Esther led her terrified sister back to the other side. "You stay with me." Gladys again clenched the hand that had become her lifeline. Up the bank, down the track, past the shallow pond, and into the trees they went. Gladys never released her grip on Esther until they were safely home, where the floor remained level and no water crept up to scare a body to death.

Grandma Lindstrom

"Where's Mama?" asked Esther. She and her siblings had arrived home from school to find Laura gone and a tall, stout, gray-haired lady with a stern countenance stirring a pot of something at the kitchen stove. The woman turned and spoke, but her words did nothing to solve the mystery. It became obvious this woman spoke not a single word of English. The Larson children recognized the woman's speech as one of the Scandinavian tongues, as many of their neighbors still spoke their native languages. Though many of the surrounding families were bilingual, Laura and Fred had resolved that their family would not be. In fact, Laura had a saying that her children heard often: "We live in America, we speak American."

So now the children who spoke only English stood gazing helplessly at the stranger in their home who spoke only Swedish. By the use of gestures and body language, the woman communicated that their mother was gone and they were to go about their normal chores.

All five pounced on Fred when he arrived home. "Papa, who's she? Where's Mama?"

"Mama's sick. She had to go to the hospital down in St. Paul. This is Mrs. Lindstrom. I hired her to take care of you till Mama gets back. You kids behave and do what she says."

The children all knew Laura was subject to sickness, and often took to her bed when she became too ill to function, but they were not kept apprised as to the nature of their mother's maladies. In later years they discovered that, in addition to heart weakness and other conditions, Laura suffered two miscarriages after Laurence's birth, but at the time, pregnancy and childbirth were considered unfit subjects to discuss with youngsters.

"What should we call her?" asked Gladys, indicating the strange woman in the kitchen.

"Just call her Grandma," replied Fred.

So Grandma she was, although most communication consisted of tugging on the woman's long skirt and leading her to whatever the kids needed help with. In addition to the language barrier, the old lady was almost completely deaf, which probably would have made the skirt tugging necessary even had they spoken the same tongue.

Grandma Lindstrom always had two kettles simmering on the stove. One held a "fruit soup" consisting of water, sugar and a variety of dried fruits, and the other contained a vegetable soup. Meals may not have been exciting during her tenure, but they were as nutritious as was possible given the limited money and foodstuffs available.

On school mornings, Esther and Gladys did their best to get ready and out the door without attracting the old lady's attention. Unfortunately, they never quite made it. Uttering a word that obviously meant "Stop," Grandma Lindstrom would pull the two over near the water bucket. Scooping water out with her hands, she thoroughly drenched the girls' hair. Then she pulled and slicked as if trying to create ponytails from the girls' short bobs. She wasn't satisfied until the hair lay back flat and sopping wet against their heads.

Released, Gladys and Esther scuttled out the door and down the road. As soon as they were out of sight of the house, Alice took over. Grabbing her sisters, she did her best to rearrange the hair, bringing the soggy locks back to their original position. "Ugh, why does she *do* that?" Alice demanded rhetorically. "You look like a couple of wet hens with your hair skinned back like that!"

Gladys and Leonard may have unwittingly caused Grandma Lindstrom to quit her job at the Larson house. One day, Gladys wandered into the small room under the stairs that was used as a pantry. There stood Leonard, his back to the door, intent on something he obviously didn't want known.

"Whatcha doin', Leonard?" Gladys asked.

Leonard jerked around, revealing a small plume of smoke. "I found these matches," he said.

Gladys, repelled yet intrigued by the forbidden objects, moved closer. Together the two experimented with burning small fragments of papers, tiny wood chips and anything else they could find that would ignite easily. Emboldened by that success, Leonard snatched a larger piece of paper that lay nearby. He touched it with a match; instantly a flame bloomed and grew, gobbling the paper in a matter of seconds. Leonard jerked his hand away, dropping the flaming paper to the floor, where the fire began seeking any other combustible substances in the immediate area.

For a split second the two kids stood frozen in shock, then Gladys, finding that her legs still worked, tore through the house, shouting, "Grandma! Grandma!"

"She's outside!" yelled Leonard, catching sight of the old woman working the pump in the front yard.

Gladys raced out the door and grabbed Grandma's skirt. One look at Gladys's terrified face brought Grandma into the house with all the speed she could muster. By now the smell of smoke filled the house, so Grandma had a good idea what might be happening. Fortunately, she had retained her hold on the water bucket. Hastening to the pantry, she heaved the entire hard-won contents of the bucket on the small but growing blaze.

Relief washed over the kids as they realized that Grandma had prevented their home from burning down around their ears. That feeling didn't last long, though, as Grandma treated them to a long and fierce tongue lashing in Swedish. They didn't need to understand the words; there was no mistaking the message.

Grandma Lindstrom was gone the next day when the kids got home from school. As their mother returned shortly thereafter, they never knew if the fire drove her out, or if she had planned to leave anyway.

Ho-Ho-WHO??

The December night pressed in around the Larsons'
cabin set some eight miles from International Falls,
Minnesota, a town holding the well-earned nickname of
"Icebox of the Nation." The kitchen cook stove and living
room heater did their best to keep out the encroaching cold.

As usual, Fred sat at the kitchen table, playing solitaire.
Gladys and Esther sang "Silent Night" as they washed the
dishes. What else would one sing on Christmas Eve? Eight-
year-old Esther carried the melody while Gladys experimented with an alto line. Esther felt a tiny pang of jealousy
at her younger sister's ability to find the harmony without
anyone teaching it to her. Esther loved to pick out tunes on
the various musical instruments around the house — the
pump organ that sat against the living room wall, harmonicas, and even Fred's button accordion, but was too shy to
try to sing harmony. Gladys was the opposite; while vocal
harmonies came as naturally as breathing, she resisted playing an instrument. "I can't," she'd say, and refused to try.

In the living room, Laura played the same tune on the
violin with Leonard paying close attention. Having learned
the *solfege* method — better known as do-re-mi — in school as
a child, she now explained to her son how it worked. "First
you have to find your key," she instructed, and sang a few
notes of a major chord. "Do, mi, sol. Now you know where
to start the song. Sol, la, sol, mi. Sol, la, sol, mi," she sang the
first couple of phrases of the familiar carol. "Now you try it."
She handed the violin to Leonard and casually announced,
"I have to step down to the neighbors' for a minute."

The kids thought nothing of this, as Laura kept up with
the goings-on around Clark's Colony, and always extended
a helping hand to anyone in need. Everyone carried on with
his or her activities. Alice, having finished her evening

chores, sat in a chair she'd pulled close to the heater, warming her toes as she buried her nose in a book. Six-year-old Laurence, apparently feeling that the singing and violin playing didn't create enough racket, lifted the lid on the Edison phonograph. He opened the lower door and pulled out a drawer containing the cylinders. Finding no Christmas carols in the bunch, he selected "The Stars and Stripes Forever," and inserted the cylinder into the machine. Grabbing the handle on the side, he cranked with all his might. A full wind-up could sometimes keep the machine going through two whole songs. He set the needle onto the cylinder, and Sousa's march joined the cacophony filling the small house.

Suddenly someone pounded on the front door. Laurence, who was closest, rushed to open it. In walked the St. Arnolds, an older couple who lived a short distance down the Clark's Colony road.

"Hello," Mr. St. Arnold greeted them. "We just thought we'd stop in and wish you a merry Christmas." He looked around. "Where's Laura?" he asked.

"She went down to the neighbors'," Fred answered. "She oughta be back soon."

"Well, we'll wait so we can see her," said Mrs. St. Arnold.

The two sat down in chairs where they could watch Fred as he played cards. The St. Arnolds didn't have children and seemed to enjoy coming over to feel the energy given off by the youngsters at the Larson home.

With company in the house, the children ceased their singing and Leonard put the violin back in its case. The march ended and Laurence put the cylinder back on its spindle. Mr. and Mrs. St. Arnold chatted with Fred, who continued playing solitaire.

A muffled but definite thump from upstairs caught everyone's attention. "What's that?" Gladys wanted to know. The St. Arnolds glanced toward the stairway and smiled, as if they knew what was coming.

Fred gathered his cards and reshuffled. "Aaaah, it's nothin'," he grunted. "Laurence, play another song."

Laurence picked out a cylinder. This was another favorite, "Red Wing," a sad song about an Indian maiden whose true love died in battle. He inserted it into the phonograph.

Another thump from above again brought everyone's eyes to the stairs. "It's Santa Claus!" Laurence squealed. Sure enough, down the steps trod the jolly chap himself, sporting a cottony white beard and clad in a red cotton flannel suit that looked a lot like some material that had been lying around the house in recent days. A gunny sack slung over his shoulder completed his outfit. "Ho, ho, ho!" he boomed. "Have you been good boys and girls?"

The children edged closer, awed by the thought that Santa was actually standing in their home. Mrs. St. Arnold quietly moved over and shut off the phonograph.

"Let's see what we have in the sack," Santa said, his voice cracking and sounding—ever-so-slightly—like Mama. "Here, Laurence, a ball for you."

Wide-eyed, Laurence accepted the ball. He hefted it in his hand, then gave it a mighty bounce. The ball sprang up with satisfying vigor, and Laurence lost interest in all else as he bounced and chased his new toy around the house.

"Esther, Gladys, come and get your babies," Santa continued, pulling out two rag dolls. The one with light brown yarn hair he handed to Esther; Gladys received the brunette. The girls hugged the dolls to their chests. Holding hers out to admire it, Esther noticed that the doll's dress looked like it had been made from the same material as one of her own dresses. How on earth did Santa know?

"Thank you, Santa," she said shyly.

Reminded of her manners, Gladys echoed, "Thank you."

"You're very welcome," replied Santa. "Well, Leonard, what do I have for you?" Santa dug around inside the gunny sack. "Hmmm…I know there's something in here." He pulled out a soft brown object, revealing a long tail with a white tip.

"A monkey!" whooped Leonard, grabbing his gift and giving it a squeeze. The sock monkey grinned back, black button eyes shining.

"And last but not least," continued Santa, "this is for Alice." He pulled a pair of woolen stockings out of his bag. The rest of the children felt a little sorry for their big sister, getting something to wear when everyone else got toys. Stockings played an important role in women's lives, as wearing anything but dresses to school was unheard of. With temperatures that often hovered near 40 degrees below zero in the winter, several good pairs of stockings were an indispensable part of all the girls' wardrobes. Still, in the opinion of the younger set, they didn't make a very festive present.

Alice seemed pleased though, as she said, "Oh, thank you, Santa." She put the slightest funny emphasis on the name, almost as if she didn't think this was truly Santa. Who else could it be, stopping by on Christmas Eve with gifts for everyone? He even knew their names, and brought presents that were just what they each wanted.

Santa moved as if to head back up the stairs when Laurence spoke up. "What about Papa? Didn't you bring any presents for him?"

"Aaaah," Papa growled, staring down at his cards. "I don't need no present."

"Sure, I have something for Papa," declared Santa. He walked over to the table. Putting both arms around Papa's neck, Santa nuzzled his cheek, practically obscuring his face with the huge white beard. "Merry Christmas, Papa."

"Aaaah," said Papa again, though his face turned a little red, and a smile played around his mouth.

"Well, it's time for me to go," announced Santa. "My reindeer are waiting on the roof." To a chorus of good-byes he picked up the gunny sack and made his way back up the stairs.

With new toys to play with and the marvelous visit from Santa to discuss, the children easily overlooked the series of mysterious noises that once again emanated from the upper floor. Mr. and Mrs. St. Arnold watched with pleasure as the kids inspected their gifts, Gladys and Esther already mentioning possible names for their new babies. A few minutes later, Laura entered the house. "Brrr! It's cold out there," she stated. "Hello," she greeted the St. Arnolds.

"Mama, Santa Claus was here!" Gladys rushed to tell her. The children gathered around, showing her their new treasures. Mama made appropriate sounds of appreciation, and asked a few questions, as if making sure that each was satisfied with his or her gift.

Once the first rush of excitement was over, the children again faded into the background until the St. Arnolds said their good-byes and headed out into the cold.

"Well, now it's time to get ready for bed," Laura said.

One by one the children made their final trips to the outhouse and climbed the stairs, gifts clutched tightly in hand. As Esther hurried in from the privy, the glow from the windows illuminated a curious sight: a ladder leaned against the side of the house, leading up to the bedroom window. Now, who put that there? Too cold to puzzle out the answer, she rushed inside and soon forgot about it as she collected her baby and headed upstairs. Oddly enough, when she visited the outhouse the next morning, she found a few fluffs of cotton, very similar to Santa's beard. Had Santa actually used their toilet? Although she'd never thought about it, she supposed the old guy needed to stop at the occasional outhouse during his all-night flight around the world.

After seeing the children upstairs, Laura turned to her husband. "Did Santa have anything for you, Fred?"

"Aaaah," Fred replied yet again, and dealt out another hand of solitaire.

Kids in front of house in Clark's Colony. L-R: Leonard, Laurence, Esther, neighbor girl, Mrs. St. Arnold, Gladys, Alice.

Alice's Plan

"Alice, you're in charge until I get back," Fred told 13-year-old Alice. He helped a wan-faced Laura into the car then turned to his offspring. "You kids mind Alice. I'll be back tonight." The five children watched solemnly as the car pulled away, carrying their parents. They had become somewhat accustomed to Laura's trips to the hospital, but they still worried.

The first day their mother was gone, everyone was subdued. They did chores, helped with meals, and waited for Papa to come home with news. He returned late in the evening, and informed them that Mama would be fine, but would have to spend a few days in the hospital.

When they were younger, Papa had felt they needed Grandma Lindstrom to look after them in Laura's absences. Now that Alice was a teenager, their parents considered them old enough to look after themselves while Fred was working. The girls were well acquainted with the kitchen, and pitched in to help put their simple meal of beans and bread on the table. Everyone knew what his or her chores were, so the basic work got done.

The next day after Fred had gone to work, Esther approached her big sister. "Alice, let's do something fun. Ple-e-e-ase? Let's play a game."

"No, we've got work to do," responded Alice, playing perfectly the role of Big-Sister-in-Charge.

Esther wouldn't let it rest, though, and kept pleading until Alice finally declared, "Esther Pester, go do your chores and leave me alone!"

Esther protested but obeyed, and for a time no more was heard about play. Then, unexpectedly, Alice announced, "I've got a plan. If you all get your chores done quick, I'll tell you what it is."

She couldn't have picked a better way to motivate her brothers and sisters to get their work done. Everyone loved Alice's plans. She always came up with original ideas for fun things to do. In record time, the dishes were washed, the floors swept, the house dusted, the beds made and Long Pete's garden weeded.

Alice looked at the little faces gazing at her expectantly. "What's your plan?" burst out Gladys.

"Let's see if Laurence will fit through the heat register," said Alice, indicating the hole directly above the cook stove, meant to convey heat up to the family's sleeping quarters. Because it was summer, the stove was allowed to go out when not needed for meals.

As always, the immediate reaction to Alice's plan was not, "Is this such a good idea?" but "How could we not have thought of this before?"

Alice directed the action. "Leonard, you stay down here and catch Laurence. The rest of you come up with me."

Laurence, Gladys and Esther eagerly scampered up the stairway, impatient to put The Plan in motion. Six-year-old Laurence scooted to the edge of the hole and dangled his legs through. He could see big brother Leonard standing on the cook stove, ready to catch him as he dropped down.

Grasping Laurence under his arms, Alice carefully guided him down into Leonard's waiting hands. "Hey, that was easy. C'mon, Esther Pester, let's see if you can do it."

Esther, still thin and tiny at age 9, slipped through the hole almost as easily as Laurence. Gladys, younger but slightly larger than Esther, was next. She, too, fit through the hole with no problem. Leonard, not to be left out, deserted his post on the stove, and climbed up to have a go himself. In short order, the kids discovered that, by hanging onto the side of the hole by their hands, they could drop onto the stove without anyone to catch them.

When the novelty of this pastime began to wear off, Esther noticed that Alice hadn't gone through the hole. "Try it, Alice," she urged. "It's fun."

Alice eyed the hole skeptically. She knew she was quite a bit bigger than her siblings, but was still adjusting to her newly developing shape. They were having such fun, and it looked so easy. Surely, if she wriggled herself just right... She threw her legs over the side of the hole. At first, everything seemed to be going fine, until her hips refused to go through. She wriggled a little more. Her hips settled more snugly into the hole's frame.

"I'm getting stuck. Help pull me back up," she grunted. Leonard and Gladys each grabbed an arm, and tugged. "Ow! That hurts!" exclaimed Alice. "Go downstairs and see if you can pull me down."

In a flash, the four siblings scrambled back down the stairway. Gladys, always ready for a laugh, cackled at the sight of Alice's legs, bare except for sagging socks and rundown shoes, dancing in the air above the stove. The ridiculousness of the situation struck the others, and they all giggled helplessly as they tried again to dislodge Alice from her prison.

"It's not funny!" came Alice's voice from the attic, which only caused another burst of hilarity. Over the next hour or so, a number of solutions were tried, with no success. Alice remained firmly stuck in the hole. As time went by, an even larger problem began to intrude into the children's brains: Papa. Whatever was he going to think or do about this escapade? Though Papa usually left care and discipline of the kids to Laura, with her gone, they didn't know quite what to expect. Were they all going to get spankings? Would he have to tear the ceiling out to loose Alice? Leonard, Esther and Gladys decided it was time to put their heads together. They needed a "plan" of their own for Papa's arrival.

Leonard looked at the clock. He knew his dad always caught a ride as far as the Clark's Colony turnoff, then walked home from there. He also knew it was nearly time for Papa to show up. "Gladys, you take Laurence with you and go meet Papa. Esther, you keep helping me try to get Alice unstuck." The kids knew if anyone could keep them out of trouble with Papa, it would be his favorite, Laurence.

Gladys and Laurence dashed out the door and down the road, where they could see Papa trudging home after a long day's work, never guessing what mayhem awaited in the house. The two ran to meet him with shouts of greeting and huge smiles. Laurence took Papa's hand and beamed up at him as he waited for Gladys to gather her courage.

"Papa," Gladys began. "Alice is stuck."

"Stuck? Stuck where?"

"In the register," she replied.

Fred's strides lengthened until his children could scarcely keep up. Panting, the two tried to fill in the gaps as they ran. "We were playin' this game, and Alice got stuck in the ceiling."

As this explanation did little to clarify the situation, Fred entered the house with an extremely grim expression on his face. There on top of the cook stove stood Leonard, grasping Alice's ankles and shoving upwards with all his strength. Esther huddled on the stairs, looking scared and guilty. What had been a midday lark had become something much more serious. What if nobody could get Alice out? Would she be stuck in the ceiling forever?

"For crying out loud! What have you kids been up to!" Fred didn't wait for further explanations. Kneeling on the stove, he put his shoulder under Alice's feet. "Keep your knees stiff," he told her. He shoved with all his strength, but the only effect was another loud, "Ow!" from the regions above. "Leonard, you stay down here and push. I'm going to pull her out from upstairs."

Up the stairs marched Papa, followed by three chastened youngsters. "How on earth did you get in there!" he demanded of Alice. Again not waiting for an answer, he grasped her under the arms. "Push, Leonard!" he hollered, at the same time giving a mighty heave.

Leonard pushed, Fred pulled, Alice screeched and the watching siblings winced. In moments, Alice was free and receiving a blistering lecture on how short she had fallen in her duties as Person-in-Charge.

Knowing she was at fault, Alice took the scolding humbly, until she could wait no longer. "I really hafta pee!" she gasped, and fled to the outhouse.

For all his stern looks and bluster, Fred refrained from any additional punishment. He probably felt the kids had learned their lesson. No doubt he and Laura enjoyed a good laugh later on, when he recounted the episode to her.

Drought and Depression

In the fall of 1930, Fred stepped out of the house into the cool air of early morning. He shouldered his shotgun and moved toward the thickly wooded area behind the house. Laura's voice echoed in his head, "We need food for these kids. You have to get some meat!"

Yes, he recognized the need. Since the stock market crash of the previous year, jobs had become increasingly tight. Added to that, Minnesota lay in the grip of the worst drought it had seen in decades. Farms that once supplied much of a family's sustenance as well as livelihood now baked under a relentless and blistering sun.

The effects of these combined crises hit home for the Larsons on the day Fred, who had worked at the local dairy for several years, came home and said, "The dairy doesn't have work for me. They laid me off."

Like most men in the area, he now took any odd job that was offered. If there was a ditch to be dug, Fred stepped up and earned a few dollars. Thanks to his wide experience with livestock, he got called when neighbors needed help with butchering or had an animal in distress. No one had money, so in payment he usually received a portion of meat from a butchering, a gallon of milk when a cow calved — welcome supplements to the family's meager food supply. Laura knew how to take these offerings and stretch them to the limit. A ham hock became the stock for a pot of beans; beef might end up in a soup supplemented with vegetables harvested from Long Pete's garden.

Now Fred shook his head. Why was it that he could look at a cow or a pig and see its potential in terms of roasts, bacon or burger, but when it came to deer… If only Laura wouldn't nag so much. He did the best he could. He understood her concern for the kids; it bothered him that there were days when there was barely any food. Thanks to his contacts at the dairy, he sometimes got the skim milk left over when the cream had been taken for butter. Laura's voice came again, "Blue milk! It's not fit to feed the kids." The economic hardship was wreaking havoc on Fred and Laura's relationship. He knew she often didn't feel well, and she had ongoing concern for the well-being of the children. He just wished she wouldn't take all that frustration out on him.

Several hours later, he was ready to head home. Not a single deer had shown its face. Fred didn't know whether to be relieved or disappointed. "At least," he told himself, "Laura can't blame me. I tried."

Just then Fred froze. In a clearing ahead of him stood a buck. He watched as it grazed, oblivious to his presence. Slowly he crouched down and brought the butt of the gun to his shoulder. Sighting in on the deer, he aimed at the spot containing the vital organs, which he knew would bring it down quickest, with the least distress to the animal. The last thing he wanted was cause pain to this innocent creature, this magnificent beast that had never done him any harm.

Fred's arms fell to his knees and his head dropped onto his arms. Silently he cursed himself in English and Norwegian till he ran out of words. He couldn't kill an animal so beautiful, so wild and free. But he had to. Once again Laura's voice sounded in his head, desperation making her shrill, reminding him of their need for food.

He'd do it...he'd just do it and get it over with. He lifted his head and started to raise the gun. The buck was gone. Shouldering the shotgun, he turned toward home, disgusted with himself and with the world.

Laura faced him as he came through the door, as he knew she would. Hands on hips, she greeted him with a sarcastic, "It was too pretty again, wasn't it?"

The country had never faced a crisis like the Great Depression. Uncertainty and fear of what the future held colored everyday life. Would the government survive? If money was worthless, how were folks supposed to buy necessities?

Most of the Larson children were too young to understand the enormity of the situation, but their mother comprehended it well. "Don't waste that," became a common admonition. No food was left on plates at mealtimes, worn-out stockings were unraveled and the yarn re-knitted. Clothing was patched until patches would no longer hold, then the cloth was cut into pieces for rugs or quilts. Cardboard boxes, paper grocery bags, even the waxed paper inserts from cereal boxes—all were kept and used in ways for which they were never intended, but which saved the family from being forced to buy products they couldn't afford.

Oatmeal was a staple for breakfast, as one of the few items cheap enough to stretch the family's dollars. Esther had a particularly difficult time with this dish.

"Esther, finish your cereal and get going; you're going to miss the bus," Laura would scold.

Esther eyed the sodden gray lump lying in a shallow pool of blue skim milk. She hated oatmeal; she hated skim milk. But she knew better than to try to leave her meal uneaten. Why couldn't she keep this stuff down? Every time she swallowed, the wad came back up into her throat. Then she had to swallow it again, with it now tasting a hundred times worse than it had the first time. Over and over she fought her nausea until, through sheer will power she managed to keep it down. Snatching up her coat and books, she raced down the road to the bus stop.

Some days she found herself gazing at the bare pantry shelves and wondering, "What are we going to eat tomorrow?" At times there was nothing to take to school for lunch. The kids knew on those days that Laura would walk the 2½ miles into Ranier in the morning, and barter something—perhaps some blueberries she had canned during the summer or a day's house cleaning—to obtain a few ingredients for a loaf of bread. Some friends who lived near the school allowed her to use their oven. At noon she walked over to the schoolyard, where her kids met her and received their portion of the bread she had baked.

Fred took any odd job he could find, from working on machines at the paper mills in the Falls to digging ditches. After he'd completed one particular job, his employer showed himself to be in no hurry to pay. This was unacceptable to Fred, who needed every dollar feed his family. For a week, he walked or caught a ride into International Falls each day and tried to get his wages. Every day the man had an excuse why the money wasn't available. Food dwindled until there was none. On Friday, the kids waited in vain for Mama to appear with bread for their lunches. That night, dinner was a small bowl of oatmeal. After no breakfast on Saturday morning, Fred and Laura loaded the kids into the car which they rarely used and drove into the Falls.

"You kids wait in the car," ordered Laura. Fred went to find his erstwhile employer to again demand his wages. The children watched as Laura went around the back of an office building and climbed the stairs to the living quarters of some friends. She must have thrown herself on the mercy of her friend, because soon she returned with a sandwich for each of the kids. To the hungry children the two pieces of brown bread pasted together by some sort of filling represented a feast. "Don't eat this too fast," their mother cautioned. "Give your stomachs time to get used to the food. Otherwise you might get a stomach ache."

Esther snatched her sandwich and wolfed down a large bite. Then, heeding her mother's words, she forced herself to slow down. Taking a smaller bite, she savored the taste. The rough texture of the bread filled her mouth. As she slowly chewed, she tasted butter. She couldn't remember how long it had been since she'd had butter. Her tongue mashed the smooth fat against the roof of her mouth, reveling in the way it coated her palate. From the looks on her siblings' faces, she knew they were enjoying their sandwiches just as much. Laura climbed back into the car, her face showing how grateful she was that, at least for today, her children had something to eat.

In a while Fred showed up, a look of satisfaction on his face. "He paid me," he said. It was all they needed to hear.

"Take me to the store, Fred," Laura directed. At the Red Owl grocery store she stocked up on as many staples as Fred's windfall would allow—flour, sugar, coffee, beans and of course, more oatmeal.

At the end of an early summer day in 1932 Fred returned from his daily trip into the Falls.

"I've got a job near Ray over by Lake Kabetogama," Fred informed Laura. "It's gonna last a coupla weeks."

"That's good news," Laura replied. "What'll you be doing?"

"Digging ditches on da road crew."

"Well, maybe we'd better come along, since it's a short job. There's good berry picking around there, too." In days before money had gotten so tight and gasoline such a precious commodity, the family had often driven to the area near the town of Ray to pick the blueberries that grew in abundance there.

Laura knew from other jobs Fred had worked that ditch digging was a hot, dirty, crushingly hard job. He'd come home so tired at the end of a day that he could barely stay awake to eat, let alone make himself a meal. She needed to be there to cook for him.

A few days later Fred and Laura loaded the four younger children into the car and headed south toward Ray. Alice, who was now sixteen, had a job cleaning rooms on another project in the Lake Kabetogama area. The family doubted they would see her though, as they all knew they were there to work, not socialize. Alice wanted to prove she was a good worker, so she could find another job quickly when this one ended. As with many of her peers, necessity had forced her to drop out of school as soon as she was old enough to get a job.

Arriving in Ray, Fred pulled up to the vacant house he'd arranged as a temporary home for the family. Although it contained little besides a countertop and wood cook stove, Laura said, "This'll do. It's not far from where you'll be working, and we don't need much for the short time we'll be here."

The children helped haul in the bedding and boxes of supplies. Their mother had planned carefully so she had all the necessities for life away from home. Besides some basic food items she brought the kids' school lunch buckets, a few pots and pans, a large mixing bowl, many cases of canning jars, and enough plates and flatware for the family.

Gladys and Esther laid their blankets side by side, so they would be sleeping together, just as they did at home. Each set her doll's cradle next to her side of the bed, so they could be tucked in at night.

Laura soon had a fire going in the stove, and heated some leftover soup she had brought along. A small piece of bread completed the simple meal.

Fred was already gone when the children got up in the morning. After a bowl of the hated oatmeal, Esther helped her mother and Gladys clean the dishes and get settled into the house. Leonard and Laurence set out to find firewood. Despite the summer heat the cook stove needed a continual supply of fuel.

Laura got out her big mixing bowl and quickly combined ingredients for several loaves of bread. Once the dough formed into a lump, she laid a cloth over it. She set it on the counter and left it to rise. Supervising the kids, organizing the house and hauling water from the pump in the yard kept her busy for the hour until time to check the bread again.

The dough was mounding up, nearing the top of the bowl. Laura plumped it onto a floured board and kneaded it expertly. With a small amount of lard she greased a couple of bread pans and divided the dough between them. Again she covered it with the cloth then left it to rise.

She carried in some of the kindling that Leonard and Laurence had gathered and started the fire in the cook stove. Once the flames caught, she fed in some larger pieces of wood. This was the tricky part—getting the fire going at the right temperature to bake bread without burning it or having it come out underdone.

When the bread had risen sufficiently, Laura slid the pans into the oven. Her mouth watered at the aroma of baking bread that wafted through the house. Her empty belly rumbled, seeming to accuse her. She knew her children's stomachs often sounded the same way. At times she nearly panicked, wondering how on earth she was going to keep all those mouths fed. Having Alice working away helped a little, but Leonard was a teenager, and never seemed to get enough to eat. The girls and Laurence were still small, but they all had big appetites.

As soon as the finished bread was slightly cooled, Laura began slicing one of the loaves. She made the entire loaf into sandwiches for Fred's lunch.

Just before noon Laura handed two heavy lunch buckets to Gladys and Esther, along with a quart-size jar of water. "Hurry over and give this to Papa, then bring the buckets back. Be careful not to tip the jar so the water doesn't spill."

The girls walked along the road with the hot sun burning down on their heads, the buckets seeming to grow heavier with each step. "I don't know how Papa can eat this much," declared Gladys.

"He's working awful hard," replied Esther.

Up ahead they saw the work crew, and spied their father among the laborers. His plaid shirt was darkened with sweat; when he took his hat off to wipe his face, his hair lay plastered against his head. He accepted the lunch buckets with little more than a grunt, and started wolfing down the sandwiches. Although they were just bread with a thin layer of jelly holding them together, Esther's mouth watered for a taste. Every once in a while Papa stopped eating and guzzled down a huge drink of water, then attacked the sandwiches again. Finishing off the first bucket, he turned to the second. This held a small jar of soup and still more sandwiches. Fred ate his entire meal in silence, then handed the empty buckets back to his daughters. Turning, he headed back to the ditch. He picked up the shovel and went to work.

Watching him eat had whetted the girls' appetites. With the buckets now empty, they jogged back home and arrived, hot and hungry. Laura gave them each a sandwich made from thin slivers of bread, and even less jelly than Fred's had contained. They devoured this meager repast and wished for more, though they knew better than to ask. Papa was the worker, so the majority of food had to go to him.

After lunch, Laura handed the buckets to the girls. "Go pick blueberries," she ordered. "I'm going to make more bread."

This became the daily routine during the weeks spent at Kabetogama. Each day at noon the girls took Papa's lunch to him while Leonard and Laurence collected enough wood to keep Laura's fire going. In the afternoon the kids all took the buckets into the woods and picked blueberries. Between bread baking, Laura processed the berries, making some into sauce and some into jam. Now they were able to spread a thicker layer of jam onto their sandwiches, but Laura still cautioned them against waste. "We need to save up most of this for later," she told them.

When Fred's job ended, they packed up the car and headed home, a few dollars in the family's collective pocket, and many jars of processed blueberries riding with them. In addition to helping them eke out meals through the winter,

Laura would also use the berries in trade for groceries if money ran out entirely.

Clean Clothes and Clean Souls

The day before wash day often found Leonard in the woods behind the house, searching for the perfect tree for firewood. He usually looked for a tamarack, as it was a harder wood and burned longer and hotter than the softer pines. If he could find a tree that was already down, it saved him the trouble of felling it, but sometimes there weren't any handy. In this case, he and either Esther or Gladys took the Swede saw and, one on each end, sawed the tree down.

If the tree wasn't too big, the kids joined forces and pulled it closer to the house. Larger trees had to be sawed up where they fell. This also called for teamwork. Once Leonard had the tree limbed, the girls helped him move the saw horses to wherever the tree lay. Grunting and groaning, they lifted the tree and laid it across the saw horses. Esther quickly took her position on one end of the saw. She hated the other job.

"Alright, Gladys," Leonard would say. "Hop up on the log."

Gladys straddled the log near one end, bracing herself with her hands, legs wrapped the trunk. Her task was to keep the log from rolling back and forth with the strokes of the saw.

Leonard eyeballed the log and prepared to saw a length that would fit into the stove. Esther gripped her end of the saw. Alternately pushing and pulling, she and Leonard dragged the saw through the hard wood of the tree. Gladys rode the trunk as if it were a pitching boat on a stormy sea. When the log listed in one direction, she threw her weight the opposite way. Sometimes a knot or a defect in the wood caught the saw and caused the log to roll almost all the way over. When this happened, Gladys's feet flew up and her body gyrated as she strove to bring the tree back into balance.

"Keep it steady, Gladys," Leonard commanded.

"I am! You quit making it roll so much," she retorted.

This process continued until the entire tree was cut into stove-sized rounds. The kids then lugged these to the woodshed. The next day Leonard split the chunks into smaller pieces, which Laurence carried into the house, while, inside, the girls helped gather and prepare the wash. Laura added sticks of wood to the fire, heating the stove to an uncomfortably hot temperature. A water reservoir on one end of the stove held several gallons, but not nearly enough to wash all the family's clothes. To supplement, Laura filled a huge boiler set on top of the stove.

When Laura could see the water steaming in the boiler and small bubbles forming along the sides, Leonard or one of the girls helped her dump part of it into the galvanized washtub, and more into a similar pan for rinsing. During the winter, washing took place indoors, but most of the year it was done in the back yard.

Adding lye soap to the wash water, Laura swished it around and dumped in the first batch of dirty clothes. She positioned her wash board in the tub and gingerly snagged a piece of clothing out of the nearly-scalding water. Then began the tedious process of scrubbing each item up and down on the corrugated tin wash board. As the water cooled slightly and her skin became accustomed to the heat, she plunged her hands in for longer periods of time. She tossed each article into the rinse water where the girls snatched it up, wrung it out, and dropped it into a basket. When the basket was full, whoever wasn't occupied at the moment hauled it to the solar-powered dryer. This consisted of a network of ropes strung around the back yard. Here each item was handled again as the girls pinned it to the clothesline. From there, the wind and sun took over.

Once the clothes had flapped in the breeze and dried sufficiently in the sun, the next step in the laundry process began. In those days before synthetic materials, virtually all outer clothes required ironing in order to be presentable. The wringing process, while effective at removing water, also created a great many creases and wrinkles which were not removed by drying on the clothesline. Laura's iron was literally a heavy chunk of iron, formed in the familiar rounded wedge shape, similar to that of the modern iron. Unlike today's irons, Laura's had no electrical cord. There actually were three irons, which all used one detachable handle. A trigger-like latch on the handle controlled a hook underneath, which slipped into a groove on the top of the iron. When it was time to iron, Laura put the three irons on the back of the cook stove to heat up. Leonard or one of the other kids had to keep the large wood box beside the stove well-stocked. Even in the heat of midsummer, Laura (or, after a few years, her daughters) stood next to the sweltering stove where the irons sat. It was necessary to keep the stove free of ash and any other debris which could be transferred from the iron to the clothing. To avoid black streaks on her newly-laundered clothes, Laura scrubbed the stove well before ironing. She also made sure her ironing board — a wooden contraption with folding legs — did not become a receptacle for books, coats or other paraphernalia that might leave a residue behind that could transfer to the clothing.

While many people of that era felt the need to press their bed linens as well as their clothing, Laura avoided that by being extremely particular about how she hung the sheets out to dry. She stretched and pinned them tightly to the clothesline, then brushed the wrinkles out by hand before leaving them to the care of the elements. These extra steps forestalled the necessity of firing up the irons yet again.

With all these tasks, doing the laundry was a long, hot and tiring process. Laura was rarely in the best of moods on wash day, and that usually affected the spirits of the children as well. Short tempers and terse, snappy comments made the day one of the least favorite in the week.

On a typical wash day in the early spring, the routine was suddenly broken by a knock on the front door. Irritated, Laura wondered, "Now who can that be?" She opened the door, to be greeted by two neatly dressed young women. Acutely aware of her reddened hands, sweaty hair hanging in her eyes, and apron-front soaked by wash water, Laura nevertheless greeted them politely. "What can I do for you?"

"Hello," said the taller woman. "I'm Miss Johnston and this is Miss Proctor. We're the new missionaries for the church in Ranier."

Wash day immediately sank to the bottom of Laura's schedule. She called, "Girls, finish the wash. I'm going to talk to these ladies."

Laura loved the Bible and took every opportunity to read and study it. As with many people of Scandinavian descent, she had been raised in the Lutheran church; however, even as a child, she had gone to different churches with her friends. Thanks to these early experiences, she had no prejudice for or against any religious group. Anyone who offered to study the Bible was welcome. Because of Ranier's small size and spread-out population, maintaining a church was nearly impossible. If missionaries came in spring, as these ladies had, they usually left by winter, finding it too difficult to keep the building warm enough for services. Attendance also dropped off dramatically as the brutally cold temperatures discouraged even the hardiest and most devout church-goer from walking to town.

Now Laura listened eagerly to the two young women who sat in her living room. They were recent graduates of Bible college, and Ranier was their first assignment.

"We want to have a Vacation Bible School after school gets out in May," said Miss Johnston. "We hope your children will come."

"They'll be there," began Laura, then had a thought. "Why don't you hold VBS right here? I know a lot of families wouldn't be able to send their kids into town for it, but if it's right here in Clarks' Colony…"

"That's a great idea," enthused Miss Proctor. "Are you sure it won't be too much trouble?"

"No, I'd love it," replied Laura. "And we'll be at church on Sunday, too."

During the long stretches of time when there were no church services in town, Laura encouraged her family to read and memorize sections of the Bible at home. Many Sundays found the family gathered in the living room. Laura called these get-togethers "playing church," but they were her way of getting her kids to read the Bible and sing hymns, and to involve Fred, as well. She encouraged the children to sing, and especially loved it when Esther and Gladys sang duets. Since Laura had learned to read shape notes as a child, she could figure out all the melodies in the song book. The children learned more songs from their mother than they did from attending church.

On Sunday, true to her word, Laura gathered the family for the trip into town for church. Since this was the first church service with these new missionaries, she convinced Fred to go along. He and Laura climbed into the front of the Model T, with Laurence on the bench seat between them. The car didn't have a back seat, so the rest of the kids sat in the trunk—what they called the rumble seat. Papa gave them a stick to keep the trunk lid open, and they sat facing rearwards, their feet dangling out the back.

At the church building, the new missionaries greeted the congregation and led some favorite Sunday School songs. Then Miss Proctor asked, "Is there anyone who'd like to sing a special selection?"

Esther scrunched down in her seat; she knew what was coming. She felt Laura's hand prodding her shoulder. "Gladys and Esther have a song," she heard her mother say.

"Wonderful!" responded Miss Proctor. "Come on up, girls."

On shaking legs, Esther made her way to the front of the small church. Only the knowledge that Gladys was beside her — and of the punishment she'd receive from Mama — kept her from fleeing out the door. She felt Gladys's hand groping for hers and clutched it tightly.

At times like this, her nearsightedness was almost a blessing, as it kept her from seeing clearly the many eyes staring at her. She took a deep breath and began to sing, "On a hill far away stood an old rugged cross..." She couldn't help wishing she were on that hill far away. Together, the sisters finished the song and thankfully made their way back to their seats.

Mama leaned over. "I could hardly hear you," she whispered. "Next time you need to sing out a little more."

Next time! Did there have to be a next time? Esther enjoyed church and singing as much as the next person, but did she have to be the center of attention?

When school let out for the summer, Laura opened her home for the missionaries to lead daily Vacation Bible School, what they referred to as DVBS. The young women drove out from Ranier each day to hold the meetings. About a dozen neighborhood children showed up to participate. Due to lack of chairs and space, the stairway became a seating area for the children. Miss Johnston played the pump organ while Miss Proctor led the group in singing songs such as "Jesus Loves the Little Children" and "I Have the Joy, Joy, Joy, Joy Down in My Heart." Then came a period of Bible study. They learned about Jonah, David, and other heroes of the Bible. The teachers challenged the kids to memorize a daily Bible verse. They taught songs that helped learn the books of the Bible, and had them practice looking up and reading scriptures. All this happened in such a positive atmosphere that the students couldn't wait to come the following day.

After two weeks the DVBS ended. Miss Proctor and Miss Johnston again expressed appreciation to Laura for opening her home, and drove back into Ranier. Laura saw them off reluctantly, knowing that in a few short months, bad weather and scarcity of congregants would cause these devout young women to move on to larger towns, once again leaving the people of Ranier with no designated public place for worship.

Summer on Rainy Lake

On Memorial Day 1934, Esther's family went into Ranier to watch the local parade and take part in the festivities. There they met Aunt Helen and her brood.

"Esther!" her cousin Lila accosted her. "I have a job!"

"You're so lucky," Esther eyed her with envy. Lila, who was several years younger than Esther, told her that she was to accompany a young woman whose husband worked surveying the lakes surrounding Ranier.

"Eula's from Michigan," Lila preened a little, self-consciously proud of the fact that she could call an adult by her given name, "but during the summer she lives on an island up Rainy Lake. She gets lonely 'cause her husband's gone all day, so she wants someone to keep her company."

"Is she gonna pay you?" asked Esther.

"I don't think so." Lila paused, then added, "Three months…that's a long time to be away from home."

To Esther's surprise, a short time later her mother and Lila's mother approached her with a young woman in tow. "Esther," said her mother, "this is Eula Davis. She needs a companion for the summer. How would you like to go up Rainy Lake with her?"

Surprised, Esther greeted the newcomer then asked, "What about Lila? I thought she was going."

"I didn't realize that Lila was only twelve," said the woman. "I think it would be better if my companion was a little older, and your mother told me you are…"

Esther impulsively interrupted. "I'm almost 14. Sure— I'd love to go," she said.

"Well, our boat is over at the landing, and we'll be leaving soon so if you want to go…"

Esther was already tugging her mother toward their car. "Be sure to pack your swimsuit." Eula called as they left.

Esther could not believe her good fortune. At home, she threw some clothes into a paper bag. An adventure! Besides, although her parents would never say it aloud, having one less mouth to feed for a few months could only help the difficult financial situation they were in.

Back in Ranier Esther clutched her sack of belongings as she walked down to the boat ramp where Mrs. Davis and her husband waited. The boat was a simple skiff, but Esther felt a thrill as she climbed in. Her first boat ride! The adventure had already begun.

"This is my husband, Ken," said Eula. "Ken, this is Esther."

As the boat skimmed across the water, Esther lifted her face to the breeze. The trees along the shore blended into a blur of various shades of green. Eula smiled at Esther's obvious enthusiasm, and Esther grinned happily back at her.

Finally Ken slowed and turned the boat toward a small island covered by the same green blur of trees. "We're almost there," yelled Eula to Esther over the roar of the engine. Her husband landed the boat and helped the two women onto a narrow, sandy beach. The three of them quickly unloaded personal belongings and other supplies, including enough food to last for the next three months. Ken, who had work to do even on a holiday, got back in the boat and roared away up the lake.

Eula and Esther filled their arms with bundles and started up a path through the trees. Reaching a clearing, Esther saw that their home for the summer was going to be a tent. The lack of electricity and indoor plumbing did not faze her, as she didn't have those amenities at home, either.

Inside the tent, to the left of the door, a double bed took up most of the space. In the back corner was a small cot. Along the right side of the tent stood a small camp stove, a rough table and chairs, and a few boards for shelves. Obviously, this was a tent for eating and sleeping, and not much else. This state of affairs agreed with Esther, as the tent's air felt close and uncomfortably hot. Esther deposited her small bag of belongings on the cot, and helped put the rest of the supplies away. Both she and Eula were anxious to get outside into the fresh air.

That evening at dinner, Ken smiled at Esther. "I'm glad you came to stay with Eula," he said. "It gets lonely for her up here."

When Esther tried to help with the dishes, Eula shooed her away, saying, "I'll clean up; you go outside and play."

What a novel concept. At home, everyone was expected to help with chores. Play was reserved for whatever time remained after the work was done. Esther walked down to the lake through the warm summer darkness. Wading along the edge of the water, she thought about Eula's promise that they'd go swimming tomorrow if the weather was nice. This was going to be the best summer ever.

The next morning, Esther was sleepily aware of Ken and Eula talking quietly as Eula got her husband off for the day. She dozed a while longer, and by the time she got up, Ken was gone and Eula had pancakes ready for Esther's breakfast.

True to her word, once she'd cleaned up the breakfast dishes, Eula said, "Let's go exploring. I'll make some sandwiches; be sure you have your swimsuit."

Esther slipped on the knitted woolen swimsuit she'd gotten in preparation for the seventh grade. As she'd now be attending junior high school in International Falls, she needed it for the swim classes she planned to take. She chuckled as she thought about poor Leonard, who made up excuses to stay home — or blatantly skipped school — on swim class days. Esther loved the water, and looked forward to having swim lessons as part of her school day. Now she donned a light blouse and skirt over the suit, and called to Eula, "I'm ready."

Down at the lake's edge, the small skiff they had used the day before floated on a mooring rope. Eula pulled the boat to shore and the two climbed in. The older woman fitted oars into the oarlocks. "I like to row instead of using the motor. It's so much quieter, and we're not in a hurry to get anywhere."

The two took turns rowing lazily through channels and around islands. When they grew hot from this exertion, they jumped over the side into the chilly lake for a swim. Eula was glad to discover that Esther actually knew how to swim. "I won't worry so much about you drowning now," she laughed.

Every once in a while Eula would say, "We're in Canada." Esther found out that they often crossed the border from the U.S. to Canada and back. It seemed odd to think that just floating in a boat could take them from one country to another.

One sunny morning, Eula produced buckets before heading down to the boat. "I saw some blueberries yesterday. Minnesota has such nice, big blueberries. I want to pick a bunch for pancakes and cobbler. Ken likes to eat them with milk and sugar, too."

Eula scanned the bank as the two paddled through the quiet water. Esther knew she was more help with the rowing than berry hunting, since she could barely see the shore, let alone spot the bushes that held the berries. "There's a patch," exclaimed Eula, and they pulled the boat in to shore.

While Eula crouched down gathering blueberries, Esther searched a little higher. Blueberries were okay, but she hoped to find her own favorite. Spotting a Juneberry tree, she made a beeline for it. The purple berries hung dark and lush. Reaching up, she picked and ate, picked and ate, and then ate some more. About the time she'd eaten as many as she could reach, Eula called to her. "Esther, I've almost filled my bucket. How are you doing?"

Esther looked at her empty bucket. "I haven't got any in the bucket. I ate 'em. They sure are good."

"Well, these mosquitoes are about to drive me crazy," Eula said, swatting at the little pests swarming around her head and arms. As Esther came back toward her, she said, "Look at you! They aren't even bothering you!"

Esther shrugged. "I don't know why; I guess they don't like me."

Eula laughed. "You're so tiny, if they come at you from the side, they probably can't see you! C'mon, let's get back in the boat."

On weekends, Ken didn't have to go to work, but his interest in surveying the lakes remained. "Let's go for a boat ride," he'd suggest.

As if they hadn't been boating practically every day, Eula and Esther eagerly clambered into the skiff. Ken preferred to cover a little more distance in the course of the day, so he fired up the motor. Off they went, passing in a few minutes areas that the women spent entire days exploring. With his guidance they saw expanses of the lake that they wouldn't have gotten to otherwise.

Sometimes in the evenings, Esther would get bored with the adults' conversation. After all, how can a 14-year-old girl concentrate on shop talk about the survey crew when a beautiful lake lay just yards away? Slipping out of the tent, she went to the outhouse to put on her swimsuit, then headed for the water. The gently sloping lake bottom gave her the choice of wading or swimming, and the water was shallow enough that it remained somewhat warm from the heat of the day. She paddled through the peaceful water, watching the daylight fade. Flipping onto her back, she floated, allowing the water to rock her gently. Finally, when darkness fell, she made her way back to the tent, already anticipating tomorrow, and another day to swim and play.

Though Esther missed being with Gladys that summer, she greatly enjoyed her status as companion to a grown-up. Many peaceful days were spent in the boat with Eula, swimming, singing, playing harmonicas, or just drifting quietly along the lake.

All too soon, their time was gone. September was almost upon them, and Esther needed to get home for school. Eula seemed even more reluctant than Esther was for the summer to end.

The women collected their belongings and packed them in the boat, and Ken ferried them back to Ranier. Dropping Esther off at home, Eula hugged her and said, "Thanks for a wonderful summer. I'm really going to miss you."

Esther, although she wouldn't have said so to Eula, looked forward to being home. This had been her first extended stay away from family. Though her home life wasn't perfect, with frequent tension and arguments between her parents and the usual sibling squabbles, it was still her family. And nobody, regardless of how sweet and kind, could compete with the bond she shared with Gladys. She knew, though, she would always remember with fondness her special summer on Rainy Lake.

Just days after Esther's return from the lake, Dr. Mary appeared at the house. "I've got four beds at the hospital in the Falls," she told Laura. "We can get all four kids' tonsils out, but we have to move fast."

The very next morning Dr. Mary whisked Leonard, Esther, Gladys and Laurence off to the hospital. There the offending tonsils, which had caused much of the illness amongst the Larson youngsters, were removed. Whether this wonderful lady pulled some strings to get the family a discount or paid for the operations herself will never be known. What is known is that Esther's health improved dramatically following the surgery; in fact, she had perfect attendance that school year, despite having a longer bus ride and a more challenging school day. Was her relaxing summer of rest, exercise and good meals partly responsible? Perhaps having the time to build up her strength, then getting rid of the poisonous tonsils, worked together to improve her health. Now, if she could just do something about her aching teeth and poor eyesight…but those would have to wait for a while.

School in International Falls

Just after Labor Day 1934, Esther, Gladys and Leonard boarded the bus that would take them to the junior high school in International Falls. Since Leonard cared very little for school and played hooky as often as he dared, he was now only one grade ahead of his sisters. Gladys struggled with her classes, and was glad she shared a grade with Esther.

Esther anticipated each day for a special reason besides school. Eula, her friend from this past summer, was staying at a hotel in the Falls while her husband finished up his work on the lake. Each morning Esther climbed off the school bus and made a beeline for Eula's hotel. The two visited for a few minutes until Esther had to dash back so as not to be late for school. She knew she may never see Eula again after the couple went back to Michigan, so she cherished these moments.

One afternoon Esther arrived home to find her mother with a strange look on her face. "I had a visit from Eula," Laura told her. "You must have really impressed her. She told me that they can't have children of their own, so she and Ken would like to adopt you."

Shock ran through Esther's body. "Adopt me? No!" she exclaimed. "You're my parents. I don't need new parents." She felt sorry for the young couple, and was grateful for the idyllic summer she'd spent with them. But leave her own family and live with someone else forever? No, thanks!

Laura must have explained the situation to Ken and Eula, but it never made a difference in the daily visits. The couple left shortly afterward, and Esther didn't hear from them for many years.

All the kids from Ranier attended the upper grades in the Falls, so Esther saw several of her friends as she entered her first junior high class. Seventh grade was a big change from the Ranier school. She had to move from room to room for the various classes, and had different teachers for each subject. It embarrassed her to explain to each teacher why she had to walk up to the blackboard whenever they wrote something. "I can't see it," she explained. Over the years she had developed an excellent memory, as she took in as much as possible to minimize the number of trips she made to the front of the room.

The highly-anticipated swim class turned out to be a bust. Coming into school from tiny Ranier, Esther didn't understand how to arrange her schedule to take full advantage of the most popular classes like swimming. Consequently, she only managed to get a class in the pool every few weeks. The instruction itself proved disappointing, as the teacher had the girls sit on one side of the pool and, a few at a time, swim to the far side. Esther decided she learned more on her own out on the lake than from school.

In place of the swimming, Esther found herself enrolled in gym class. This, too, lacked any real relevance to Esther's active lifestyle. For some reason, the teacher seemed to consider human pyramids a good athletic effort, and required one nearly every time the class met. Esther felt a stab of sympathy for the large, sturdy girls who always got stuck on the bottom row. On hands and knees, they braced themselves for the onslaught to come. The next row of girls climbed onto their backs, left knee and hand on one girl's back, right knee and hand on another's. Row after row, smaller and smaller girls climbed into position. Once everyone else was in place, with the pyramid shifting as the girls strove to maintain balance, tiny Esther scampered up over all those rumps to take her place on top. After a quick pose to satisfy the teacher, she scrambled down, knowing she had the farthest to fall should the pile collapse.

As they rode the bus home one afternoon, Gladys and Esther sat trying to ignore the leers from Hector, an older boy who lived a short distance up the main road from their stop. He seemed to enjoy harassing them, especially on days that Leonard skipped school. Now, he moved to the seat behind them and murmured flirtatious comments. At each stop several students disembarked, till finally only the two girls and Hector remained.

Nerves on edge, Esther leaned as far as she could away from the grinning face. Gladys turned around and snapped, "Why don't you just leave us alone?"

"Oh, that wouldn't be any fun," their tormentor replied.

"Here's your stop," Esther announced with relief as the bus slowed.

Leaning around the edge of the seat Hector called to the driver, "I'm getting off at the next stop today." He leaned back as the bus picked up speed, a self-satisfied smirk on his face.

At their stop, Esther and Gladys exchanged a quick look which said as clearly as words, "We're sticking together, no matter what." The two hurried down Clark's Colony road, trying to ignore the ominous presence behind them. Just as they got out of sight of the main road, Hector spoke, "Hey girls, what's your hurry?" He grabbed Gladys's arm. "Let's go check out the bushes, Gladys. It's pretty nice in there."

"No!" Gladys writhed, trying to free her arm. Esther launched herself at Hector, kicking and punching.

The boy pushed Esther away. "You go on home like a good girl," he told her.

When Esther renewed her attack, Hector changed tactics. "Oh, you're the one that wants to come with me, huh?" He released Gladys and gripped Esther around the waist, lifting her off the ground. Now it was Gladys's turn to defend her sister. Grabbing Hector's coat collar, she pulled him backwards and at the same time banged her lunch bucket on his head. Esther whirled her arms and legs like windmills, not knowing or caring which part of her abductor's anatomy she hit. Hector swung his free arm at Gladys. As his hand flailed near her face, she opened her mouth and chomped down on his wrist—hard.

"Ow! You little…" Hector used a couple of words the girls weren't supposed to know, then dropped Esther to the ground. "Run on home to your mother, little girls," he sneered. "You don't know how to have any fun." His attempt at a dignified exit back toward the main road was marred, however, as his gait more closely resembled a limp than a saunter.

The sisters didn't wait to watch his progress. Shaking, they raced down the road toward home. Not sure if Hector had followed them, Gladys gasped, "Let's go to Pete's."

Long Pete's house lay a little closer than their home. They knew the bachelor was at work in the Falls, but hoped Hector, if he was still chasing them, wouldn't know it. Never breaking stride, they dashed up the path to Pete's house. Esther jerked the door open and the two tumbled inside and slammed the door behind them. For several minutes they heard no sound but their rasping breaths as they struggled to calm their pounding hearts. Finally, Gladys peeked through the window and said, "I don't see him. He must've gone home. Good riddance."

Grateful to each other for their narrow escape, the sisters hurried to the safety of their own home. Now they understood a little better their mother's frequent warnings: "Don't trust men. They'll try to take advantage of you." Unfortunately, the girls didn't consider reporting this attack to their mother or any other authority. They looked at it as part of life that had to be faced, and felt they had dealt with it as well as anyone could.

The next morning the girls glared at Hector as he boarded the bus, as if daring him to approach them again. For his part, Hector pretended to have forgotten their existence, and if he moved a little gingerly, with something less than his usual swagger, only the three of them knew the reason why.

"I'll get it!" Gladys yelled as someone knocked on the back door one Saturday morning. She opened the door.

"Hello," said the tall stranger standing outside. "I'm Stuart Bronson. Is your mother home?"

"Yes, she is. Mama!" Gladys called.

Laura came to the door.

"Hello, ma'am," the man repeated, "I'm Stu Bronson. I wonder if I could interest you in some fresh fruits."

"Well, we probably don't have money for any, but I'll take a look," Laura had trouble telling anyone 'no' straight out. After all, you never knew if someone needed money even worse than you did. She was used to traveling salesmen, especially in the summer, as they marketed their wares to the visitors who owned lake homes. Every once in a while, like Mr. Bronson, they would try their luck selling to locals.

"Come in," Laura invited. She poured the man a cup of coffee as he set out a variety of pears and apples.

Mr. Bronson swigged a mouthful of coffee. "Ahhh," he said contentedly.

Laura inspected the fruit, then said, "I'm afraid we can't get any fruit today."

"Well, I thought I'd check," Mr. Bronson replied. He didn't appear too disappointed that he hadn't made a sale. Neither did he appear to be in any hurry to leave. He stretched out his long legs and leaned back in his chair, as if prepared to spend the day.

Laura made polite conversation for a few minutes, then turned back to her task of peeling potatoes and carrots, preparing a soup for the evening meal. As Esther and Gladys worked around the house on their own chores, they got tickled by Mr. Bronson's continued presence, long after he'd nursed his cup of coffee to the grounds. They began to make guesses between themselves as to how long he'd stay.

Amusement eventually turned to discomfort for Esther; it seemed as though every time Laura's back was turned, he ogled the two girls in a most unsettling way. He seemed especially attracted by Gladys's quick wit and vivacious personality, and kept trying to draw her into a conversation.

"Oh, darn, we're out of salt," Laura said. She reached into a jar where she kept her few precious coins. "Gladys, here's a nickel. Run to the summer store and get me some."

The summer store was a forerunner of today's convenience stores. It catered mostly to the summer lake visitors, carrying many basic staples. It also helped out the local residents, as they didn't have to walk or drive into Ranier if all they needed was salt.

Gladys accepted the coin and departed. Esther, with every nerve screaming "Danger!" kept a surreptitious eye on their unwanted guest. She'd seen the way his eyes lit up as Gladys headed out the door alone. Sure enough, less than a minute later Mr. Bronson stirred.

"Well, I guess I'll be on my way. Thanks for the coffee," he said to Laura. He quickly gathered up his wares and headed for the door.

While he exchanged a few more pleasantries with her mother, Esther slipped out unnoticed and headed to the special shortcut the kids had made through the woods. This path paralleled the well-worn trail everyone else used. She barely reached the cover of the trees before she heard Mr. Bronson hurrying down the main path. Peeking through the branches, she saw him, long legs eating up the distance like some huge, malevolent spider. His big feet hit the ground with a slap, slap, slap as he hastened along.

Esther didn't waste another instant. She had to get to Gladys. Her slight form zipped down the shortcut without a sound. Mr. Bronson was making enough noise for both of them, which made it easy to keep track of his progress. Once she knew she was well ahead of him, she quit worrying about noise and simply ran. Soon she spied Gladys ahead of her. As expected, Gladys was taking the shortcut. Esther overtook her sister and grabbed her arm.

"Quick, we gotta get outta here," she panted. "Mr. Bronson's trying to catch you."

"What? That old puke!" exclaimed Gladys.

"Here he comes; get down!" Esther squeaked.

The girls flattened themselves on the ground and peered through the bushes. Moments later, Mr. Bronson strode by, those huge feet still thumping the ground with each step.

As soon as he moved out of earshot, Esther grabbed Gladys's hand. "Let's go," she urged.

"The old puke," Gladys said once more for good measure, then the two fled back home down the shortcut.

Bursting into the house Esther gasped, "Mama! Mr. Bronson was chasing Gladys, but I caught up with her first."

Laura, having grown up around threshing crews and other rough types, possessed a fairly extensive vocabulary of salty words. Now she threw out of few describing their erstwhile guest. "Did he see you come back?"

"I don't know," said Esther, "We were just running. He might have heard us."

"Go get Pete," Laura commanded.

The girls hurried over to their bachelor neighbor's place and quickly filled him in on the situation. Never averse to a cup of Laura's coffee and perhaps a cookie or a slice of cake, Long Pete willingly accompanied them back to the house. His solid presence calmed their fears until enough time passed so they were fairly sure Mr. Bronson had given up the chase. Then the girls went to the store—together—and got the salt.

Moving to Alaska

On a spring morning in early April of 1935 Fred, as had become his custom, set out for International Falls. The family was in desperate straits and he needed to find work. He trudged along the road until finally a passing motorist picked him up.

"You can drop me off at da courthouse," he told the Good Samaritan.

A group of men milled around the area outside the courthouse, all looking for work. This had become the gathering place, where hopeful men showed up each day. Employers knew that they could be sure to find willing help here.

Today there was a buzz of conversation and an air of excitement. "What's going on?" Fred asked a man next to him.

"They're wanting folks to go to Alaska," the man replied. "Can you imagine?"

Fred could imagine; anything seemed better than facing his family each evening with nothing to show for his day. He walked into the courthouse. "What's dis I hear about going to Alaska?" he asked a man who seemed to be in charge.

The man looked at Fred doubtfully. "We're looking for young families," he said, emphasizing the word "young." "How old are you?"

"I'm 42."

"We want people no older than 35." The man moved as if to dismiss him, but Fred persisted.

"I'm as strong and able as any t'irty-five-year-old, and I've got experience dose young guys don't have."

"Well," the man reluctantly turned his attention back to his persistent client. "Tell me a little about yourself."

Fred quickly told about his family, stressing the fact that his wife and children were hard workers who would be great assets.

"Do you have any special skills?" the man asked next.

"I've lived on a ranch and worked on threshing crews. I keep da machinery running at da paper mill here in da Falls, and I fix da neighbors' cars when they break down. I do some carpentry, and have worked in dairies, I help out with livestock when they get sick or have trouble during birth and I do butchering. I've dug ditches on road construction projects…"

"Okay, okay," the man laughed. "You sound like you can handle just about anything that comes up. Fill out the application and we'll see."

Although Fred spent another jobless day, he returned home with a sense of hope he hadn't felt for a long time. "Laura, I got an application for us to go to Alaska," he told his wife. "It's part of President Roosevelt's plan to get people back to work. They're gonna ship us up there, and we'll get a piece of land and everyt'ing we need to start farming."

"I can't believe that," said Laura. "The government is going to give us all that if we move to Alaska?"

"No, they're not *giving* us anyt'ing," Fred hastened to clarify. "Everyt'ing will be charged to us, and we'll have thirty years to pay it off. They say the land in this Mat…Matanuk…Matanuska Valley…" Fred stumbled over the unfamiliar word, "…is good farmland. They want people who know about farming to come up and cultivate da land and start growing crops. They expect it to be self-sufficient in just a few years."

Laura caught Fred's excitement and felt a glimmer of optimism herself. "Well," she said, "It can't be any worse than it is here. With you not able to find work, and this awful drouth*…let's do it."

* *'drouth' was the word for 'drought' in the vernacular of that area of Minnesota*

"We have to be accepted first," Fred cautioned. "They're looking for young families. They don't want da parents to be over thirty-five."

This silenced Laura briefly, but she wouldn't let the opportunity slip away through lack of effort on her part. "Well, I think we should still try. The kids could be a big help at their ages, and we're not *old*." That evening they filled out the application that would drastically change their lives.

The Matanuska Colonization Program had been dreamed up in the previous few months by a government desperate to get the country out of the doldrums of the Great Depression. Reports of the rich farmland lying idle in Alaska's Matanuska Valley had circulated through the nation's capital. Why not take some of the Midwest families who needed jobs and put them there to work the soil and build new lives? It sounded like the perfect match. The government organizers planned to transplant one hundred families from Minnesota, then a few weeks later another hundred from Wisconsin and Michigan. They told their representatives at the county welfare offices to look specifically for those of Scandinavian or other northern European heritage, possibly feeling that the ability to withstand cold temperatures was embedded in the genes. They apparently expected an inborn talent for tilling the soil as well, though many of the people selected had never farmed in their lives.

Fred made his usual trip into town the next morning, taking the completed application with him. A few days later he received the welcome news that the family had been accepted into the program. This time Fred headed home with his mind churning with thoughts of all the preparation and planning that needed to be done in the next few weeks.

"Well, did you hear anything?" Laura asked when he stepped through the door.

"We're going to Alaska!" he replied. "We leave on April twenty-fifth, and there's a lot to do before then. We gotta figure out what we're gonna do with this house and the car. And all of us have to have complete medical examinations, including eye doctor and dentist."

Since the tonsillectomies of the previous fall the children's health had improved, but their eyes and teeth had never had any professional attention. Laura's ill-health—much of it brought on by anemia—had also stabilized over the past few years. The doctors had prescribed an iron-rich cure which seemed to have helped, though probably few could stomach it. As often as she'd been able to get hold of some raw beef liver, she had ground it up and drunk the slimy result. She told her kids when they grimaced at the sight, "The hardest part is getting started. After that it all just kind of slides right down."

Esther's eye test confirmed that she was extremely near-sighted. She received her first pair of glasses and felt like she'd been given the world. Looking up at a tree, she studied the individual twigs on the end of a branch. "Is this what everyone else has seen all the time?" she asked herself in amazement. She saw people around her with distinct faces and bodies, not just colored blurs. And the biggest thrill, she could now read what teachers wrote on the blackboard. No more traipsing up to the front of the classroom and trying to memorize everything.

The dentist found her upper teeth were badly decayed and needed fillings in nearly every one. They, along with several more fillings in the lower teeth lent a silvery glint to her smile. Once the dentist finished working on her, Esther went to bed without a toothache for the first time in her memory.

With the departure date looming, the house whirled with activity. The car and house were deeded to nineteen-year-old Alice, who would not be moving to Alaska with the family. For several years she had been working at a variety of jobs, and had recently accepted a position as nanny for Ed Dahl, a widower with 2 children.

Laura agonized over what to bring along. Any furniture worth selling was put on the market. One thing she knew: her Singer treadle sewing machine would make the trip with them. Nearly every garment the family wore had been created on that machine.

Coupons arrived for purchase of traveling outfits. Alice drove Laura and the girls into the Falls to shop at the JC Penney store. There they picked out clothing that seemed capable of standing up to the harshest climate the Frozen

Top Gladys, Leonard and Esther ready to leave for Alaska; Bottom, Alice, Gladys, Esther and Laura.

North might throw at them. Everyone—including Fred and the boys—received the same outfit, which consisted of woolen jodhpurs, white cotton shirts, and sturdy leather boots that laced up to the knee. Gladys and Esther each bought a woolen coat and beret. Alice, though she wasn't going, got into the spirit of the day and bought a matching outfit for herself. "For when I come to visit you," she promised.

As news of the Matanuska Colonization Program spread, it caught the imagination of people throughout the country. Many people considered such a move to the north a romantic adventure. Church groups held clothing drives to donate clothing to the colonists. Esther and Gladys each received a new dress, which they gratefully added to their scant wardrobes.

The days leading to the family's departure were filled with sadness as well as anticipation. The older folks knew it might be the last time they'd see some of their relatives. Alaska was far away and still known by such names as Seward's Folly or Seward's Icebox. Most people thought everyone in Alaska lived in igloos.

When the day finally arrived, Uncle Franz and Aunt Helen, their children and other relatives gathered to say good-by. Helen took pictures. Leaving Alice was especially difficult for the Larson kids. Not only was she their big sister, but she had been a sort of mother figure during the many times that Laura had been bed-ridden or in the hospital due to illness.

Night was falling as the train pulled out of the International Falls station. During the ride south, the Larsons met another colonist couple—Gilford and Catherine Lemmon were newlyweds, spending their honeymoon on this trip to Alaska. Catherine was a school teacher and was confident she would easily find a job in their new home.

Upon reaching St Paul the next day, Esther, Gladys and their brothers gazed in awe at the huge depot and crowds of people. They had rarely visited International Falls except to go to school. They had certainly never seen a city like this.

"There's Aunt Julia," called sharp-eyed Gladys as their aunt came smiling to greet them. Everyone—even Laurence—received her kisses.

"C'mon out to the car," she said. The family piled into her vehicle and soon the kids were enjoying their first look at the capital city of the state in which they'd lived their whole lives. Office buildings towered over streets that ran in all directions. "How," wondered these country cousins, "do people find their way through all those roads?" The impressive Minnesota capitol building brought gasps of wonder. Esther kept her face against the window, thrilled anew with the glasses that allowed her to see all the marvelous sights.

Aunt Julia took them to her home where they spent the night. The next morning — April 26 — she drove them back to the station, where the specially-designated train waited to convey them to San Francisco.

Noise and confusion filled the station. Babies and toddlers cried and clung to their parents or siblings. Older children gaped, wide-eyed, at the chaos. The braver ones left their parents' sides, then had to be found and brought back to the family group. The majority of the colonists were either newlyweds or parents of very young children. Fred and Laura, whose children were mostly teenagers, were among the oldest of the colonists. A festive and optimistic atmosphere enveloped the station. Everyone looked forward to the new beginning that awaited them up north.

Finally the luggage was loaded. Everyone climbed aboard and the train chugged out of the station, headed for California. Esther and Gladys enjoyed the activity and sense of common purpose among the colonists on the train. They were drawn to the babies and young children, and the harried mothers quickly recognized potential babysitters in the two girls.

The train trip to San Francisco took three days. For the girls, it was a great adventure, seeing parts of the country they had only read about. Daily one-hour stops gave the colonists time to stretch their legs and wash the most urgent of laundry items — usually diapers. Unfortunately, the sisters missed out on much time off the train, as someone was sure to call, "Oh, Gladys, oh Esther, would you mind watching my Johnny/Molly/whoever for a little while?" Those "little whiles" ate up any time the girls might have spent exploring. They remained behind, in diaper draped train cars, keeping youngsters entertained until the parents returned.

As the train pulled into San Francisco, a cheering crowd greeted the astounded colonists. These Midwest folk who days before had been jobless and penniless were now treated like celebrities. Newspaper reporters roamed around, asking for statements from anyone who would talk to them. Buses and taxis took them on tours of the city and transported them to hotels where they would spend the night. Esther and Gladys missed most of the shows, dinners and tours arranged for the group, because they were once again babysitting.

After two days, the group prepared to board the *St. Mihiel*, the steamship which would transport them to Alaska. It became obvious in short order that they wouldn't be getting underway anytime soon, as huge cranes swung back and forth, lifting bulldozers, trucks and all manner of heavy objects and lowering them into the bowels of the ship. The Larson kids strained to see what sorts of cargo would be making the trip with them. Laura had crated up her trusty treadle sewing machine, but they were unable to spot it in the chaos of loading. They watched in awe as tons of cargo entered the ship. How on earth could it hold so much? Was there going to be room for the people?

Finally, the colonists received the go-ahead to board. Each family was assigned a room based on need and number of people, with priority given to those with babies and younger children. The Larsons and the few other older families received the least desirable lodging, down in the steerage area with all that cargo they had watched being loaded. The excitement of seeing the stuff deposited on board faded as they realized that the crates were to be their bedroom walls for the voyage.

Still, what's an adventure without a few rough patches? Everyone pitched in and staked out their sleeping areas. Once the Larsons selected their spot, Gladys and Esther lay out their sleeping bags side by side in the cramped quarters, glad they would be on board the ship for only a few days.

As evening fell on May 1, 1935, the *St. Mihiel* finally headed out of the harbor. Esther stared as they passed the partially-completed Golden Gate Bridge. Everyone was talking about this marvelous project, which still had a couple more years to go before it would open. Esther had never seen an undertaking so huge and impressive. She hoped she could come back someday and see the finished product.

There were two main routes that ships took for the trip to Alaska. The Inside Passage meandered through the islands and fjords of southeastern Alaska, offering breathtaking views of water, mountains, trees and wildlife. The Outside Passage was a straighter route, with little sighting of land between California and Alaska. Because the *St. Mihiel* was on a mission rather than on a cruise, the crew took the Outside Passage. So these passengers from the Minnesota prairies saw virtually nothing but water for the entire journey.

The families settled into their quarters, then found they had little to do but socialize. Meals were cooked and served buffet-style by a staff of kitchen help, who then collected and washed the dishes. Mothers with young children still had to keep clothing and diapers washed, but compared to the mountain of tasks they had faced back home, life was easy. Laura loved visiting and soon knew the names and histories of a number of her fellow colonists. Esther and Gladys were still in demand for babysitting. Fred found he had a lot in common with the men—many of them first-generation Scandinavians like himself—as they discussed the work that lay ahead of them in Alaska. Leonard, feeling himself at the age of 16 on the verge of manhood, joined the men's conversations. Laurence found children near his age to play with.

Altogether, the population of the *St. Mihiel* was larger than some of the hometowns these people had left back in Minnesota. In addition to the 285 colonists, four hundred men hired by Roosevelt's Civilian Conservation Corps were on board. The colonists came to refer to these men as "the transients," since their purpose was to assist with building roads, barns, homes and co-op buildings, after which they would return to the Lower 48. There were doctors and nurses to care for any passengers who became ill, and reporters and photographers from various newspapers came along to record this historic occasion.

One evening as Esther and Gladys headed for the stateroom of the children they were to babysit, strains of music caught their attention. Intrigued, they followed the sound back to the dining hall, where the tables had been pushed back and a fiddler and concertina player had started a lively polka. The girls would have loved to stay, but duty called. They headed reluctantly off to babysit, and were accosted by several women making their way toward the music. The girls' small group of charges swelled to a dozen as the grown-ups prepared for a night of dancing and fun. Though they kept the children busy with story books and games like "Ring Around the Rosie," the girls felt slighted for not being able to join in the dancing. On many a winter night back in Minnesota they had kept warm by dancing polkas and schottisches around the house while Laura or Leonard fiddled and Fred played his concertina.

When the dance finally ended in the wee hours, the girls crawled wearily into their sleeping bags. A few hours later they were awakened by an unfamiliar sensation. A giant hand seemed to be bouncing the ship up and down like a bathtub toy. They soon realized that the *St. Mihiel* was being battered by a vicious storm. The Outside Passage to Alaska was notorious for bad weather, as the route took the ship through the unprotected waters of the Gulf of Alaska. Esther and Gladys turned out to be surprisingly good sailors, unaffected by the seasickness which befell the majority of the passengers. Mothers too sick to care for their children once again cried out for help from the girls. The staff of nurses on board staggered from room to room giving what aid they could as the ship plowed its way through the raging sea.

On May 6, after what seemed like some of the longest days of their lives, the *St. Mihiel*'s passengers sailed into the calm of

The St. Mihiel.

Resurrection Bay near Seward, Alaska. From this point the colonists would board a train for the remainder of their journey to their new homes. Then came an unwelcome announcement: due to a few cases of measles among the youngsters, all children had to remain quarantined on the ship for a couple more days. In those days, contracting measles was nearly as common as a catching a cold; most adults had experienced the disease sometime in their childhood, and so had developed immunity. It was decided that the men, not posing a threat to the health of others, would board the train and head for the Matanuska Valley, where they'd get started unloading supplies and organizing the temporary homes. The women and children would stay behind until the quarantine was lifted.

Huge cranes moved into position to remove the freight from steerage. This presented a problem to the families like the Larsons who had been forced to set up camp below deck: they needed to move immediately or risk having something extremely large and heavy dropped on their heads. A quick shuffle amongst those in the cabins on the upper deck provided room for the displaced. Since the transients and other men were leaving, every cabin had at least a bit more room. Esther and Gladys squeezed in with the Otto Peterson family and their 5 kids. Laurence stayed with another family, and Laura with still another. Fred and Leonard headed out with the men.

Once the men had left with Caterpillars, trucks, and all the larger worldly possessions of the ship's inhabitants, life turned dull for those left behind. The children who didn't have measles chafed at being stuck aboard a ship that now seemed more like a prison. The Larson kids, having already had measles, received special permission to go ashore, as long as they were accompanied by their mother. Gregarious Laura soon made friends among the townsfolk in Seward. When a local woman invited them to her home for coffee, they went willingly, thrilled to talk firsthand with a "real Alaskan."

The quarantine ended on May 10 and the train stood ready for boarding. Mothers, children, and all personal luggage that hadn't gone ahead with the men crammed onto the huffing train for the several-hours-long ride to Anchorage. Esther, appreciating anew the glasses that opened up her vision to the world, gazed in awe at mountains that seemed to poke up through the clouds to Heaven.

What a party greeted them in Anchorage! Horns honking, people cheering—it was like the reception in San Francisco, on a smaller scale. Cars ferried the group from the train station to a community hall where a luncheon awaited them. Anchorage had gone out of its way to give their new neighbors a taste of Alaskan foods, serving moose, caribou, salmon, and all manner of wild berries and other native plants. Esther thought back to a month ago, when her family had rarely known where their next meal would come from, other than the fact they could be pretty sure it would contain little more than beans or oatmeal. Now here she was, being urged to eat her fill and more of all these exotic foods.

After lunch, the colonists were again loaded into cars and buses for a tour of Anchorage. At the time, the business district stretched from the docks and train station on 1st and 2nd Avenues to 6th Avenue. Beyond that point a few gravel and mud roads ran out to the various homesteads and residential areas of the town.

Soon it was time for the colonists to re-board the train and continue on to their new homes in the Matanuska Valley. Excitement mingled with apprehension as they looked forward to getting settled, wondering what challenges awaited them.

Esther and Gladys spent as much time as possible staring out the windows at scenery so incredible as to appear unreal. It seemed that the train was going to drive all the way to those mountains that jutted up in front of them.

The train stopped at the railroad junction of Matanuska to drop off a bag of mail. Any passengers who so desired were allowed to step off the train and stretch their legs. Esther took advantage of the invitation. She stood next to the train and gazed around at the tiny settlement. She saw a combined store and post office, a hotel and community building that seemed to be closed, and a few homes scattered around.

The train pushed on to its final destination — Palmer, Alaska. Peering out the window, Esther saw another crowd waiting to greet the train. This time, many of the faces were familiar, as they were the husbands and fathers who had left Seward ahead of them.

Beyond the crowd sat what looked like a city completely constructed of white wall tents. A deeply rutted street of

Palmer Tent City.

89

mud ran between the train tracks and the tent town. Though these newcomers didn't know it yet, they were about to get their first taste of an Alaskan phenomenon—spring breakup.

Fred located his family through the crush of reunions going on around them. "I've got a place for us," he said. He led them to a tent on one side of the camp. "We're gonna need to get a couple more beds, but we'll only be staying here until the drawing for property. The toilets are over there." He waved his hand toward the back of the tent city, where a row of outhouses stood amongst the spruce and birch trees.

First Palmer Hospital.

The tent was nearly as large as their home back in Minnesota. A sturdy wooden floor and wood studs held the canvas securely. Inside, the standard issue items—a double bed for the parents, a set of bunk beds for the kids, a stove, table and chairs—stood ready for the family. Food, blankets and basic supplies—including a pile of coal for the stove—had also been supplied for the travelers. Laura and the kids dropped their belongings onto the beds. They had been told that supper would be served to them that evening at a railroad car set up as a dining room. They all trooped over and squeezed into the dining car. There they received another bountiful meal surrounded by the cheerful sounds of their fellow colonists, relieved that the long trip was over, and excited to start their lives in this new land. Circulating through the group, a lone man seemed to be trying to shake hands with every person in the group. "I'm Reverend Bingle," he said in introduction. "I'm the minister here, and I hope to see you at church Sunday morning." He made sure each person had directions to the church, then moved on.

After dinner everyone dispersed to their tents. Laura went to their next door neighbors, who happened to be the newlyweds, Gilford and Catherine Lemmon. "Can we have your set of bunk beds?" she asked. "We only have 2 beds for our four kids." The transaction completed, Leonard and Laurence hauled the extra beds into the Larson tent.

Not used to having nearly 24 hours of sunlight, children stayed outside, exploring and playing till late. Finally, parents called them in and the encampment quieted.

The next day everyone awoke to broad daylight, as if the sun hadn't gone to bed at all. Though a chill hung in the morning air, the sun showed every intention of warming things up as the day went on. The dining car again opened to serve the colonists breakfast. From that point on, each family would be responsible for their own meals. Esther stepped out to go to the privy and stood transfixed once again by the majesty of the mountains that loomed so nearby. The birch trees with their tinge of early spring greenery stood out against a blue sky. Was this place real, or some fairy-tale land? The acrid smell of coal smoke from nearly 100 chimneys bit her nostrils and assured her that she was still firmly on planet Earth. Wet mud squished onto her shoes as she made her way up the path to the outhouses. Not exactly a magic carpet ride. Still, the sense of adventure lightened her steps.

Laura quickly set about organizing her tent. Several railroad tankers filled with water sat on the tracks a short distance from the tents. She sent the girls out to get water, while Laurence collected some wood to supplement the coal for the stove. Leonard and Fred helped with the unloading of supplies and setting up more tents. A second contingent of another hundred families was expected from Michigan and Wisconsin in less than two weeks, and they would need places to stay.

Sunday morning found a large number of worshipers at Rev. Bingle's church. A warm feeling flowed through them as they sang and prayed, thanking God for the chance to come to this new land.

The sun that shone so brightly on the first days of the colonists' life in the Valley eventually gave way to clouds and rain. The mud paths between the tents turned to ribbons of goo. The road next to the railroad tracks became mushier with each vehicle that passed over it. Such was the glory of breakup. Though the surface of the ground might appear to be dried by the warm sun, frost lay only a few inches below. The procession of tires disturbing the slumbering frost transformed the entire area to the consistency of pudding. Men spent as much time pushing stuck vehicles out of the mud as they did off-loading supplies. By evening they were covered from head to toe with muck. Reverend Bingle proved himself a servant of the people as he always seemed to show up when an extra hand was needed, getting as wet and muddy as everyone else.

On chilly, rainy days, the cook stoves which had made the tents unbearably hot in the sun, now worked just to warm them to an acceptable temperature. Huge mosquitoes lurked outside, waiting to gorge themselves on the blood of these newcomers. Every bed soon wore a gauzy dress of netting to keep the pests from continuing their nefarious work through the night.

Even with these inconveniences, the overall feeling among the colonists was one of optimism. The group in charge of the project—the Alaska Rural Rehabilitation Corporation (ARRC)—so far seemed to have planned well for their protégés. In a couple of weeks the land drawing was to be held. At that time, each family would know which plot of land they would live on, and the building of homes could begin.

On a day when there was some free time, Esther and her siblings donned their jodhpurs, high boots and wide brimmed hats and set out to explore their new surroundings. Leonard led the way, as he had already been asking around and knew a little about the layout of the land. They roamed over to watch the wide Matanuska River flow past. "Careful with this river," warned Leonard. "I heard that a person can drown easy in there. You think it's not deep or there's not much current, but it fools you. It's that grayish color 'cause it's got glacier silt in it."

The kids eyed the opaque water uneasily. It certainly didn't look like the clear waters of the lakes and streams back in Minnesota. Esther backed away from the edge. Laurence, ever the fisherman, longed to throw a hook into that watery expanse and see what came out.

Leonard pointed toward the north. "There's gold mines up that way." He paused, watching his siblings' eyes widen. Gold mines! This truly was Alaska. "I been talkin' to some guys from the mines," he continued. "I'm gonna get a job up there."

Back at the tent city, Fred and Laura pored over house plans. The ARRC offered five different designs for homes, featuring from one to three bedrooms. Laura pointed to a two-story, three-bedroom style. "I think this'll be the best one," she said. "The girls will have a bedroom, there's one for the boys, and one for us. And the kitchen's good-sized."

Fred nodded. "Yeah, and I want the three-sided logs. I like that look."

On May 23, everyone gathered for the drawing of 40-acre farm tracts. (The men from the Wisconsin and Michigan contingent showed up on May 22, just hours before the drawing. Their women and children would follow shortly.) The colonists had worked out a system to decide who would draw in what order, and families watched eagerly as the process began. The ARRC representatives—Don Irwin and Colonel Otto Ohlson—mounted a homemade platform with several other dignitaries. Col. Ohlson clutched a shoe box with 204 slips of paper, each with the description of a tract of land. One by one each man stepped up and drew a paper out of the box.

When Fred drew his slip of paper, he made his way through the crowd around a large map of the Matanuska Valley which had been tacked to a post nearby. He located his tract, then went to where Laura and the kids awaited his news.

"We got Tract 24," he informed them. "Looks like we're a ways out of town. We're out past the experimental farm, over toward Wasilla, so we'll be living in Camp 2. There's a transient camp out there and they'll help us build."

Esther was disappointed that their land wasn't closer to Palmer, but she was anxious to get moved out of the tent and into a house. She'd heard about the experimental farm. She knew it was run by the University of Alaska in Fairbanks, and that it conducted experiments in both farm crops and dairy, to find out what things would and would not adapt well to the Alaskan climate.

The family once again packed up their belongings and prepared for the next phase of life in the Far North.

Building the Farm

Westward out of Palmer and on down the road, Fred drove his new team. The two horses were part of the basic set of supplies provided to each colonist to get them started in Alaska. Laura had visited the commissary to stock up on essentials before this move to an area closer to their new property. A dizzying array of goods packed the shelves of the commissary, with credit extended liberally. Still, Laura and Fred both knew that a day would come when every penny they charged now would need to be repaid. At this point, 30 years seemed far away to many of the colonists, but the Larsons were already watching the total accrue. They were not about to let it get so out of hand that they'd be unable to repay their debt. Laura stuck to the basics — sugar, flour, coffee, yeast, canned fruits and vegetables, a sack of beans and some canned meats. That would be enough to get started.

Fred and Laura sat in the front of the wagon, while the four kids rode in the back, holding onto the sewing machine and other items that threatened to slide around with the lurching of the vehicle. With each step, the horses sank several inches into mud and the wagon wheels flipped filthy water onto everything in the wagon. Now and then a wheel dropped into a particularly deep pothole, stopping the wagon's forward motion. The kids jumped off the back of the wagon and put their shoulders against it. When Fred hollered, "Push!" they pushed, and kept pushing till the thick goo relinquished its hold and they could move on.

After nine miles of this sort of stop and go motion, Fred turned up the gravel road that headed toward the town of Wasilla. As the main thoroughfare leading to the experimental farm and Wasilla, this road was firmer than the one they'd just traversed and showed signs of recent grading. The weary horses seemed to perk up as their hooves encountered the more solid surface. A half-mile from the intersection they pulled into Camp 2.

Camp 2 consisted of a couple dozen tents—similar in size and furnishings to the ones back in Palmer—set up at Charlie Merino's farm. Charlie was a homesteader who had offered his land as a temporary squatting place for the colonists until their homes were built. Once again, a row of privies stood near the wood line to accommodate the needs of the group. A large pump in the yard marked the well where the colonists could get water. The first order of business was to pump a bucket of water, heat it to a tolerable temperature, and wash off the coat of grime acquired on the trip from Palmer.

Laura with guitar at Camp 2.

Once settled in their tent, the Larsons set out to get a look at their 40 acres. Their land lay only about a half-mile from Camp 2. Arriving at their tract, the family discovered the land was heavily wooded with spruce trees, interspersed with a few birches. All those trees presented them with both good and bad news. The good news was that they had a

Sawmill at Camp 2.

ready supply of logs for building the house and barn. The bad news was that all those trees had to be cut down — by hand. The men from the nearby transient camp were available to help with the heaviest work, but there was plenty of hard work to go around.

The Larsons' choice of a home with 3-sided logs proved to be a popular one. Three sides of each log were squared off so they fit tightly together. The outside of the house would show the rounded side of the logs, while the inside wall was flat. All of the materials needed for each model were listed so that, once a pattern was chosen, the builders knew how many and what size boards they'd need to complete the job. There was no need to choose a barn design; only one pattern was available. Every barn built by the ARRC looked identical to every other barn.

With help from the transients, the residents of Camp 2 set up a saw mill in Charlie Merino's front yard. As each colonist drove a load of logs down, the logs were sawed to the specifications of their particular house design.

Shortly after the move to Camp 2, Leonard left the family nest. He was sixteen and had no intention of returning to school, as he figured he'd already learned everything he needed to get a job. He badgered the men he'd met from the mines until he managed to get hired on as kitchen help. He expected to help cook, but for a time his main job was washing dishes. It was a job, though, and for a youngster who had never had much opportunity to earn money, it seemed too good to pass up.

Back at the farm site, the men cut and limbed trees, accumulating a huge pile of brush in the process. Fred pressed Esther, Gladys and Laurence into service to clear away the mess. The kids rode in the wagon as he drove the horses back up to their land. On one of their first trips, Esther met with a mishap. As Fred drew the horses to a halt and the kids jumped off the back of the wagon, Esther yelped as a piercing pain shot through her foot.

"Are you hurt?" demanded Gladys, swooping down beside her.

Fred looked back from his seat on the front of the wagon. "What happened to you?" he asked.

Esther clutched her left leg. "I hurt my foot," she groaned.

"Let me take a look at it," said Fred. After examining it, he said, "I think your ankle's broken, but I don't know. Let's get you onto the wagon seat."

Esther stood up, feeling another rush of agony to her foot. She gave a tentative hop. The pain in the jostled joint almost knocked her to the ground again. With Gladys and her dad supporting her she made it to the wagon seat, where she waited in misery while Gladys and Laurence cleared brush and Fred, with help from some neighbor men and several transients, filled the wagon with logs.

Back at the camp, Esther held onto Gladys's shoulder and hopped to their tent. There the two girls filled in their mother on the happenings of the morning.

"Well, I don't know what we're going to do about it; I can't get you to the doctor in Palmer in the shape you're in," said Laura.

Laura made Esther as comfortable as possible, elevating the leg and applying cloths soaked in the cold water from Charlie Merino's well. There was no ice to be had, but the water from deep underground came out at a near-freezing temperature.

That evening Fred showed up with an oddly shaped branch that he'd whittled and fashioned into a crutch. "Here," he said, "See if this helps."

Esther leaned on the crutch. "I think that'll work," she said.

Once she got a rag wrapped around the top to cushion her armpit, the crutch became her third-best friend that summer, the first still being Gladys, and the second, that marvelous pair of glasses.

Years later, when Esther broke her hip, the medical staff noted that her left foot toed in slightly. As it couldn't be connected with the current break, they postulated that it was due to a previous injury. In all likelihood, it happened when she broke her ankle that first summer in Alaska and had to let it heal without proper medical attention.

Work at the property, which they already referred to as "the farm," continued through the summer. One of the first orders of business was to put in a well. Fred hired a local man with well digging experience to help. With a combination of shovels, augers, and buckets to dump the dirt, the well slowly sank deeper. Unfortunately, the water under the Larsons' property lay far beneath the surface. By the time they hit a usable water table, the hole was over 300 feet deep. If anyone in the family was homesick for Minnesota, working the hand pump reminded them of what they'd left behind, as the struggle to get the pump primed and then keep it going was almost as big a challenge as it had been at Clark's Colony.

The sight of the house going up brought renewed energy to the family. A tent was fine for a temporary shelter, but everyone was eager to get a permanent roof over their

The Larsons hauling water on their tract. L-R: Gladys, Laurence, Blackie the horse, Fred and Esther (on crutch).

heads. Once the logs were sawn to the proper size, the house-raising process went quite smoothly for Fred and the transient workers.

In addition to the two horses, any colonists who desired them received a couple of cows to help build the farming utopia envisioned by the project's planners. Fred's real interest lay in dairy farming, and his previous experience with it gave him confidence that he could make dairying profitable. He immediately requested three cows. Over time he managed to acquire several more from folks who had gotten them, then decided they did not want to be bothered caring for the animals.

Laura researched the regulations for setting up a business to sell milk and cream. One major requirement was that all milk had to be processed in an area separate from the living quarters. An edict from the colony honchos stated that all milk and related products were to be sold to the co-op creamery in Palmer, from whence it would be re-sold to individuals, stores in Anchorage, or to the mines. A slight glitch in this plan was that the creamery was not yet built, and the settlers were anxious to get busy earning some money. They'd worry about selling to the creamery when it got built. For now, they'd find customers on their own.

Even before the house went up, Fred built the milk house. Since it wasn't needed yet for processing milk, it would provide a small but adequate living area for the time being. The family moved out of Camp 2 and set up housekeeping in this structure until the house was finished enough to live in.

The farmhouse – unfinished.

So went the summer of 1935. Esther, either aided by the crutch or hopping on her good foot, helped Laura and Gladys wash clothes, clear brush and debris, milk the cows, and prepare three meals a day for the hungry building crew, all from the cramped confines of the milk house. Laurence, as often as he could get permission, took a pole and line down to one of the nearby lakes or streams and fished.

A woman from the Extension Service of the University of Alaska in Fairbanks went from house to house (or tent to tent as it often happened) instructing the women on preparing and cooking the native plants and animals they found outside their doors. Homemakers' clubs sprang up across the Valley, as women from the various camps sought support and ideas from their neighbors. Laura was an active member, and even wrote a theme song for the club from Camp 2. Borrowing the tune from "Home on the Range", she entitled it "Home on the Farm":

> There's a place that we love;
> It's the home that we've made,
> It's a place for our loved ones to dwell.
> How we make these homes bright
> With our love, work and might,
> Is a story I gladly will tell.
>
> The Homemakers' Club
> Has taken the rub
> Out of most of the farm women's life;
> They sew, cook and can,
> They knit, plant and plan,
> Prepare for the cold winter nights.
>
> Chorus:
> Home, home on the farm,
> Where the homemakers practice their art,
> The place to abide, and close to our side
> Our families all do their good part.

By late summer, the shell of the house was up and ready for occupation. Though bare studs served as room dividers for a time, the family was happy to again be living in a "real" house. Esther and Gladys shared one of the bedrooms upstairs, and Laurence had another. Their parents' room was on the main floor, along with the kitchen and living room. There was no electricity, and an outhouse furnished toilet facilities.

In mid-August word came to the colonists that Wiley Post and Will Rogers were in Alaska, and would be making a brief stop in Palmer the following day. The bus that ran from Wasilla to Palmer would pick up anybody who wished to see them.

Laura jumped at the chance. Though she wasn't an aviation buff, she followed the news and knew that these two men were on a historic trip. Besides, it's always fun to rub elbows with somebody famous. She and the kids boarded the bus and rode into Palmer for a day of socialization.

A carnival-like atmosphere prevailed as the crowd assembled in Palmer. Colonists whom the family had gotten acquainted with over the past few months gathered, greeting each other like long lost friends. People swapped stories of the hardships and successes they met as they worked on their individual tracts of land scattered throughout the Valley.

Suddenly someone yelled, "Here they come!"

All eyes turned skyward toward a small dot that slowly grew larger. The plane landed in an open field and everyone pressed forward to see the celebrities. Three men climbed out. Will Rogers was instantly recognizable to most of the group, as they had seen his movies or read his humorous writings. Wiley Post, with his eye patch, was nearly as well-known, especially to those with an interest in aviation. A local pilot who flew them from Anchorage was the third occupant of the plane.

Because of the crowd, Laura and her children only caught glimpses of the famous men talking and joking with those lucky enough to get close to them. All too soon the three men re-boarded the plane and roared off into the sky. "Well," said Laura, "even if we didn't actually get to talk to them, I'm glad we came. This is history."

She didn't know how true her words were. The next day, a neighbor dropped by the farm with news. "I just heard that Will Rogers and Wiley Post died in a plane crash up around Barrow," he said.

The Larsons felt almost as if they'd lost a member of their family. "We just saw them yesterday," Esther said sadly. "They seemed like such nice people, and so alive. I can't believe they're dead." A somber mood hung over the family for several days as they contemplated the harshness and potential for tragedy in this rugged land.

September arrived; it was time for the kids to head to school. Esther was disappointed to learn that the Palmer school was not yet completed. She, Gladys and Laurence would have to attend school in Wasilla. Since the Larsons' farm was located near the road to Wasilla, this wasn't an inconvenience, but Esther still didn't like it. In her mind, her family had come to Alaska to live in Palmer and she considered herself a resident of Palmer. She'd go to school in Wasilla for now, but she fully intended to transfer as soon as she could.

Many of the colonists lived too far away to make the daily trip to Wasilla for school. These groups set up temporary schools near their tracts of land where the kids could attend until Palmer got its school built.

While their children settled into the routine of school, Fred and Laura worked to turn the farm from a money "taker" to a money maker. Thanks to their contact through Leonard, they had learned that the gold mines would pay for daily milk delivery. A few residents of the nearby settlement of Matanuska also agreed to buy milk. Soon Fred had a group of customers who put in orders for milk several times a week.

Once the family moved into the farm house, Laura prepared the milk house for processing milk. She scrubbed every surface and set up the separator and churn. Once the lakes froze over, Fred cut chunks of ice and stored them under sawdust in the shady back corner of the milk house. He purchased an ice box from the co-op and positioned it near the stored ice. The ice box had two compartments — a top one which held ice and a bottom section for the milk.

Fred also added a room onto the end of the milk house to be used as a laundry shed.

Building the barn.

Though the barn remained unfinished till the following year, it provided some protection for the cows and horses as the weather turned colder. With the milk house set up, the dairy business began in earnest. Twice each day, Fred milked the cows and brought the buckets of warm, fragrant milk to the milk house. There, Laura strained it to remove any impurities, poured some into large cans, and put the rest into the separator. From one spout came cream, and from the other issued skim milk, that hated drink from Minnesota days. As skim milk was thought at that time to be of little nutritional value, it was sold at a cheap price for feeding calves.

Cream was the money crop. Laura poured about a gallon of it into her square glass churn. The lid of the jar held a handle above and metal paddles below that stuck down into the cream-filled jar. Laura cranked, watching as the cream went from a thick, smooth consistency to a whipped froth. Finally, small flecks of yellow appeared and the froth turned to thin liquid. Another few minutes of cranking gave the tiny bits of butter time to merge until they became one lump floating in a shallow sea of bluish buttermilk.

Laura set the buttermilk aside, knowing that Fred considered it a special treat. She went to work on the butter. Placing the lump into a bowl of cold water, she began mashing, turning, and squishing the mass with a wooden spoon. All traces of milk had to be worked out, otherwise the butter would quickly turn rancid. If any sign of milkiness appeared in the bowl of water, Laura dumped it and refilled it with fresh water. When satisfied that the butter was as pure as she could make it, she pulled out her wooden butter mold. Packed as full as possible, the mold held one-quarter pound. Laura turned the chunks out onto waxed paper, and wrapped them securely. She made sure the lids were secured on the cans of whole milk and, along with the pats of butter, stored them in the ice box until Fred's next milk run.

On delivery days, Fred loaded the wagon with the cans of milk, cream and butter, hitched up the team, and set off on his route. After only a couple of trips with the horses and wagon, Fred returned to tell his wife, "This isn't gonna work, Laura. It takes too darn long to drive the horses all the way to the mines and back. I can't get anything else done. I'm gonna have to get a car."

Laura protested, knowing this would add to their ever-growing debt, but Fred eventually convinced her. With the work that had to get done and long distances between destinations, a car was the only way to make it work. Though the roads were little more than muddy tracks and vehicles got stuck on a regular basis, a car would still save time in the long run. Fred got a good deal on a Chevy coupe with a rumble seat, and this became his delivery vehicle.

As the days got shorter and nights turned frosty, the colonists realized that those cows and horses they'd received would need to be fed through the winter months when they couldn't find their own food. Everyone had been so busy this first summer, building homes and clearing property that very little planting had gotten done. There was some grass they could harvest for hay, so the men joined forces to help each other put up at least a portion for their livestock's winter feed. The ground was too wet for the hay to dry, so they drove long poles into the ground and stacked the hay on them. The rest of the animals' food supply had to be shipped up from the Lower 48, at a huge cost.

Top right, The Larsons' farm near Palmer.

Bottom: Laura and Fred in front of the farm house.

School in the Valley

Despite her initial objections, Esther enjoyed her year of school in Wasilla. Many of the colonists' children were in the same situation she was, attending school in Wasilla while they awaited completion of the Palmer school. Because the Larson property was on the main road near the experimental farm, the bus picked them up in front of their house and transported them the seven miles to school.

At home, work kept Esther and her siblings too busy to go gadding about, so school gave her an opportunity to form friendships with kids near her own age. Because of her small size, the fact that she was several years older than the others in her class never became an issue. Esther was a late bloomer and fit in well with her eighth grade classmates in that most awkward of ages between childhood and adulthood. While

Laurence, Esther, bus driver and Gladys, ready for school, 1935.

some of the girls were showing interest in boys and fussing with hair and makeup, recess gave them all a chance to be kids. A hill near the school furnished entertainment during the winter, as everyone took turns using sheets of cardboard as sleds.

By the fall of 1936 the Palmer school opened. Esther was now in 9th grade and excited to start high school. Still determined to attend the school of her choice, she lobbied until she convinced Gladys and Laurence to join her. They had to walk a mile down to the main road (which is now the Glenn Highway), where the three caught the bus into Palmer.

At her new school Esther soon struck up a friendship with a girl named Sally, whose parents were also colonists. They lived on the far side of the Valley from the Larson tract. Instead of trying to farm, Sally's father set up a saw mill operation, which provided lumber for the building projects going on around the Valley, a good income for him, and employment for many of the younger men.

Sally was an only child and seemed hungry for contact with girls of her age. She and Esther could not have been more different in temperament. Shy, hard-working Esther wouldn't dream of trying to call attention to herself, while Sally was outgoing, flirtatious and always ready for a good time. They complemented each other, as Sally encouraged Esther to come out of her shell a bit, and Esther's cautious nature kept Sally's most outrageous inclinations in check.

Before long, Sally began inviting her new friend to visit her at home, and there Esther became acquainted with her parents, Ted and Marta. They also took a liking to Esther, and encouraged her to come as often as possible. Finally, Sally's mother wrote to Esther's folks, suggesting that Esther stay with them for the remainder of the school year, as a companion for her daughter and to make it easier for her to go to Palmer School.

Esther may have been naïve, but she was far from stupid. She realized that Sally's parents had ulterior motives for inviting her to live with them. For one thing, the saw mill operation needed an extra pair of hands during meal times. Sally's mother prepared meals for the saw mill workers and Sally was supposed to serve; however, Sally considered flirting with the men infinitely more important than feeding them. Esther who, when she had a job to do, kept her head down and her feet moving, made a much more dependable waitress than her friend. She also could, as she put it, "slam through a pan of dirty dishes" while Sally made one giggling trip through the mess hall. The girls helped with breakfast before they went to school and with supper in the evenings. Esther knew she was being used as unpaid help, but figured it was worth it to be able to attend the school she wanted.

Sally's fascination with the male of the species was evident to everyone. As Esther said to herself, Sally would chase anything that wore pants. Sally's parents knew this made her an easy target for unscrupulous men, but they still had trouble clipping the wings of their only chick. This was where Esther came in. If Sally wanted to go out with a fellow, her folks figured there was safety in numbers. As long as Esther chaperoned, Sally would have to behave with some degree of decorum.

The school year passed happily for Esther. She enjoyed school, both the academic and social sides of it. Sally's parents treated her well and she reciprocated by working willingly for them.

Summer of 1937

Esther wrapped her arms around a 2-gallon metal can filled with milk and lugged it out to the car, which stood with the side door open, ready to receive its load. She shoved the can into the area behind the back seat and went to the milk house for another can. Her dad met her on the way, carrying a wire basket filled with glass bottles of milk. Without speaking the two continued working until all the milk containers sat ready for transport. They then loaded handmade pats of butter and cartons of eggs from Laura's chickens. Then Esther slid into the passenger's seat, while Fred took the wheel.

Once the school year ended, Esther had said good-by to Sally and returned home to help on the farm. One of her jobs was to accompany her dad on his daily milk deliveries around the Valley.

Without appearing to, Esther watched her dad carefully as he pulled out of the yard. She had a goal for this summer that Fred knew nothing about. She was about to turn 17, and she was determined to learn to drive the car. Fred seemed to take it for granted that the girls wouldn't be interested in operating the car, especially considering Laura's past experience.

Several years before they left Minnesota, a moment of distraction had caused Laura to stop driving. As she drove home from Ranier one day, the men working in the gravel pits caught her attention. Some of them were family friends; they waved at her and seemed to be clowning around, gesturing with their arms and making faces. Laura waved back, laughing. Suddenly, she realized that their arm-waving was not a salutation but a warning, as her car dived off the road and into the deep ditch. Unhurt except for her pride, she suffered the laughter and teasing of the men as they helped to push her car back up onto the road. Laura drove home, parked the car, and never drove again.

Now Fred drove the eight miles of gravel road into Wasilla, stopping occasionally while Esther scooted out and delivered a bottle of milk or some eggs to their regular customers. On past Wasilla, another eight miles brought them to the Fern Mine, where Leonard worked. He came out to greet them and helped unload the milk cans.

After two years on their Alaska farm, Esther's parents knew that this dairy business was losing money. What they earned barely covered the cost of keeping the animals, not to mention the expenses for the family. The great hopes of the organizers of the colonization program were not panning out for all of the participants. Many of the original colonists had left, with reasons ranging from homesickness to inability to make a living. Fred and Laura knew they had nothing to return to in Minnesota, so continued to do their best with what they had, hoping that someday they would turn a profit.

When Esther and her dad returned home, she got out of the car, knowing that soon Fred would leave to help out over at a neighbor's property. When he left, she slid into the driver's seat and tucked her coat behind her back in order to get close enough for her feet to reach the pedals.

She reached for the key, which her dad always left in the ignition. What better place to leave it, where you'd always know where to find it? Theft was not a big problem at the time, and everyone left keys in cars and doors to their houses unlocked. Looking at the floor, she moved her feet to the clutch, brake and gas pedals. She'd memorized every move her dad made when he drove, so it shouldn't be too difficult.

Esther pushed in the clutch and turned the key. The car obligingly hiccupped to life. Carefully she pushed the gear shift into the position Fred always put it when he started out.

Grasping the steering wheel with both hands, she slowly eased her foot off the clutch. The car frog-hopped a couple of times, then died. Undaunted, Esther started it again. This time she pushed tentatively on the gas as she let out the clutch. The car gave a bigger lurch, and once more expired.

This wasn't quite as easy as it had seemed from the passenger's seat. For several more minutes Esther started, clutched, gassed, and killed the motor. With each try, though, she felt a little more comfortable with it. Now she had an even better idea what to watch for.

The next dairy run found her scrutiny of Fred's driving techniques more intense than ever. "Ah," she thought, "that's how he keeps the motor from dying," as Fred smoothly coordinated his foot and hand movements. She took note of the sounds of the motor before, during and after each shift, and memorized her dad's manipulation of the clutch, brake and gas pedals.

Over the next week she practiced every day. She thought she was doing this on the sly, not knowing that in the house her mother and Gladys were tracking her progress, hooting whenever the car lurched, causing her head to snap back and forth like a paddle ball. "Look, Mom," said Gladys one day, "she's figuring out how to go frontwards. Oh, now she's backing up." The two stood, heads together, staring out the kitchen window. The car lunged backwards, and the watching pair whooped again as the Chevy coughed and quit. But Esther didn't quit. The watchers heard the motor start again, and this time, the car rolled smoothly backwards. There wasn't a lot of room for maneuvering in the yard, but Esther took advantage of what space she had, guiding the car the few yards forward and back. By the end of the week Laura and Gladys had lost interest, as good driving wasn't nearly as much fun to watch. Esther always took care, at the end of her self-taught lesson, to park the car in the exact place Fred had left it. Why she thought her dad would object to her driving is not clear; perhaps, like all teens, she couldn't resist the idea of doing something just a little sneaky.

Once she'd mastered the technique, she continued to move the car back and forth in the yard every day. Her chance to branch out finally came one afternoon when Fred entered the house. "I need to go into Palmer to see about a job at the new creamery in the morning. I'm not gonna have time to go up to the mines. I can take the bus into Palmer, but who's gonna do the deliveries?"

Esther piped up, "I'll take the milk to the mines."

"You!" Fred brushed aside her offer. "I need somebody who can drive the car, not just help with the delivery."

"I can drive," Esther persisted.

"Nah, you can't. When did you learn to drive?"

"I've been practicing in the yard."

Unconvinced, Fred said, "Come and show me."

The two walked to the car, and Esther slid into the driver's seat and tucked her coat behind her. Carefully she started the car and backed it around. Now was not the time to get rattled and make the car do its leap frog act. At Fred's direction, she eased out onto the quiet main road. The car responded smoothly to her hand and foot commands, and after a while her dad said, "All right. From now on you can deliver the milk by yourself."

Esther knew that Fred was impressed and trusted her driving. Her family was not given to handing out compliments, and Esther knew those few words were the closest Fred would come to praising her driving.

That first trip presented some challenges, as the farm yard was a great deal flatter than the road up to the mines. Still, she kept in mind what she'd learned from watching her dad — how the different sounds of the engine meant time to shift, and how well-coordinated movements made for greater success. And if she killed the engine a few times in those early days, well, no one was around to tell on her.

Esther got extra practice driving when Fred decided to take part of his dairy herd up toward the mines, where they'd have better grazing. Most of the cows he moved were pregnant so were "dry" — not producing milk at the time — but some were still milking. Fred raised a tent as a temporary shelter, and when not working at the creamery he often slept in the tent. When he was unavailable, Esther would drive Laurence or Gladys up to watch the herd. Before long, Esther taught both Gladys and Laurence how to drive.

Later that same summer, a letter arrived from Alice. Correspondence from Alice always caused a stir of excitement, as the family would be sure to hear the latest goings-on with friends and family back in the International Falls area.

Over the past two years, Alice's letters had expressed a deepening affection for Claude and Margaret, the two children she was caring for, and respect and liking for Ed, their father and her employer. Now Alice wrote that she was coming to Alaska for a visit and was bringing her youngest charge, Margaret, with her.

"Oh," said Esther, "it would be so nice to see everyone back there again…Gladys Thomas, Mary Jean Anderson…" She named a couple of her special friends. "I wonder what's happening with them."

Her mother didn't say much at the time, but a few days later she brought up the subject. "Esther, how would you like to go back to Minnesota with Alice and go to school there for a year?"

How would she like it! Esther could barely contain her excitement. Although Alaska was a beautiful place, to go back and spend time with the kids she grew up with, go to school with them again, roam her old haunts…it was a dream come true. Wouldn't her friends be surprised to see her! The following days saw her performing her chores as usual on the farm, but her mind had already transported her back to Minnesota.

Alice and Margaret arrived in early August. Margaret, whom they had met before leaving Minnesota, was only a few years younger than Esther. Alice seemed to have a special glow about her which couldn't be completely explained by the excitement of reuniting with her family. She soon burst out, unable to contain her joy any longer: "Ed has asked me to marry him!"

"You're getting married?" shrieked Gladys.

"I thought Ed was an old man," put in Esther, realizing only after the words were out how tactless they were.

"He's quite a bit older, but he's been wonderful to me and I want to marry him," Alice stated firmly. In fact, Ed was a year older than Fred, which made him 21 years older than his intended bride. To a teenager like Esther he must have seemed ancient, but Alice, who was mature beyond her years, clearly didn't see a problem.

Laura had reservations, but her daughter's confident demeanor eventually convinced her that Ed would be good to her and make her happy. Though her own relationship with Fred was becoming increasingly rocky, she still felt marriage was the best way for a girl to ensure a secure future.

Alice and Margaret wanted to experience all this new place called Alaska had to offer in their few weeks of vacation. They plunged into the farm work, helping to herd the cows, take care of the chickens, work in the milk house — all the preparation and clean-up involved in a home dairy operation. Laurence showed them his favorite fishing holes in the nearby rivers and streams. Leonard even took some time off from his job at the mine to spend time with the visitors.

A day of blueberry picking turned into a special outing as Margaret, Laura and all five of the Larson offspring decked out in jodhpurs and boots for a foray into the wilds

Above: Esther, Gladys, Alice, and Alice's step-daughter, Margaret, ready to go berry picking, 1937.

Right: Leonard and Esther clowning around.

of the berry fields. They hung canning jars on their belts to collect their harvest, and shouldered shotguns in case any bears should prove foolish enough to intercept the rowdy crew. As Laura surveyed the group she knew she needed pictures to remember this special day. Everyone hammed it up for the camera, filling the farm yard with laughter and joking. At one point Leonard lit a cigarette and Esther—who, like her mother, strongly disapproved of smoking—scolded him for falling prey to the habit. Why she hung a cigarette out of her own mouth remains a mystery, but Laura's snapshot of Esther grasping Leonard by the ear captured the spirit of the moment.

In addition to enjoying the time with her big sister and future step-niece, Esther continued to anticipate going back to International Falls for the school year. All her plans came crashing down when Laura called her aside and told her, "We're not going to be able to send you back with Alice. I'm sorry we got your hopes up, but we just don't have the money. Maybe we can try again next year."

"But you promised! You said I could go. I've got it all planned out!" The pain-filled cries rushed to her mouth as Esther stared at her mother in hurt and confusion; however, in the Larson home talking back to an adult was not tolerated. So the words stopped, unspoken, like bitter stones weighing down her tongue. Laura continued trying to explain the situation, obviously hoping to soften the devastating blow.

Esther swallowed the angry words, feeling them settle into a hard lump deep inside. She knew money was tight, and the milk and eggs they sold didn't cover the family's expenses. She never should have planned to go. She wished her mother had never suggested it. She nodded and agreed with her mother that she was right, that it would be better to plan a trip when the family's financial situation improved. With clenched teeth she did her best to put on a brave face. And when the tears finally came, no one saw them except the animals in the barn.

The day Alice and Margaret left, Esther stood with the rest of the family at the depot in Palmer, waving at the train as it chugged off toward Anchorage. Anger and sorrow churned inside as she watched it leave. She should be on that train! She should have been allowed to go with them. She had never felt the unfairness of life as she did in that moment.

Alice wrote letters telling of her wedding plans, and the pictures that eventually arrived showed her and Ed and the children beaming with happiness. Esther was glad for Alice, but the lump of resentment remained inside her for a long time.

Letting Go of Disappointment:
"It Could be Worse"

Esther reluctantly returned to Palmer High School for her sophomore year. The disappointment of not going back to Minnesota affected her attitude for a while, then her common sense took over. She had suffered a severe disappointment; now it was up to her to deal with it. Life would go on, and sulking wouldn't get her anywhere. And as Laura had said, maybe next year there would be enough money for her to go.

Her friend Sally provided a welcome distraction for her unhappiness. Just a few days into the new school year, Sally again invited her to come and stay with her. After receiving the okay from her folks, Esther agreed. As before, in addition to being companion and confidante for Sally, Esther worked mornings and evenings serving food for the sawmill workers. Being used to hard work, she took it in stride, realizing that by keeping busy she kept the blues from enveloping her. Besides, there was always Saturday night to look forward to.

Most Saturdays brought a dance either at Palmer High School or at the community center down in Matanuska. Sally never wanted to miss out on any social function that would involve boys, and Esther, who loved to dance, was glad to go along. Ted, Sally's father, usually took them to the dances, while Marta preferred to stay home.

Sally made the most of the dances, laughing and making eyes at every boy in sight. Esther had a natural grace and sense of rhythm, so she never lacked for partners. Before Ted left them to their own devices he always said, "Now, remember to save one dance for me." Sometimes Esther had to turn down invitations in order to keep an opening for her friend's dad, but she always honored his request.

A high point at nearly every dance came when the Simpsons performed. Regardless of whether the dance was a polka, schottische or waltz, their steps remained consistent. Flapping his arms, Mr. Simpson trotted in rhythm with the music, while his missus hopped alongside like a plump little chickadee. Their abandoned twirls endangered anyone in the immediate area, so the rest of the dancers obligingly cleared the floor while this couple enjoyed their dance.

Esther also looked forward to the weekly dances because they gave her an opportunity to see Gladys. Though she didn't mind staying with Sally, she missed sharing life with her sister. The two usually managed to spend a few minutes during the dance, catching up on each other's lives.

One evening, Gladys pointed out a fellow who appeared to be a few years older than the majority of the merrymakers. "See that guy over there? The one who's almost stepping on his own feet? That's Lionel Haakenson. He's been staying with us and working on the farm for Papa for several weeks. He seems like a nice guy, and a really hard worker. He sometimes speaks Norwegian with Papa. I guess his family back in North Dakota spoke only Norwegian at home until his older sisters started school."

Esther looked in the direction indicated by Gladys. She saw a man in his mid-twenties with blue eyes and light brown hair that he wore combed back from his forehead. He shuffled his feet, looking confused as he strove to follow the rhythm of the lively polka. He obviously came for the socialization. He danced because that's what one did at a dance, but he seemed to prefer standing around visiting and joking with everyone.

"I know him a little bit," Esther replied. "He worked at Ted's saw mill for a while. In fact, he brought Sally and me to the dance one night when her dad couldn't come." Her cheeks reddened at the memory of that episode. "Sally made me ask him if he'd pick us up for the dance. He said 'sure' and picked me up right then and carried me out the door! He was joking around, but I was so embarrassed!"

Gladys laughed. "Well, I can tell you he's probably not looking for a girlfriend. He has a picture of a girl back home—Gwilet..." she chuckled at the unusual name. "I thought her name was Violet when he first said it, but he corrected me. He keeps her picture beside his bed. It's got a thumbprint worn in one corner where he's picked it up so much."

Esther spent little time thinking about the new guy from North Dakota. She had a cadre of regulars she could count on to dance with. A young man named Irv recently had started showing her special attention, and she returned his interest. Unlike some of the other guys, he never needed to be scolded for smuggling a bottle into the dance, or for using bad language or getting too fresh.

Sometimes when she and Gladys chatted, the news from home was less pleasant. Their mom and dad were fighting all the time it seemed. Leonard was doing a lot of drinking, being around those mine workers. One week Esther noticed Gladys was distracted and starry-eyed.

"Uh-oh," thought Esther, "She's got a crush on someone." Gladys's vivacious personality drew men to her. She had a happy-go-lucky attitude that at times seemed to keep her from considering the long-range consequences of her actions. Esther felt obligated to keep her younger sister from blundering innocently into a situation which could ruin her reputation.

She watched Gladys surreptitiously as everyone danced with various partners. One man kept coming back to Gladys, and the two seemed entirely too friendly, especially considering that the guy was married. This was the last straw—she had to get back home where she could keep a closer eye on her sister. Sally's parents would just have to look after their daughter themselves.

She maneuvered so that when the dance ended she was near Gladys. Knowing better than to confront her directly about the folly of getting involved with a married man, she came at the problem from a different angle. She grabbed Gladys's arm and spoke quietly but urgently. "Tell Mama to write Sally's mother a letter saying she needs me at home. I want to come home!"

Surprised, Gladys questioned her, but finally agreed to relay the message to their mother.

Less than a week later, Esther returned to the family farm. She had to go back to walking the mile down to the intersection to catch the school bus to Palmer, but she was at peace with the decision. Though she couldn't make her parents' relationship get better or keep Leonard from drinking, she chaperoned Gladys as diligently as she had Sally, and soon managed to separate her sister from her ill-chosen swain.

Dark Days

The summer of 1938 passed with little time for play. As he had the past summer, Fred relocated part of his dairy herd to graze up near the mines, and his kids took turns staying with them and ferrying milk home, where Laura prepared it for sale.

Nothing more was ever mentioned about school in Minnesota; still Esther began her junior year that fall with a sense of relief, glad to be back in school where she could immerse herself in friendships and studies. For a few hours each day she could forget the tensions building at home.

The farm, which according to the optimistic program planners should now be self-supporting, continued to lose money. One of the main reasons for this was the difficulty in marketing the produce. To earn enough money to feed both the animals and the family required a large number of customers—customers which were spread out from the mines north of Palmer to Matanuska. With all of the colonists vying for the same customer base, it had become obvious to Fred, despite his expertise in the dairy business, that he couldn't make a living with his small herd. His job at the creamery in Palmer helped bring in some money, but it, combined with the milk and egg income, barely supported the family. It also took him away from home for many hours, preventing him from making improvements on the property or keeping the buildings and vehicles maintained. And always, the specter of that 30-year loan loomed large in his thoughts. The stress of once again having money problems affected his relationship with Laura, as they bickered and sniped at each other out of sheer frustration.

Laurence was put in charge of caring for and milking the cows, while Laura and the girls processed the milk and took care of the chickens and eggs. All the produce now was required to go to the co-op creamery — recently named "Matanuska Maid" — so Fred packed the milk, butter and eggs into the car and took them with him when he went to work.

During that winter, Matanuska Maid offered Fred the job of manager for the newly-formed Anchorage distribution branch. In order to be near the job he moved into Anchorage and lived in rooms above the business. Laura, Esther, Gladys and Laurence remained on the farm, pouring all their efforts into trying to turn the dairy and egg business into a profitable production.

One spring day the kids came home from school and found Laura in a rage. She had somehow discovered that Fred was seeing Mrs. Hartfield — a married neighbor woman with a gaggle of daughters. "No wonder he was so anxious to get out of here and take that job in Anchorage!" she shouted. "Well, she's welcome to him. Let's see if he can support all her kids when he can't take care of his own!"

Stunned, the children stared at each other as Laura continued her rant. Esther's heart felt that it had not only dropped into her feet, but continued down to the depths of Hell. How could her father do this? He was married to her mother. He had no business carrying on with another woman. What was to become of the family? Even though Fred showed little affection to his kids and left the discipline to his wife, he was still the head of the family, and was always ready to help in his quiet, brusque way. Now his three youngest children stood as if frozen in place. The spell was broken when Laurence threw his lunch bucket across the room and rushed out the door.

School limped to its close with very little interest shown by any of the Larsons. Gladys was the first to face the fact that, without the money Fred brought in, the farm was not going to support them. "I'm gonna go see about getting a job in Palmer," she announced soon after the end of school.

Within days, she had secured a job working in the kitchen at the barracks that housed school teachers and other government employees. Though, as an entry-level job, it brought in only a few dollars a week, it was money and every penny helped.

Following Gladys's example, Esther also applied for work at the barracks. Unfortunately, the boss took one look at her delicate form and turned her down, convinced she wasn't up to the job. Esther returned home and continued working on the farm with her mother and Laurence. Instead of driving the milk route up to the mines, she now drove her wares directly to the Mat Maid creamery in Palmer.

About this same time, Esther suffered another blow when her boyfriend, Irv, showed up at her door. Irv had moved to Palmer about the same time as the colonists, and now split his time between working in the Valley during the winter and fishing Bristol Bay in western Alaska in the summer. She and Irv had gotten acquainted over the past few years, first as part of a larger group of friends, then as an "item." Content with having a Christian boyfriend who treated her with kindness and respect, Esther enjoyed his company but refused to think far beyond their immediate uncomplicated situation.

Her feelings of security in that relationship ended with a painful meeting. When he arrived it was obvious Irv had something on his mind. She invited him to the kitchen, where they could talk a little more privately, without her mother or siblings listening to every word.

"I've been thinking," he began. "I'm going home to Wisconsin to visit my family when I get back from fishing this summer. How about we get married and you can go meet them too?" Esther opened her mouth to respond, but he rushed on. "The World's Fair is going on in San Francisco. We could take the boat to California first and then go back to Wisconsin."

San Francisco! She would love to know if that bridge she'd seen as they left had ever gotten finished. Esther hated what she had to do, but knew she had no choice. In view of her parents' problems, marriage was not her favorite institution right then. And she had a second reason.

"I can't marry you," she told Irv. "I'm going to graduate from high school before I think about getting married."

Irv looked down at the table for a long moment; finally he raised his eyes to Esther. "Well, I guess I'll see you when I get back then." He leaned over and gave her a kiss, walked to his car, climbed in and drove away. Esther knew in her heart that, in choosing education over marriage, she had sent Irv an unmistakable message. He was ready for marriage; she was not. He would not wait around for her. He would interpret this as the end of their relationship.

When September rolled around, none of the Larson kids considered returning to school. Survival was their focus. Still, Esther considered her schooling on hold rather than finished. She knew, without a doubt, that she would someday receive her high school diploma.

The farm had become a dreary place where its inhabitants stayed simply because there was nowhere else to go. Laura continued to fume over Fred's infidelity. Laurence, with no stable force in his life, expressed his hurt and confusion in anger. He and his sisters argued almost constantly. It often seemed to Esther that the only time he was content was when he was working with the cows and horses. He loved animals, and treated them with much more kindness than he did the humans in his small sphere.

Such chaos could not go on indefinitely. Early in 1940 Laura gave in to the inevitable and acknowledged that the farm was not going to bring in enough money even for her family's simple needs. And, after some time of reflection, she knew that she would never agree to a divorce. When she'd married Fred, she had taken him, among other things, "for better or worse." These past months were definitely in the "worse" category, but now it was up to her to make it better. She wouldn't let this other woman waltz in and take her husband without putting up a fight.

With that in mind, Laura packed her clothes and boarded the train to Anchorage. Sometime previously — probably during the optimistic early days in Alaska — she and Fred had bought a small house a few blocks out of the main Anchorage business district. It had been sitting vacant, but Laura decided to make it her base of operations in her quest to restore her marriage and remove Fred from the clutches of Mrs. Hartfield.

Gladys had quit her job at the barracks to help out at home. Now she, Esther and Laurence remained on the farm. The plan was for them to carry on the dairy and egg business, but other issues soon intruded, making that scheme unworkable.

Over the past months Laurence had grown from the easy-going baby of the family into a surly young man. Not quite 16, he was already nearly 6 feet tall, wiry and strong. He decided, once Laura left, that he was boss of the farm. Perhaps, with the disintegration of his parents' relationship, and feeling as if they had both deserted him, he clung to the farm as the one thing in his life he did control. Whatever the reason, the heavy-handed bullying from their younger brother didn't sit well with the girls and they let him know it. Unfortunately, their resistance merely caused him to focus all his anger on them.

The first time it happened it took the girls by surprise. Gladys came in from the chicken coop to be greeted by Laurence's challenge, "Did you get that coop actually clean, or did you slop through it like you usually do?"

Gladys snapped, "The coop is a lot cleaner than you ever got it."

"What about the barn?" Laurence demanded.

"That's your job," Gladys shot back. "You need to do something around here."

Laurence's fist flashed out and connected with Gladys's cheek; she reeled backwards until the wall stopped her.

"What do you think you're doing!" Esther blazed to her sister's defense. "Don't you hit her!"

Laurence swung around and his open hand caught Esther across the mouth. "I'm in charge here! You might's well get used to it." He slammed out the door and headed toward the barn.

Shaken, Esther and Gladys stared at each other. This was a side of Laurence they'd never seen. Though sullen and quick with angry words, he'd never lashed out at them physically before. Finally, Esther pulled out a couple of dish cloths and dipped them in the water bucket. She wrung out the cold water and handed a cloth to Gladys to put on the bruise that was already showing on her face, and applied the other to her own swollen lip.

Similar scenarios continued to play out over the next days. No matter what his sisters did Laurence found something to criticize, and seemed to look for excuses to knock one or the other of them around. The final showdown came on a rainy February day.

Esther lifted the burner off the cook stove and poked a piece of wood into the fire box. Discovering the fire had gone out she pulled the match box from the shelf above the stove and stuffed some paper under the wood. Laurence sat at the kitchen table with a pile of bent nails and a hammer. Taking each nail, he hammered it straight so it could be reused. He looked up. "It's about time you started making something to eat."

Esther didn't bother to turn around. Though she fully intended to prepare a meal for everyone his tone raised her hackles. "What makes you think I'm cooking for you?" she sneered. "Gladys and I do all the work around here. You can find your own food."

Pain exploded through her back as Laurence slammed the hammer between her shoulder blades. The impact drove her forward into the stove shelf and knocked her glasses off. The unlit match fell harmlessly into the fire box. Esther clutched the shelf with both hands, feeling tears prick her eyelids as she fought for breath. She sensed Laurence's presence behind her, as if he was waiting for her to say something—anything—that would give him a reason to hit her again. She remained silent until she heard him go out the door.

Carefully she moved her shoulders then tilted her head from side to side. Despite the pain, nothing seemed to be broken. She replaced her glasses with shaking fingers.

"That's it," she told herself. Wincing, she put on her coat and headed out to the chicken coop, where she knew she'd find Gladys. She made sure Laurence was out of earshot in the barn then said, "I've had it. I'm leaving." She recounted the incident and ended by saying, "I'm going to Anchorage. I don't know how, but I'm gettin' out of here."

"Let's just take the car and go," said Gladys. There was no need for discussion about whether the sisters would go together; as always, if one needed support the other was there to provide it.

"No, we can't do that…Laurence would hear it and stop us. We need to sneak out somehow."

That night, once they were sure Laurence was asleep, they made their move. They donned several layers of their warmest shirts and the woolen jodhpurs that had served them well since they'd arrived in Alaska. Overshoes, coats, mittens and wool berets completed their outfits. Each carried a flashlight and a small bundle of extra clothes.

Cold rain hit their faces as they picked their way along the road. Southcentral Alaska was in the grip of one of its winter "warm" spells, when daytime temperatures neared 40 degrees and hovered just below freezing each night. A thick layer of ice and snow always covered the roads throughout the winter months, but now the daily freeze-thaw cycle turned them into sheets of ice.

When planning this escape, the girls had been confident that they would hitch a ride soon after hitting the main road toward Anchorage. Now, walking along a pitch black roadway, the probability of anyone else taking the notion into their heads to set out for Anchorage at midnight in an icy rain seemed less and less plausible. After an hour, Esther noticed her flashlight growing dim. Soon Gladys's also gave out, and the girls continued through the blackness. A white ribbon of crusty snow along the shoulder of the road glowed faintly in the dark and afforded a little traction for them to walk.

Though the rain was light, a breeze drove the chill through their coats and shirts. They shivered, but knew there was no turning back.

Before long, despite the seriousness of the situation, Gladys's ready sense of humor bubbled to the surface. "What do you think Laurence will do when he gets up in the morning and we're not there?" She imitated his gruff growl, "Hey! Get up and make me some breakfast!" She resumed her normal voice: "Won't he be surprised to find out he's talking to himself! Let's see how he likes doing all the chores without his slaves."

Laughter warmed them for a while, but a long, dark road still lay before them. "There's gotta be some place we can get out of the rain." Esther shivered.

Gladys thought for a few moments then exclaimed, "I know! There's that cabin near the Knik bridge. Remember when we were there right after they finished the bridge? It's an old cabin that nobody lives in, but the door was unlocked."

Esther knew the bridge was 12 miles from the farm; still she picked up her pace. Though it wouldn't be a warm and welcoming haven, it was at least a goal to reach for. Besides, they'd covered at least half the distance already. Hugging their clothing bundles and the useless flashlights the girls plodded on. Finally, after nearly four hours, they saw the bulky outline of the Knik bridge through the darkness. The girls located the cabin and staggered inside, to be greeted by nothing but four log walls and a frozen dirt floor. They huddled together through the rest of the night, cold, unable to sleep, but thankful to be out of the rain. As soon as it was light they walked back out to the road, and soon were able to flag down a driver who took them into Anchorage.

Upon arriving in the city, the girls walked to the small house at 7th Avenue and East K Street where their mother was staying. (At that time, the streets running north and south were simply designated by letters in alphabetical order. All streets to the west of A Street were referred to as 'West B, C, etc.; and those east of A were labeled East B, C, etc. This got confusing as Anchorage grew, so the streets to the east were eventually given Alaskan place names Barrow, Cordova, Denali, and so on.)

Laura wasn't home when they arrived, but the door was unlocked. They went in and soon had a fire going. They dried their clothes and crawled into the bed for a much-needed sleep.

They awoke to the sound of their mother's voice, "What in the world are you doing here?"

Esther said, "We couldn't stay there with Laurence. He's just too mean."

She and Gladys related what they'd gone through over the past several weeks. Laura was appalled to think that one of her children could behave so cruelly. She inspected Esther's bruised back then declared, "I'll take care of him next time I get out to the farm."

The conversation turned to the ever-present problem of making money. Laura had found a job at a nearby laundry. Gladys and Esther made plans to start job hunting the next day. As usually happened when the Larson women got together, before the evening was over Laura pulled out a harmonica and ukulele. She and Esther played instruments and all three sang. Their troubles faded to the background, temporarily quieted by music and laughter. But they all knew the hurt was still there, waiting to once again slice through their hearts when they were least prepared for it.

The next morning, before starting her job hunt, Esther decided to pop down to the creamery and say hello to her dad. The family hadn't seen much of him since the split, and though she disapproved of his shenanigans, she missed having him around.

She tramped the icy roads up to 4th Avenue and turned west. This was where downtown Anchorage truly began. Here the road was paved and flanked by well-shoveled sidewalks—a sharp contrast to the shoulderless, snow- and ice-rutted roads just a few blocks away. Esther gripped her woolen coat tightly around her as she hurried past restaurants and bars, and variety, clothing and drug stores that lined the street. When she reached the dairy, Fred seemed happy to see her, and they chatted for a few minutes. She told him about Laurence's behavior, and Fred agreed that she and Gladys had good reason to leave. Though apparently concerned about his favorite son's actions, Fred made no mention of helping to sort out the problem. He still clung to the Old World belief that discipline of the children was the mother's job. Any correction Laurence received would come from Laura.

As she visited with her father it seemed to Esther they covered just about every topic except the one uppermost in her mind: how could he leave his family like he had? Didn't he realize how much they needed him? Didn't he care about their pain?

Finally Esther said, "Well, I'd better be going. I need to start looking for a job."

"Okay," replied Fred. "See you later. Good luck." He turned back to his work.

As she left the creamery, Esther came face to face with Mrs. Hartfield. She glared at the woman on whom she blamed all the current chaos in her life. Mrs. Hartfield's face creased in a friendly smile and she spoke warmly, "Hello, Esther, it's good to see you. How have you been?"

All the hurt and anger surged up in Esther. She snapped, "Don't you pretend to be my friend! You should be home taking care of your own family and let my father take care of his." Shocked and a little embarrassed by her rudeness, she turned and rushed down the street, away from her dad and away from Mrs. Hartfield, but she couldn't run away from the feelings of loss.

Her frame of mind didn't improve over the next days, as her job hunt wasn't successful. She applied in cafés, grocery and dry goods stores—anywhere she heard about or even thought there might be a job opening. She was soon on a first-name basis with the woman at the employment agency, as she checked in each day. As had been the case in Palmer, employers looked at her doubtfully and wouldn't even give her a chance. But giving up was not an option. This was not a game—this was her life. She needed work and knew she was a good worker. All she needed was an opportunity to prove it. Someday, someone was going to recognize her worth and give her that chance. But where was that someone?

Beaver Trapping on the Nushagak

"C'mon, Esther, just ask Mrs. Carson for a job," Gladys urged her. Soon after arriving in Anchorage, she had landed a job at the laundry where their mother worked. "Mom and I are both there, and she knows we're good workers. If the Ostrich can do it, you won't have any trouble at all. She works so slow, she looks like she's wading through molasses!" Gladys loved to tell stories about her co-worker, a tall woman with long legs and a long neck.

Now Esther approached the woman who owned the laundry. "I'm Esther Larson. Would you have a job for me?" she asked.

"Oh, yes, you're Laura's daughter. Gladys's sister." Mrs. Carson eyed the bespectacled young woman in front of her. She saw a girl in a neat shirtwaist dress under her old but serviceable wool coat, whose small bone structure belied her height of 5'4", making her seem tinier than she actually was. Esther awaited her answer with a shy but hopeful smile.

The woman sighed. She hated this part of her job. "Honey," she said, "I'd love to hire you, but I just don't think you're..." she searched for a word, "you're not *robust* enough."

The words hit Esther like a physical blow. Her throat swelled and her eyes stung, but she refused to let this woman see her cry. "Thank you," she managed, and fled from the building.

Hurt turned to anger as Esther marched down the road through several inches of new snow. "Not robust enough," she muttered. "What does 'robust' have to do with anything! That ostrich woman Gladys talks about, I could work circles around her!"

She stamped along for a few more minutes, feeling the anger melt away to be replaced by the real underlying emotion: fear. Fear that no one would ever hire her. Fear that because of her the family would starve. The unreasonable fear that her inability to get a job would be the final straw in dissolving her parents' marriage.

Like the woman at the laundry, all the employers Esther had applied to took one look at her slight frame and dismissed her. "Too petite." Words she'd come to hate. They had no idea what a good strong worker she was.

"I'm going back to that employment office, and I'm gonna get a job, no matter what it is!" she told herself.

Ida, who ran the employment agency, looked up as Esther came in. "Hello, Esther," she greeted her. "I thought you were checking into the laundry where your mom and Gladys are working."

"I did…I'm not 'robust' enough." Esther struggled to keep her voice from shaking. "I want to apply for that job I heard about on the radio this morning—the man in Dillingham who needs a babysitter for his kids. I've been a babysitter. I'm good at that."

"Oh, yes, it's a very sad story. This man—Larry—lost his wife to TB, and two of his kids died from pneumonia, all this past winter. He has two boys left—a five-year-old and a one-year old. But I don't know if you want to go there." Ida looked concerned. "Dillingham is on Bristol Bay—way out in the southwest part of the state. You can only get there by plane or boat. And you'd be cut off from just about all communication."

"So the guy won't see me until I get there? He won't know how 'un-robust' I am? I'll take it," Esther declared. "What do I need to take with me?"

"Well," Ida said doubtfully, "I'd guess you'd better take all your warmest clothes. If you're sure about this, I'll make arrangements for the plane."

Exultantly, Esther returned to the small cabin she shared with Gladys and their mother. Packing didn't take long. She carefully folded the slacks, jodhpurs and flannel shirts she used for berry picking and other expeditions into the woods. The simple cotton dresses which were her typical daily wear could stay in Anchorage. Putting the pants, shirts, a few toiletries—and of course, her harmonica—in a sturdy cardboard box, she wrapped string around the box and tied it securely.

When Laura and Gladys returned home that evening, she greeted them with her news: "I've got a job babysitting in Dillingham. I leave tomorrow."

The next morning, Esther walked to the employment agency where she met Ida, put her box into the trunk of Ida's car, and rode with her to Spenard Lake, where the ski planes were tied down. There, Ida led her out on the ice to a small red and white airplane and introduced her to the pilot. "John, this is Esther. You take good care of her, you hear?"

John promised to do that, and loaded the box into the plane as Esther climbed into the passenger compartment and found a seat. The plane held six passengers, and all the seats were filled for this flight. Esther felt a little nervous as this was her first airplane ride, but John's air of confidence quickly allayed her fears and she relaxed to enjoy the experience.

As soon as it was airborne, the plane banked sharply and headed west. Esther craned her neck to peer out the window at the expanse of water below. It took a few moments before she identified it as Cook Inlet. This was a very different view of the inlet than anything she'd ever seen before. Leaving the inlet behind, the plane flew between tall mountains through an area she later discovered was Lake Clark Pass.

Just beyond the pass a large body of water appeared. Esther leaned over to her seat mate. "What's that?" she asked, pointing out the window.

"That's Lake Clark," came the answer. Esther watched as the long, narrow lake passed below them. Then an even larger lake came into view. To her surprise, John soon brought the plane smoothly down onto the ice. He climbed out to perform his baggage-handler duties. Esther looked out at a small group of houses that seemed to be the only signs of civilization. Several of the passengers disembarked here, collecting their gear and heading off toward the houses. Esther leaned forward as John resumed his seat. "Where are we?" she asked.

"This is Lake Iliamna," replied John, "A lot of my passengers live along here."

From there, the plane made stops at several more tiny settlements, setting down on lakes or snow-covered runways to deliver mail and supplies, and to pick up or drop off passengers. Esther enjoyed the stomach-lifting feeling as the plane came in for a landing, and the rush and roar of the engine as it took off again. Between stops, she watched in awe as miles of tundra speckled with small lakes crept by below. Long ribbons of rivers meandered across vast uninhabited spaces.

Whenever a solitary cabin came into sight, John swooped low over it. Esther chuckled as, at each cabin, someone popped out like a jack-in-the-box in response to the noisy plane. Sometimes these folks waved that all was well and John flew on. A certain sort of signal let him know they wanted him to stop. In those cases, he landed on the nearest spot that was snowy and flat enough. Esther had lived in Alaska long enough to know that these small planes were many Bush-dwelling Alaskans' only link with the outside world, and they depended on them. John knew everyone who lived along his route, and looked upon them as family.

When they reached Dillingham, John set the ski plane down on a small ice-covered lake and jumped out to open the passenger door. The other passengers—all residents of the area—disappeared, leaving John and Esther alone by the plane. Esther gazed around at the village. She saw a number of small homes, a Russian Orthodox church, a hotel and a general store. A wooden walkway connected nearly all the buildings and led down to the bay's edge where stood a group of buildings that obviously comprised some sort of large commercial operation. She found out later this was the Alaska Packing Company cannery, a major player in the economic life of this community. John pointed to a small cabin a short distance down the boardwalk. "There's Larry's place," he said. "I can vouch for Larry. He's a good man."

Esther thanked John and he handed her the box containing her belongings. As she turned to leave, she felt John's hand on her arm. Surprised, she looked back at him. He studied her seriously for a few seconds, as if he had something more to tell her. Finally he said, "Listen—if Larry doesn't treat you right, you come and see me. I'll take you right back to Anchorage any time."

Well—here was an angle Esther hadn't considered. In the past, her babysitting jobs had been in a more traditional setting, where she left once the parents returned. Here she'd be eating, sleeping and living with a family that didn't have a woman on the premises. Esther's mind churned this issue around on the short walk to Larry's cabin. She was greeted at the door by a man in his late 30s with brown hair, regular features, and a friendly smile. He held a toddler, while an older child peeped out from behind his legs, getting his first look at the new babysitter. The boys, with their bright dark eyes and black hair clearly showed their mother's Alaska Native heritage.

"You must be Esther; come in. I'm Larry Lombard." The man put his hand on the older child's head and said, "This is Sonny, and this little guy is Richard." He pulled out a chair from the table and offered her a cup of coffee.

Esther was relieved to see that Larry seemed like a nice, respectful man. He obviously loved his kids, who clung to him as they stared at Esther. She sensed the sadness in him, grief for the wife and children he'd lost. At one point in their conversation Larry, still holding Richard, went to the window and pointed across the snow-covered flatness. "Do you see the little cabin over there, across the muskeg? That's where my wife had to live until she died. Because she had TB, she couldn't live with us, so I built that for her."

Esther nodded, feeling sympathy, but not knowing what to say. She knew that tuberculosis was common among the Alaska Native people, and difficult to treat.

Larry continued, "I want to send my boys back East to live with my relatives, but I have to get enough money to send them. I'm a trapper, and if I can't trap, I can't make money. That's why it's so important that I have someone who can take care of them while I'm out on the trap line." He came back and sat down, then looked intently at Esther over Richard's head. "And I promise you, you'll be as safe with me as you'd be at home with your mother."

Relief flooded through Esther. She buried her nose in her coffee cup to hide her confusion then held out her hands to the baby on Larry's lap; the child immediately reached his arms toward her. She cuddled him on her lap while continuing to visit with his father. When in the course of the conversation she told him that she had lived in Alaska for almost five years, Larry's eyes sharpened.

"Then you're an Alaska resident!" he exclaimed. "That could work out good all the way around. We'll get you a license, and we can get a limit of beaver for you, too. I was going to pay you to just stay here with the boys while I'm trapping, but this way, you can come along and we'll get twice as many beaver, and it'll work out to more money for both of us. Of course, your main job will still be taking care of the boys, but you'll be able to help me with the traps if I need you. What do you think?"

Esther, knowing nothing about the business of trapping, was willing to go along with any scheme that promised a good payday, but she had a few questions. "Where will we be trapping, and who will be there, besides us?"

"Oh, the whole town goes up there," responded Larry. "It's almost like being here in Dillingham, except we'll live in a tent instead of the house." His enthusiasm grew as he talked. "I'll get John to fly us out to Koggiung Creek as soon as possible, and we'll set up camp."

Larry went out to start making arrangements for the move while Esther settled into the cabin. She checked out the pantry—a hole underneath the floor, covered by a trapdoor. Along the dirt walls of the hole, Larry had installed shelves which held various Alaskan Bush dwellers' staples: canned vegetables, fruits and meats, evaporated milk and boxes of crackers. She also found bags of flour, sugar, dried beans and peas, packages of elbow macaroni and several cans of powdered eggs and milk.

The kitchen took up most of one side of the one-room cabin and consisted of a wood cook stove, a few rough board shelves containing dishes and cooking pots, and a round white enamel pan. This pan served multiple purposes, as it was used for bathing, hand washing and washing dishes. A few chairs around the homemade table offered the only area for sitting. Larry's bed, with its log frame, occupied most of one wall, while a cot-size area at the far end of the wall would be sleeping quarters for Esther and Sonny. Baby Richard would sleep in a basket that sat on Larry's bed.

Behind the house a shed contained firewood, dog sleds and harnesses, and various supplies for trapping. Esther loaded her arms with firewood and went in to start a meal. She'd show this man that he was getting value for his money. He'd have no complaint with her work.

As evening approached and Larry started helping get the boys ready for bed, Esther faced a new problem. She was dressed; how was she supposed to get undressed and into her nightgown with Larry in the house? Larry must have noticed her quandary, because he suggested, "If you need to change clothes you can do it out in the shed."

Esther gathered up her night gear, thankful that she'd packed her heaviest, longest flannel gown in expectation of cool weather. Though it embarrassed her to walk in front of this stranger in her nightgown, at least she was covered from neck to toe.

Larry was gone almost all of the time for the next few weeks, as he worked to catch up on the tasks he'd had to postpone while he searched for a housekeeper/nanny. There were traps to mend and a boat and camp equipment to ensure were in good working order. He spent most of his days down by the cannery, where his boat was stored. As soon as he finished breakfast, he left to work on the many tasks necessary before moving his family out to the trap line. There wasn't much time for play, but sometimes in the evening, after the boys were in bed, Larry would challenge Esther to a game of cribbage. Several times, he left for a day or two, saying he needed to get things ready up on the trap line.

The days in Dillingham went by quickly, as Esther got acquainted with the family and their routines. Determined to prove her worth as an employee, Esther worked as hard

Dillingham community well.

as she knew how. She baked bread, kept the house tidy, put three meals on the table each day and hauled water from the community well for drinking, cooking and washing clothes. With Richard still in diapers, washdays came around frequently. She couldn't help chuckling over the placement of the town's well, situated as it was at the bottom of a hill. On top of that hill sat the Russian Orthodox church with its graveyard overlooking the public water supply. "Oh well," she said to herself, "People seem to be pretty healthy here, so I guess it's not polluted."

The boys and she became quite attached to each other. They took a big share of her time, as she did her best to replace the mother they had lost so tragically. They snuggled on her lap as she taught them songs, told stories, or played her harmonica. Her heart went out to them as she saw how they drank in any affection she offered.

She knew Larry was pleased with her work, as he made several comments about the freshly baked bread and simple but nutritious meals she put together from the contents of the root cellar/pantry. It was obvious, too, that he appreciated being able to spend what spare time he had playing with his boys, instead of always being tied up with household chores.

Though shyness and work kept Esther from extensive socializing, she occasionally stopped in to say hello to the pilot John's wife, Rose. Rose had one little boy about Richard's age, and another baby on the way. Esther found her easy to talk to and Rose welcomed her, happy to have a woman near her age, with similar interests. They compared notes on child rearing, learned about each other's lives, and Rose shared recipes and hints for making do with what was available in Dillingham. She also hinted at her loneliness, with her husband's job keeping him away from home for long days at a time. On one visit, Rose put forth a proposition. "Why don't you come and stay with me? I'll pay you whatever you're getting from Larry. You can help out with the baby, and when the new one comes, I'm sure I'll need more help. You're so good with kids."

Flattered, Esther hesitated. It would be fun to stay in Dillingham and be around another woman, instead of living in a tent out on the river. Finally, though, she shook her head. "I promised Larry I'd work for him. It wouldn't be fair to leave him now."

In early April came the day for the big move to the trapping grounds. John's plane landed on the river and taxied to the dock next to the cannery. Larry had packed his skiff with the tent, traps, stove, clothing, food, and blankets that would be needed at the camp. Larry and John secured a tarp over the load then tied the skiff between the skis of the plane.

"You know you're pushing it, don't you," John informed Larry. "It's getting awful late in the year for me to be landing on the river on skis. I need to get to Anchorage and change to floats."

"I know," Larry replied, "But I couldn't get everything ready till now."

John shook his head, letting his expression speak for him.

Esther lifted the boys into the plane then climbed in behind them. Larry joined them and in a moment the plane taxied down the river and roared into the air.

The noise of the engine discouraged small talk as they flew along the route of the Nushagak River. When they approached a small stream known as Koggiung Creek, John buzzed the creek then yelled back to Larry over the roar of the engine, "I can't land there—the ice'll never hold us. I'm gonna try that little lake over there." He motioned toward a snow-covered dot a short distance away.

They buzzed the lake once, then John carefully set the skis down onto the ice. "It's mushy," he informed them. "You're gonna hafta get your stuff unloaded in a hurry, 'cause that ice isn't gonna hold this crate for long."

John and Larry quickly unlashed the skiff, while Esther jumped out of the plane. She was shocked to find a thin layer of water on top of the ice, and knew that John wasn't kidding. Turning, she pulled Richard out and helped Sonny to alight. By this time the men had the skiff loose. Without another word, John jumped back into the plane, started the motor, and roared down the lake, spraying water as he went. His erstwhile passengers watched till they saw him safely airborne then turned their attention to getting off the lake.

Larry grabbed a tow rope and began dragging the skiff. Esther, seeing that Sonny needed help navigating the slippery surface, set the baby in the skiff, and reached for Sonny's hand. In this way, the small group headed for the safety of the shore. From there, they followed a tiny creek toward the larger stream, which Larry told her was Koggiung Creek. Richard, upset by the unfamiliar activity, started fussing so Esther picked him up and carried him.

Each step was a struggle, as their feet broke through the rotting snow, and willows and alders blocked their way. Larry followed the river, as this presented a smoother surface for towing the boat, although he had to climb over fallen trees and duck under overhanging bushes. Esther and the boys sought somewhat easier walking by going around the bushes. Sometimes this strategy was successful; sometimes it wasn't. At least they had little trouble keeping track of each other, as they crashed and sloshed noisily along.

Esther watched Sonny, trudging along without complaint, trying so hard to be grown up. She thought about something Larry had told her. All through the past winter, while Larry worked at the cannery and a procession of people had tried to help take care of the boys, Sonny had had a special job. Every day the cannery cooks would prepare a plate of food. Little Sonny walked down the boardwalk that circled the town and made his way to the cannery. He picked up the plate and carried it to his sick mother, alone in her cabin on the other side of the muskeg.

Until her health deteriorated to the point that she had to be hospitalized, he never neglected his job. Respect for this brave little boy welled up in Esther.

"Once we reach the Nushagak," Larry told her, "we'll have to walk quite a ways to the first campsite."

"As if we haven't walked 'quite a ways' already," thought Esther, but, determined not to complain, she shifted the baby to her other arm, and slogged on.

A wet, weary foursome finally arrived at the campsite about five o'clock that evening. There were flat, cleared spots where tents had once stood, each with a fire pit of stones beside it, but no people.

"Huh," said Larry, puzzled. "I thought everyone would be here by now. Oh well, they'll be coming soon." In this, Larry proved to be mistaken, as no other families ever showed up during the time Esther spent on the river.

But now was not the time to worry about where everyone else was. Esther had four hungry people to feed. She scooped water out of an open spot in the river. Sonny and his dad brought some wood; Esther got a flame going in one of the fire pits and set a pot of water to boil. Then Larry said casually, "I'll take Sonny and go down the river a ways and look for more firewood."

Esther correctly interpreted this as his subtle way of saying he'd be gone for a while. The only toilet facilities took the form of the nearest tall bush, so privacy was hard to come by. She was thankful that she'd gotten a job with such a sensitive man, who went out of his way to show respect and consideration for her.

She put together a quick meal of macaroni and canned corned beef, making it creamy with evaporated milk. When Larry and Sonny returned Larry pulled a box out of a tree and unloaded cans of food.

"I took this stuff up here a while back," said Larry. "I've got stuff stashed at all the sites we'll trap at."

Esther was surprised that the cans hadn't frozen, but she figured Larry must know enough about the weather to know when it was safe to leave the food outside.

After supper, Larry showed Esther an oven he had fashioned out of a 5-gallon can that had once held cooking oil. He demonstrated how to position it over the fire pit so she'd be able to bake.

While Esther washed the dishes, Larry busied himself setting up the wall tent. Esther had seen him pulling dried grass that was sticking up through the snow, but hadn't really paid attention to what he was doing. Now she saw that the grass was heaped into the areas inside the tent where they would sleep. She spread blankets over the heaps, and the beds were made. Larry and the boys had a larger area, and she had a small heap near the foot of their bed.

Everyone was exhausted after their full day of slogging through mud and slushy snow, so they soon fell into bed and went right to sleep. Sometime during the night, Esther awoke to hear Sonny say, "Daddy, I gotta go potty." The straw mattress rustled as Larry rolled off and took his son outside. She drifted back to sleep, glad that Larry was willing to take care of this chore himself.

The next morning after breakfast, Larry approached her carrying a trap. "Fish and Game'll be checking on us during the season, and they'll want to be sure that everyone who has a license knows how to trap. Let me show you how to set it." He showed Esther how to pull up the jaw of the trap and hook it open. "Now you do it," he directed. It took a few tries, but Esther soon got the hang of it.

"Good; now I'll show you where you'd set a trap." Larry led the way, carrying Richard in one arm and a trap in his other hand. Esther and Sonny followed, each carrying a trap. They stopped in an area of chewed-down trees where quieter water pooled off to the side of the main river. "See that kinda smooth area, like something's been dragged there? That's a beaver trail. They drag their tails, so they make that kinda track. We'll set the traps right here along these tracks."

Larry set a trap, then directed Esther as she set and positioned one. Once the traps were in place, the group returned to camp. Larry and Sonny again disappeared, giving her a chance to take a toilet break before turning to the task of preparing lunch. By the time they returned she had some canned beans bubbling over the fire and had even managed to bake a pan of biscuits. "You certainly are a talented gal," Larry told her.

Esther soon found out that trapping was a time-consuming business. Larry spent most days and even many nights working on the trap line. He might show up for meals, or he might not. Esther didn't have time to worry much about what Larry was doing, though. She stayed busy cooking, washing dishes and clothes, and taking care of the boys. As she worked she sang to them. During the baby's nap times, she taught Sonny to play simple card games like Old Maid and Crazy Eights. Richard, like all toddlers, was anxious to try out his legs, so Esther kept a close eye on him, making sure he stayed well away from the river. Once in a while she pulled out her harmonica and entertained the boys.

After a few days in camp, Larry came back with several beaver pelts and announced that it was time to move upriver. Almost as an afterthought he said, "Y'know, next week is my birthday. Maybe I'll get a good catch as a present."

Back into the canoe went all the supplies, and Esther hefted the baby and got ready to move on. This move took less time than the first one, so Larry put up the tent and left Esther to finish preparing camp while he headed out to set the traps. With evening approaching, Esther knew she had to get the dried grass pulled in a hurry or their beds would be extra hard. She grabbed hands full of grass stalks, yanking it out as quickly as she could. "Ouch!" she yelped, as she felt a blade of grass cut into her hand. Stopping to inspect her injury, she found a small slit between the third and fourth fingers of her right hand. It bled a little and stung like mad, but didn't appear to be a serious wound, so she went back to her task. Sonny helped by hauling armloads of grass into the tent until there was enough to make comfortable beds.

Having found out exactly which day was Larry's birthday, Esther planned to surprise him by making a cake. With a little lard, sugar, flour, dried eggs and baking powder, she made a simple but recognizable cake. She even found some powdered sugar which she whipped with margarine for frosting.

Sonny danced up and down as they presented Larry with his cake. "Happy birthday, Daddy!" he yelled. Larry seemed flabbergasted, but pleased. After the cake was eaten and the boys were asleep, he relaxed at the table with a cup of coffee, watching as Esther straightened up around the tent.

"Y'know," he finally spoke, "We get along pretty good, and the boys really like you. Would it spoil everything if I made advances?"

Shocked, Esther stated firmly, "It sure would!" She had never considered Larry in any light except as her employer. At the age of twenty, she considered a man just shy of forty to be downright elderly. Besides, Irv was her boyfriend — or had been until recently. She wasn't in the market for a husband. She fervently hoped Larry would get the message.

Apparently he did; he sat sipping his coffee for a while longer, then got up and left the tent. He didn't come back that night, and was gone several more days. Esther didn't know if he was embarrassed, if he was giving her some time to get over feeling uncomfortable, or if he'd just gone off on the trap line as he did so often.

When he returned, no more was mentioned about advances, and they carried on as they had before. The grass cut between her fingers was an irritant, stinging when she put her hands in water and aching at night. She was too busy to worry about it, though, so she ignored it as best she could.

Over the next few weeks, they moved camp two more times. Each time her chores seemed more difficult to Esther, as the soreness in her hand refused to go away. Her fingers swelled so much it was nearly impossible to do a simple task like buttoning her shirt. Although she had never had trouble falling asleep in the past, now the throbbing of her hand kept her awake for hours. Packing water from the river, scrubbing clothes on the washboard, squeezing the can opener to prepare meals—all became excruciatingly painful. Her head throbbed, and she suspected she had a fever. Larry, since he was rarely around, didn't notice her difficulty. Even when he was there, she couldn't bring herself to show him the wound. It felt like admitting defeat, that she wasn't capable of the job she'd taken on. Anger at herself and the infected hand spurred her on when all she wanted to do was to lie down and sleep.

One morning a boat pulled up just below the bank where their tent was perched. Larry spoke for a while with the uniformed man from the boat then came in search of Esther.

"Fish and Game is here," he told her. "Like I said, they want you to prove you know how to set a trap."

Larry picked up a trap, and Esther followed him back down to the shore where the officer waited. She grasped the trap, knowing the moves, but unable to do it with her swollen hand. "I'll have to use my foot," she said. Holding the trap down with her foot, she used her left hand to pull the jaws open. After several attempts she finally got it set and stood back.

The officer seemed to have lost interest in the trap, instead saying, "Let me see that hand." Esther pushed up her sleeve; in addition to being swollen to almost twice its size, her arm had deep red streaks running up past her elbow.

Larry looked shocked. "When did that happen?" he asked.

"Oh, I cut it picking grass a while back," she replied. Just then she heard the baby crying in the tent, and hurried back to her work. The ranger spoke a little more to Larry then hopped back into his boat and roared off.

Larry came up to the tent, obviously shaken by the look of her hand. He hung around helping with anything he thought she needed. She appreciated the help as by now she was feeling so sick that she performed her chores in a daze.

The next morning she heard the drone of an airplane. Seeing a plane was always an event so, despite her aching body, she moved outside to watch it go over. She recognized the red and white of John's plane, now equipped with floats. She started to wave, thinking he was just going to waggle his wings in greeting as he flew over. It quickly became evident that John was circling, preparing to land. She walked toward the river, eager to see her pilot friend and hear whatever news he brought.

She never could have guessed what his load was. The plane taxied in to shore, the door opened, and out hopped two young women. "Gladys!" exclaimed Esther. "And Florence." Sure enough, her sister and one of their best friends stood there, laughing at her surprise. They climbed up the bank and ran to meet her.

"What are you doing here?" Esther demanded. She turned to Gladys. "What about your job in Anchorage?"

"We came to take over for you." Gladys said. "We've been working at the store in Dillingham for the last couple of weeks. John called and said the Fish and Game ranger said you needed to leave 'cause your hand is infected, but, Esther, what am I supposed to do about that Man?"

"Larry?" laughed Esther, "He won't bother you. I just can't believe he sent for you. Now you're here and I have to leave? What about the kids?"

"Let me see that hand," ordered Gladys. "Ugh! You'd better get that treated. It looks awful."

"Don't you worry about anything here, Esther," said Florence. "We'll take care of everything. You just go with John. You see those red streaks up your arm? You have blood poisoning. You can die from that."

The girls helped Esther bundle up her few belongings. Sonny and Richard watched her, bewilderment written on their faces. She felt sorry to be leaving; after getting so close to her during the past weeks, they probably felt they were losing a mother all over again. She did her best to explain why she had to leave, but knew they wouldn't understand.

There was little time to spend making them feel better, as Gladys and Florence almost pushed her toward the plane. Larry thanked her solemnly for all her help. John helped her into the plane, revved it up, and taxied out onto the river. Soon they were in the air, following the Nushagak River toward its mouth. A short distance from Dillingham, John brought the plane down on a lake in the small town of Kanakanak, where the regional hospital was located. He took her to the hospital and waited while the staff treated her. They lanced the wound but recommended that she go on to Anchorage and be treated at the hospital there. This time John didn't make extra stops but flew directly into Anchorage and got her a taxi to the hospital. The doctor who treated her told her sternly, "Blood poisoning is nothing to mess with, young lady. You barely got here in time to save your arm."

Esther found out later that her share of the beaver Larry trapped using her license just paid for her medical bills and the airfare home.

Summer, 1940

Esther spent several weeks in late May and early June at the little cabin in Anchorage with her mother, regaining her health and strength. Only during this period of recuperation did she finally realize just how close she had come to dying of blood poisoning. It was a sobering experience, and she vowed she'd never again neglect her health to such an extent.

Once she felt well enough, her thoughts turned to the necessity of finding another job. Letters arrived from Gladys every week or so. She reported that, once Larry's trapping season had finished, he was able to send his boys to live with his relatives back East. With the babysitting job at an end, Gladys had applied and started working at a hotel in Dillingham. She wrote, encouraging Esther to join her. So Esther again boarded John's small plane and returned to Dillingham.

Gladys met the plane and led her sister along the boardwalk to the hotel. She introduced Esther to Mrs. Danielson, the owner of the establishment. Then she showed her the room they would share, all the way at the top of the house, in a small space that probably had once been a closet. They'd slept in worse places, though, so Esther was content with her lodgings, especially since they came with a job. She accompanied Gladys back down to the kitchen.

"One of your jobs," said Mrs. Danielson, "will be to get everything ready in the restaurant every morning. You two will need to do most of the restaurant work because I'll be taking care of the bar. You're not to go in there. I'll bake the pies and bread for the restaurant...I wish I had someone who could take over that job..." she interrupted herself.

"I can bake bread," Esther spoke up.

"You can?" said her boss doubtfully. "You have to make twelve loaves at a time, twice a day, y'know." Esther knew the woman was mentally tagging her as a puny little runt who surely couldn't handle such a demanding job. She stuck out her chin; she'd faced down the Grim Reaper when the doctors gave up on her as a 4-pound preemie, and again in her recent brush with blood poisoning; she surely wouldn't let a few batches of dough conquer her.

She followed Mrs. Danielson to view the huge bread bucket with its crank handle that turned the paddle to mix the dough. Esther had never baked bread on such a massive scale, but she wasn't about to say anything that might jeopardize her chances to keep this job. She declared, "I can do it."

The next morning she rose at 5 a.m. Mrs. Danielson watched as she stirred yeast and sugar with warm water and set it to begin working. She measured the rest of the ingredients into the bread bucket with quick, sure movements. Before long her boss nodded, convinced the bread-making was in capable hands. Esther set the dough to rise while she and Gladys prepped the kitchen with eggs, potatoes and other ingredients that hungry customers would want for breakfast. When she saw the dough mounding over the top of the bucket she divided it into twelve loaves and set them to rise again. In an hour the smell of baking bread wafted out the door and drew in the first customers of the day.

Gladys snatched up her tablet and went out to take orders. Esther followed her and soon discovered that this was a multi-task job. There was no designated cook so, when a customer ordered ham, steak or bacon the waitress hustled to the cool room where the meats were kept. She sawed the right-sized portion off the correct type of meat, took it back to the kitchen and plopped it into a hot pan. Meanwhile, whatever else the customer wanted—eggs, toast, potatoes— had to be cooked at the same time.

By the end of that first breakfast rush Esther's head was spinning. Once they'd washed the dishes, Gladys poured leftover pancake batter on the griddle. The girls quickly downed the pancakes with cups of coffee. Then they scampered upstairs to clean the hotel rooms. As she came downstairs Esther heard Mrs. Danielson calling, "Esther, it's time to start another batch of bread."

Esther groaned inwardly, but she headed to the kitchen and prepared a dozen more loaves. A lull after the lunch crowd cleared out gave her and Gladys the opportunity to a gulp another cup of coffee and savor a bowl of the soup Mrs. Danielson had simmering on the back of the stove.

All too soon it was time to get ready for the dinner hour. At the end of the day Esther felt like *she* had been cranked in the big bread mixer. She knew that any new job seems harder at first, and looked forward to the time when she was as comfortable in the position as Gladys was.

Within a week Esther felt like a veteran waitress. She glanced up one morning from setting loaves of bread to cool and saw one of her least favorite customers sitting in the dining room. Bill — or Bill the Pill as she thought of him — was one of the many fishermen who patronized Mrs. Danielson's hotel and restaurant. He knew which tables were assigned to her and sat at one of them whenever he could. This particular fellow loved making her life difficult. She reluctantly approached his table and poured a cup of coffee. "Good morning, Bill, what would you like to eat?"

"Oh, I think I'll have my usual," Bill smirked. Esther gritted her teeth. Bill had no "usual".

"Can I get you eggs? Bacon?" she asked politely, determined not to lose her temper.

"Yeah, I'll just take some eggs."

"How do you want your eggs?"

"On a plate." More smirking.

Esther stood and waited. Finally Bill relented. "Over easy."

"Anything else?" she asked.

"Oh, just some toast."

She headed for the kitchen where she broke eggs into a pan and sliced the bread.

"Esther, I changed my mind. I want scrambled eggs instead."

Esther pushed the half-fried eggs to the side. She'd be hanged if she'd let them go to waste. She planned to eat them whenever she got a break, no matter how cold or overcooked they were by then. She quickly whipped up more eggs and poured them in the pan. She knew Bill was watching her every move from his table. She timed the toast to finish when the eggs were done, and dished them up. She carried the plate out and set it on the table.

"Oh, I forgot—I want pancakes too."

"Don't get mad," she told herself. "That's exactly what he wants."

She poured out three generous portions of Mrs. Danielson's excellent sourdough pancake batter and kept an eye on them while fixing meals for her other customers. She and Gladys dodged around each other as they raced to get everyone's meal to them quickly. She slid the pancakes onto a plate, grabbed a pitcher of syrup and took them to Bill.

"Where's the bacon?" asked Bill.

"You didn't order bacon," Esther replied.

"I'm sure I did. You just forgot."

Without a word Esther whirled around and headed to the cool room. She grabbed a huge, sharp knife and hacked a couple of slices off of the big chunk, not caring overly-much if they were the most uniform strips of bacon in the world.

"I oughta just wrap 'em around his head!" she muttered to herself.

As she expected, Bill protested because he didn't get all of his food at the same time. Knowing that he had purposely toyed with her, wasting her time and potentially wasting food, Esther offered to bring Mrs. Danielson over from the bar to talk to him. At that, Bill backed off. Mrs. Danielson worked her staff hard, but she was fair. She'd side with Esther, and Bill didn't want to lose the privilege of eating at the restaurant. When Esther grumbled to her sister about him Gladys just laughed. "I think he likes you," she teased.

Fortunately, diners like Bill were the exception rather than the rule. Most of the customers appreciated the friendly and efficient service that Esther and Gladys provided and, for the most part, Esther enjoyed her job in the restaurant.

Cleaning the hotel was a different matter. Mrs. Danielson hired some local boys to dump the chamber pots that served the patrons of each room, but on many days when Esther went to clean the hotel rooms, a strong scent of human excrement stung her nostrils. She discovered that the boys often either emptied only some of the pots, or didn't show up at all. On those days, Esther and Gladys had extra work, as they had to carry the odoriferous containers to the large outhouse behind the hotel and dump, wash and replace them in the rooms.

The girls got one day off each week. With that uncanny radar of the young, the unattached men who lived at the Seventh Day Adventist camp nearby learned that a couple of attractive single ladies were working at Mrs. Danielson's place in Dillingham. From that point on, the girls never worried about what to do with their days off. Their well-behaved new friends squired them around, showing them more of the area than they would have gotten to see otherwise. They picked berries, explored the Wood River

Esther outside the Dillingham Hotel.

area and visited friends up the river in the village of Aleknagik.

Esther noticed Gladys lit up when a certain chap came around. This fellow was not one of the missionaries, but he often stayed with them at their camp. Stan was a recent arrival from Michigan, the son of Polish immigrants. He was attractive in a brash sort of way. His abundant wavy brown hair adorned a head he carried at a cocky angle. Esther wasn't overly thrilled with Gladys's new beau, but felt it was probably just a summer crush that would end when they returned home in the fall.

Once the fishing season wrapped up in late July, Mrs. Danielson no longer needed two waitresses, and the girls flew home to Anchorage. Despite their hard work and long hours, their wages covered their air fare home, with little to spare. Still, they had supported themselves through the summer, so they considered the time well spent. The two young women faced the job market again, this time with a little more experience and confidence to draw on.

Esther and Gladys on a picnic outing.

Right: Esther, Gladys, and the car, headed for a picnic.

Below, Laura and Esther on the day of the picnic.

1940 - The Cabin

Just days after returning from Bristol Bay, Esther accompanied her mother to the farm to see how Laurence was getting along. On the way, they stopped by the combined post office and general store in the town of Matanuska. Kerwin and Ginny Frank had taken over the establishment when its previous owners, Mr. and Mrs. Krogh, retired and moved Outside—the term Alaskans use to refer to the Lower 48 states.

Matanuska was not an easy place to run a business. The area probably never would have been settled at all if it hadn't been at the junction of the railroad that ran east to Palmer and north to Fairbanks. The town sat in a flood plain that all too often filled with water. Up in the hills behind the town lay a body of water called Lake George. Each spring the lake acted as a reservoir as the snows melted and poured into it. All the excess water built up behind a dam of ice until warming temperatures melted the dam. When that happened, Lake George released its overflow, pouring tons of water into the Knik River. From there it spread across miles of flat, open land, burying everything under dirty water and gooey mud. The inhabitants of Matanuska had learned to expect such an event nearly every year, anywhere from mid-summer to early fall. Some winters, when the weather was warmer, the ice dam didn't form, so what water did pool in Lake George drained down gradually, forestalling the flood. Living in Matanuska was like playing Russian roulette, as residents tried to prepare for a flood while praying it wouldn't come.

The Franks had two young children to care for in addition to running the store and post office. To make ends meet, the couple couldn't just wait at the store for customers to show up; instead, they took orders and delivered supplies to people throughout the Valley. Ginny became the delivery person, while Kerwin tended the store, post office and children. Esther, after her experiences working for Larry and Mrs. Danielson, felt able to speak up and ask for a job. The Franks gladly accepted her offer, and even provided a small room for her to stay in. She would start as a babysitter, with some light work in the store. Esther was thrilled to have landed a job so quickly after returning from Dillingham.

Very soon Esther's strong work ethic and quick mind drew her boss's attention. Kerwin began training her to work in the post office. Esther knew this was the kind of job that could lead to long-term employment. She threw herself into learning the job with the same determination that had buoyed her through all the challenges of her life.

With a steady paycheck, Esther began thinking about getting a place of her own. She appreciated the Franks for providing a place to sleep, but she was 20 years old now, ready to put down roots somewhere. One Sunday—the only day the store was closed and she had a day off—she walked up to the main road and hitchhiked into Anchorage. She needed to talk with her father.

She walked into the creamery. "Esther!" her father greeted her. "What brings you to town?"

"I want to build a cabin," she replied.

"What d'you wanna do that for?" exclaimed her dad.

"I just want my own place. I talked to Tex Cobb, who owns the land just up the hill from Matanuska. He'll let me build a cabin there. Would you help me?"

Fred argued for a time, but eventually Esther convinced him that she was not going to change her mind. She showed him the plans she'd drawn for a simple 16 x 16-foot structure, made largely from boards that were lying unused around the farm and supplemented by materials that Esther would buy with her wages. It would not be spacious or elegant, but it would be hers.

Once Fred committed to something like this, he attacked it with vigor. Though he couldn't leave his job in Anchorage during the week, on Friday evenings he took the train down to Matanuska and spent his weekends helping Esther. He stayed with Laurence at the farm, so Laurence got to have some company and also some help with needed repairs around the farm. During the week, Esther spent any spare time working on the cabin. She was handy with a hammer and though she couldn't lift huge boards on her own, she could work on small tasks that Fred left for her to do.

It wasn't long before the roof was ready to put on. Esther held boards while Fred nailed, then the two of them tacked tar paper on top. At one point Fred stopped, sat back on his heels and said, "I t'ought you were gonna finish high school. Now you got a job so how you gonna do both?"

"I don't know," Esther replied, "but I'm gonna."

"Aaah, you'll never finish now. You're too old. Here I t'ought one of my kids would finish high school."

Esther set her jaw. "I'll show you, you old buzzard," she vowed silently.

On a rainy September day, Esther moved into her cabin. Its contents, from the wood cook stove to the single bed,

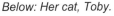
Left: Esther's cabin in Matanuska.

Below: Her cat, Toby.

were castoffs either from the farm or nearby neighbors who heard she needed furnishings. Nails pounded into the walls furnished hangers for clothing and household utensils. With a table, a couple of chairs and a built-in set of shelves to hold her few belongings, Esther felt self-sufficient at last.

Over the next couple of weeks Esther, carrying two water buckets, enjoyed the morning walk down the hill, across the railroad tracks and into the Franks' store. Each evening on her way home she stopped at the spring at the bottom of the hill and filled her buckets. On days when she had clothes to wash she made several extra trips.

Kerwin, true to his promise, continued to teach her to handle the post office. She looked forward to the day when she would wear the title of Postmistress of Matanuska, Alaska.

But the job was never to be. One morning Esther, as had become her custom, looked out of her cabin down onto the town below. Her heart froze. A swirling, surging mass of muddy water covered the town. Lake George had burst its ice dam once again. Her eyes searched for Franks' store. "Are they all right?" she thought frantically. "What can I do?" About then, the Frank family's vehicle chugged into her yard.

"We're okay," yelled Kerwin. "But it looks like everything on the lower shelves in the store is ruined. It'll probably be several days before we can get back in there, so we're goin' to stay in Palmer till the water goes down."

Esther watched their car disappear down the road, shaken with the realization that her job may have been literally washed away. All day, she couldn't keep her mind on her tasks as she kept being drawn back to the bluff to see what havoc the river was wreaking on the town below. Finally, she put on her coat and walked to the farm. A flood was big news in the area, and she knew Laurence would want to know about it. Now that she no longer lived at home, she found she could enjoy a visit with Laurence now and then, though she never intended to live with him again.

In typical non-confrontational Larson fashion, the three siblings had reconciled their split caused by his earlier abusive behavior. The girls were sure that their mother had given him a thorough tongue-lashing, though she'd never said anything to them. In place of an expressed apology, the next time Laurence saw his sisters he greeted them cordially, and seemed to go out of his way to be polite. The girls responded in kind, and the issue was considered closed.

Now Laurence and Esther walked back down to the bluff overlooking Matanuska. They stood and watched the water below, each thankful their own houses were spared, yet feeling sympathy for all those whose homes and livelihoods were being damaged or destroyed. They knew that some of the inhabitants would be stubborn enough to rebuild, but with each deluge more residents gave up and moved away from the flood plain. Without a doubt, Matanuska was a town whose days were numbered. (Because of Alaska's warmer average yearly temperatures, Lake George hasn't flooded the Matanuska area since 1966.)

A few days later, when the waters started receding, Esther again walked out to her vantage point overlooking the town. What she saw at the Franks' store shocked her more than the flood had done. The postmaster from Palmer was parked outside the store. She could see him slogging in and out of the post office end of the building, carrying bags of mail and loading them into his truck. When he had all of it, he climbed into his truck and splashed off down the road, up the hill, and past her house. Kerwin broke the news to her the next day when he and the family returned. The decision had been made that Matanuska was in too precarious a position for a permanent post office. From this point on, all mail would be processed in Palmer. Esther's postmaster job was gone.

Despite the loss of the post office, there was plenty of work to do for the Franks. Esther pitched in, mopping up and throwing out the stuff that had been destroyed by the flood, cleaning up and inventorying the goods that had been spared. She admired the toughness of the people of the town. They took the dumping of Lake George in stride, cleaned up and forged ahead. Ginny resumed her deliveries throughout the Valley, Kerwin ran the store and Esther helped out with the store while the children were at school, then cared for them when they got home. In the evening she retired to her little cabin and enjoyed the novelty of having her own place. She did acquire a roommate, Toby, a black kitten who had been born on the farm.

Though she kept busy all week, she rarely missed attending the Saturday night dances at the high school. One of several young male friends usually showed up to escort her. Sometimes her swain brought a box of chocolates. She didn't have the heart to tell these nice young men that she didn't care for chocolate, but Toby soon figured out that these gifts meant a treat for him. In the evenings when Esther snuggled in bed with a book and her box of chocolates, Toby jumped onto the bed and purred his way into her lap. Esther carefully peeled the chocolate off each candy, fed the chocolate to Toby, and ate the filling herself. It has come to light in the years since that chocolate is not good for cats but neither Esther nor Toby knew that. As Toby suffered no ill effects, they would probably opine that the dangers are overstated anyway.

One Sunday, Esther walked to the farm to check in with Laurence. On this afternoon he had a couple of friends visiting, and one was showing off his new rifle. As the guys took turns trying it out, Esther watched with interest. Finally the proud owner suggested, "Here, Esther, give it a try."

Esther had shot guns a few times, but was by no means an expert. Not wanting to admit such a failing amongst these youngsters she snugged the gun to her shoulder and brought the scope so close to her face that it nearly touched her spectacles. She squinted through the scope at a tin can set on a stump. When she was sure her aim was right, she squeezed the trigger.

The kick of the rifle drove the scope into her eye, breaking her glasses and knocking her head backwards. The boys hooted with laughter, but stopped when they saw Esther's hand pressed to her eye and blood seeping out around her fingers.

Laurence did his best to help, bringing ice from the milk house to put on her eye. Once Esther was able to remove her hand from the eye, her brother inspected it. "It looks like you've just got a cut by your eyebrow. You're gonna have a dandy shiner, though."

Esther returned to her cabin grateful that the accident hadn't been worse. At present, her main concern was the loss of her glasses. Her poor eyesight made them a necessity for daily functioning.

Kerwin expressed concern when Esther showed up for work with a black eye and no glasses. "Who'd you fight with?"

"A rifle," she replied. "It looks worse than it is, but I sure miss my glasses."

"I know a real good eye doctor in Anchorage," said Kerwin. "You go in to see him and he'll fix you right up. And stay at Mrs. Johnson's hotel. It's right near the train station, and she'll take good care of you."

Esther hated going to doctors but she needed her glasses, so a few days later she caught the train at Matanuska. She couldn't even enjoy the sights of the trip, as everything appeared as if she were looking through a window that had a waterfall streaming down the other side.

In Anchorage, she walked the short distance to Mrs. Johnson's hotel. "I'm Esther Larson," she told the motherly-looking woman at the desk. "Kerwin Frank told me you'd put me up."

"You come right in, dear," said Mrs. Johnson. "We'll take care of you. Don't you worry about a thing. Come along;

you can have the room next to my daughter. Clara!" she called. "We have a special guest."

Clara, a young woman a few years older than Esther, appeared and greeted her. The two women fussed over her, showing her how to lock her door and find the bathroom. Because of Esther's size, they probably assumed that she was several years younger than her actual age of 20, and in need of protection.

Once Mrs. Johnson went back to her duties Clara turned to Esther. "You rest for a while, then I'll take you for a tour of Anchorage."

Esther was too shy to tell her that without glasses she'd see precious little of the town. Clara drove her down Fourth Avenue through the business district, then around Spenard and Jewel Lakes on the outskirts of town. Her guide kept up a lively commentary so Esther, though she didn't see much, enjoyed the tour.

The next morning, with Mrs. Johnson's warnings not to talk to strangers still sounding in her ears, Esther set out for Dr. Halstad's office. She stepped into the small office and stood hesitantly at the counter. A kindly-looking older man appeared and greeted her. "What can I do for you?"

Esther produced her broken spectacles. "I broke my glasses and I can't see much without them. I don't have much money, though, and I can't pay for them all at one time. Can I get them on credit and pay you some every time I get paid?"

The man gave her a rather odd look, then chuckled. "I think we can arrange that." He held the broken glasses up and looked through them. "Yes, we can definitely do that."

He smiled at Esther, who smiled back uncertainly. What on earth was so funny? She didn't see anything humorous about her request. She was just relieved he agreed to give her credit.

The doctor examined her eyes and gave an exclamation as he looked into the one she'd injured. "You have a cut on your eyeball. Luckily it's small and I don't see any glass in it. It'll heal up in a month or so. Just be careful with it for now. I'll look at it again when you come back for your glasses."

Dr. Halstad said good-by and told her to come back in three weeks, when the new glasses should have arrived from the Lower 48. That seemed like a lifetime to Esther, but she had no other option. Three weeks later she again rode the train into Anchorage and, with the first payment in her purse, made her way to the office. The doctor greeted her with the good news that the glasses had indeed arrived. He seated her on one side of a small desk while he sat in the chair on the other side and checked the injured eye again. "Looks like it's healing nicely," he told her. Taking out her new frames, he squeezed and crimped and tried them on her face repeatedly until they were a perfect fit. He leaned back in his chair. "Okay, tell me how those feel."

Esther gazed around the room, able to see clearly for the first time in nearly a month. "They're perfect," she began, then blushed as she caught sight of a sign hung prominently behind the counter—a sign that until today she had been unable to read: "Please do NOT ask for credit!" Now she got the joke.

As winter set in, Toby became not only a companion and a sharer of sweets, but a bed warmer as well. The little cabin was not well insulated and, unless the stove was filled with wood and burning strongly, Esther could see her breath in the air. Water froze in the bucket and frost etched feathery designs on all the windows. The firebox in the stove was too small to hold enough wood to last through the night. Sometimes Esther awoke during the night, hopped up and replenished the wood, but most of the time she snuggled deeper into the blankets, pulled Toby close and dealt with the cold in the morning.

A problem she had not anticipated was a lack of easily accessible firewood. Aside from a few downed and rotting logs, most of the trees near her place were alders or young birches—too small and too green to make a substantial woodpile. As she had no transportation other than her own two feet, she relied on her father's infrequent visits to the area. He would swing by and dump a load of spruce, cut to the length that her stove would hold. Many of her free hours were spent splitting the rounds into chunks small enough for the stove.

At times the cold and lack of human companionship made her wonder if she'd made the right decision in building this cabin. When such thoughts crept in, she told herself sternly, "Look at you. You've got a job and a place to live. You've got a lot to be thankful for and don't you forget it."

Big Changes - 1941

In June, Gladys started talking about returning to Bristol Bay to work for the summer, and urged Esther to come with her. Esther knew Gladys had been writing to Stan throughout the winter and suspected that he was a major reason for her yen for Dillingham. She talked with Kerwin who said he was sorry to see her go, but promised her she'd have a job when she got back.

Since the girls had made plans to spend the Fourth of July with Lionel Haakenson, they postponed their departure till after the holiday. Esther spent the day trying to push Lionel and Gladys together. She suspected Lionel had a soft spot for her sister, and wished Gladys returned his interest. To her disappointment, the two laughed and joked together, but showed no inclination to become any closer. At the end of the day she conceded at least temporary defeat as matchmaker. The next morning she took Toby to stay at the farm, shut up her cabin and boarded the plane with Gladys.

Esther, Gladys and Lionel-July 4, 1941.

Mrs. Danielson welcomed the girls back, as Gladys was the best waitress she'd ever had and Esther relieved her of the task of bread making. "One of the supply boats couldn't get through this spring, so a lot of town folks are low on flour," she told them. "I put in an extra big order last fall just in case something like this happened. If that boat doesn't get here soon, Esther, you're gonna have to make some extra bread."

Within a short time Dillingham businesses and individuals began feeling the pinch. The clerk from the general store came in for bread to sell at his establishment. Even another restaurant owner bought a dozen loaves, and many local residents who had run out of flour came in for a loaf or two. Esther spent her days baking one batch after another. She didn't really mind; she'd rather do this than wait on tables any day.

The flour shortage stretched to nearly a week, and Mrs. Danielson began eyeing her own supplies with concern. "We'll have to start rationing people if this keeps up," she declared.

Before she had to put such a drastic measure into effect, the supply boat arrived. Esther stood on the front porch of the hotel and watched the residents streaming down to the dock to welcome the tardy vessel. Flour had been one of the main shortages, but everything from candy to fishing gear had also been running low, and folks felt the absence of those other items as deeply as they did bread.

The young men from the Seventh Day Adventist camp again came around, and the girls could always find someone to have fun with. Gladys and Stan made it clear they were an item, and a few weeks later Gladys came to Esther, her face glowing.

"Stan asked me to marry him," she confided.

Esther's heart sank. She didn't know Stan very well, but she felt he wasn't the right man for her dear sister. It wasn't her place to say yea or nay, though, and Gladys seemed set on her course. Esther had a question, though, that she just had to ask. "What about Lionel?"

Gladys stared at her, puzzled. "What *about* Lionel? He's a lot of fun, but I'd never want to marry him. And if you ask me, you're the one he's got his eye on."

"I doubt that," replied Esther. She couldn't help hoping that Lionel wouldn't be too crushed.

"I'm gonna go home and tell Mom and Dad," Gladys said, returning to the topic of interest to her. "We'll get married after fishing season. I want you to be my maid of honor."

Gladys flew back to Anchorage to break the news to her parents. Esther wondered how the folks would feel about their daughter marrying someone they hadn't met.

Gladys returned with her parents' blessing and another bit of good news. For Fred, the greener grass on the other side of the fence had already withered, and he had reconciled with his wife. Laura had moved from the small cabin into the creamery, and both of them spent time on the farm with Laurence when they could.

In late August of 1941, Gladys married her Stan in a ceremony performed by one of their Seventh Day Adventist friends. Stan had a job at the cannery in Dillingham and lived in a wall tent nearby. Gladys had also recently started work at the cannery, and the newlyweds settled down to married life. Esther flew back to Anchorage with a change in mind for her own life.

"This is the year," she told herself. "I have a little money saved, I have a place close to the road; I'm going to finish school."

She broached the subject to her parents. Laura, as expected, supported her dream, while Fred still expressed skepticism. "Aaaah, you'll never make it through the winter. How you gonna do that on your own with no job or nuthin'?"

Esther gritted her teeth and stuck out her jaw. "I'll make it," she retorted. "I'm gonna get that diploma."

She spent the days before school started putting up firewood with help from her dad, stocking up on food and buying a few new clothes to get her through the year.

On the first day of school she caught the bus and rode into Palmer. Her favorite teacher gave a start of surprise when she saw her. "Esther!" she exclaimed, "I'm glad you came back. Is Gladys here?"

"No, Gladys got married last month. She's living in Dillingham."

Esther looked at her classmates. These kids had all been freshmen the last time she'd been in school. Now she'd be graduating with them. It seemed odd to be 21 in a class of 17-year-olds, but Esther was undaunted. Due to the illnesses in her early years, she'd always been older than her classmates.

Life settled into a busy routine. After spending her days in school, Esther came home to a chilly house. She stoked the stove, made a simple meal from beans or canned goods, and settled down at the table to do her homework. As the days grew shorter she relied more on her lantern for light to complete her work. Though she was frugal, she saw her small savings dwindle more rapidly than she had expected. If she had a chance to get out to the farm she could usually get a few eggs or some milk; however, she grew concerned that her money might not last through the winter.

She still enjoyed Saturday evening dances at the school, and more and more often it was Lionel Haakenson who showed up to escort her. Surprisingly, he didn't seem too torn up over Gladys's marriage. Esther began to wonder if perhaps Gladys had been right—that his interest was in her.

By mid-November, Esther knew she had to face facts— her money was already gone. One frosty morning, as was her wont, she reached out of bed and pulled her clothes under the covers until they warmed up, then got dressed before getting out of bed. She got up, lit a candle, and poked a few sticks from her dwindling wood supply into the firebox. She shook the tea kettle to break the skin of ice she knew covered the water inside, and set it on the stove to heat. Shivering in the flickering light, she surveyed her empty shelves. She'd eaten her last pilot crackers—that standby of Alaskan staples—for lunch yesterday at school. Now the only things left were salt and pepper and a nearly-empty can of coffee. Her aching stomach informed her she wasn't going to be able to concentrate in school today.

Esther made herself a cup of coffee then bundled up in her warmest clothes, pulled on her overshoes, and tramped through several inches of snow down to the highway. She didn't stand at the bus stop, though. She headed up the road toward Palmer. She knew that Jerry—a friend of hers—often drove into Anchorage about this time of the morning. (In those days the road to Anchorage looped north of Palmer, then ran south along the Butte area before finally turning west toward Anchorage.) She peered into the darkness, hoping to see the vehicle. Sure enough, she soon saw the familiar outline of Jerry's truck, and stepped far enough out into the road so he'd see her.

The truck stopped. "Where are you going?" Jerry asked. "I need to go into Anchorage and see my folks."

Thankful Jerry didn't ask any more nosy questions, Esther chatted with her friend as they drove. He dropped her off near the creamery, promising to see if she needed a ride home before he left that evening.

Her parents also expressed surprise when she entered. As soon as she could, Esther maneuvered her mother to the side. "Have you got anything I can eat?" she asked quietly.

"C'mon upstairs," said Laura. She laid out what looked to Esther like a feast—bread with butter, coffee, eggs and a huge slice of ham. "Eat slowly at first," Laura warned, just as she had many years ago. "Give yourself time to get used to it."

Haltingly at first, not wanting to admit defeat, Esther confessed her troubles to her mother. "Don't tell Dad about this," she begged. "He doesn't think I can finish high school. I'm gonna do it if it kills me."

"Stay and help us here today," said Laura. "You can eat a good meal before you leave and I'll send something home with you. That'll get you through for a while."

Later, carrying a loaf of bread and a bag of beans, Esther prepared to catch her ride back to Matanuska. She was home before she happened to slide her hand into her coat pocket and discovered a dollar. She blessed her mother and clutched the bill as if it were a fortune. That, plus the food she'd brought from the folks, should get her through another couple of weeks. Esther could stretch a dollar until it squealed for mercy.

When Thanksgiving rolled around she gave extra thanks for the dinner the family had at the farm. She left with a full stomach and another basket of leftovers—turkey, bread, potatoes and dressing.

December began with snow and cold that seeped through the Celotex walls, chilling Esther through and through. She began counting the days till Christmas vacation, when she would again have an excuse to visit the farm without admitting defeat, which she was determined not to do. She boarded the bus on Monday, December 8th, and noticed an air of tension among the passengers.

"What's going on?" she asked her seat mate.

"Didn't you hear what happened yesterday?" exclaimed the girl.

"No, I didn't go out all day except to chop wood."

"The Japanese bombed Pearl Harbor in Hawaii yesterday morning. The president gave a speech on the radio and everything. We're at war. They're already calling for guys to volunteer for the military."

Esther stared at her, dumfounded. Of course she knew about the war going on in Europe. She'd heard about Fort Richardson, the military base in Anchorage, but it seemed distant and unconnected to her life. Without electricity she didn't get news on a radio, and she had no money for a newspaper. Her thoughts, oddly enough, flew immediately to Lionel. Had he heard? He had a job working for a plumber in Anchorage. Would he feel like he needed to enlist? He was older—he'd just turned 27—so maybe he wouldn't have to go. And what about Leonard? He was prime age for service. Laurence was only 17. Surely they wouldn't take anybody that young. Not her little brother.

School went on through the week, but Esther sensed that everyone was just going through the motions, keeping to the routine to hold onto some form of normality. Esther wished she had a radio. Her friends updated her daily on the constant stream of news about the war.

That Saturday evening, Esther relaxed in front of her stove, entertaining herself with some lively tunes on her harmonica. With her feet in the oven, she savored the last heat from the dying fire. She set down the harmonica and glanced at the wood box. Only a few sticks remained in it; she knew she'd have to spend tomorrow gathering what wood she could find to get her through another week. Around a purring Toby, she fingered the patchwork quilt in her lap. It had been a Christmas present from her mother several years ago. How she'd managed to save all those scraps and get them to Alaska, Esther couldn't imagine. Here was a printed cotton piece from matching dresses that she and Gladys had worn as little girls. This one was from a shirt Laura had made for Leonard. Shirts, dresses, blouses — even pants — every scrap brought back memories of someone in the family. Esther could remember specific times when they wore a certain garment. Nostalgia for those days when the family was all together washed over her.

Her reminiscences were cut short as lights from a car swept across her window. She had company. Lionel? She'd become adept at recognizing the motors of the various cars her boyfriends drove, and this one sounded like "Lucille." That's what Lionel had named his car after he'd learned it was her middle name. She hopped up and quickly spread the quilt on the bed. Dislodged, Toby followed it and settled down for a nap.

Esther hadn't heard about a dance anywhere tonight; all the talk had been about the war. But she was always ready to go dancing. Anything to escape her chilly house for a few hours. She opened the door to see Lionel's car backing up to her house. "What's he doing?" she wondered.

He jumped out and opened the rumble seat. The interior was stuffed full of split firewood — enough to last at least a couple of weeks. How can a girl resist a guy who brings her firewood? The two made short work of unloading the wood then Lionel said, "I couldn't find any dances around tonight, but how about we go visit the Moores?"

Esther readily agreed. She enjoyed the Moores. The young wife was the daughter of an old-time homesteader. Her husband worked at the local store. Between the two of them, they seemed to know just about everybody, and a visit to their place was better than a local paper for learning all the news. Like her family, the couple loved to play music and sing. An evening at the Moores' was sure to be filled with conversation, laughter and music. And the coffee and cookies would be fresh and hot.

Tonight, though, for a while the talk turned to the news on everyone's mind. Lionel said, "I thought sure I'd be called up by now, but I haven't heard anything so I'm going in this next week to enlist. If some country thinks they can come and bomb us and get away with it, they'd better think again. I wanna be a pilot and go shoot down a few of those Jap planes."

Even after the conversation moved on to less serious topics, Esther's brain kept turning that thought around. Lionel in danger? She hoped this war would resolve itself soon, but all the news made it sound like it was going to continue for a while.

Later, after Lionel dropped her off back at her place, Esther surveyed her wood pile with a heart full of gratitude. What a great guy. Candy and flowers were nice, but a stack of firewood — now that showed real thoughtfulness.

The following Wednesday evening Esther was surprised to hear the rumble of Lucille's engine as Lionel pulled up in her yard. "What's he doing here again so soon?" she wondered.

Squinting out into the December darkness she saw him striding to the door, lugging what looked like a large sack of potatoes. When he stepped inside she realized that's exactly what it was.

"I enlisted in the Army Air Corps today," he informed her. "I have to move onto the base, so I'm cleaning out my house. They'll be feeding me, but I thought maybe you could use this stuff."

"I sure can," Esther replied. She grabbed her coat and followed him out the door. Lucille again carried a full load; this time it was foods ranging from staples — flour, sugar and coffee — to luxuries like bacon and packages of store-bought cookies. The appearance of several boxes of oleo margarine and cans of evaporated milk nearly caused her to swoon. By the time they had it all inside, her shelves were overflowing. She knew that, with careful stewardship, this bounty would see her through the remainder of the school year. She flung her arms around Lionel. "Thank you for all this," she said. "I really didn't know how I was going to feed myself for the rest of the winter."

Lionel didn't seem to mind at all this assault on his person. "You're welcome," he replied as he enfolded her in a warm hug.

"Can I make you a cup of coffee?" Esther asked, reluctantly moving out of his arms.

"Yah," he responded, his Norwegian heritage peeking through. "That sounds good."

She added wood to the stove, boiled water and measured several spoonsful of coffee into the pot. When it was brewed, she opened a can of evaporated milk. She'd observed that he liked to use it in his coffee. He always called it "high-grade." With the coffee she served a plate of cookies straight out of the package. No baking required.

How easy it was to talk and laugh with this fellow. How the time flew by.

Finally Lionel said, "Well, I have to report to the base in the morning, so I'd better head home."

Esther watched Lucille's tail lights until they disappeared. What a comfort it was to have someone looking out for her. She could fall for a guy like that.

A few days later, school let out for Christmas break. Though Esther wished she had money to buy gifts for her family, she now had something in mind that she knew would be well-received. On Christmas Eve she made up a batch of sweet yeast dough, flattened it out and spread it with oleo margarine. Then she sprinkled it liberally with sugar and cinnamon and rolled the dough into a log, pulling the ends around to form a circle. With a knife she cut inch-wide slices all around the circle, leaving the inner rim of the circle uncut. She turned each slice slightly so the cinnamon swirl was visible. This was a Swedish tea ring—one of her mother's old-time Christmas traditions, though she hadn't made it for several years now.

The aroma of the sweet bread filled Esther's little cabin and made her mouth water, evoking memories of past years and what seemed to be simpler times. As soon as it came out of the oven she poured on a glaze made of water, margarine and powdered sugar. She couldn't resist sticking a finger into the icing that oozed and dripped onto the plate. As she licked the sweet stuff off her finger she smiled in satisfaction. This would be her Christmas present to the family.

Fred came over early on Christmas morning to pick her up. She scooted into the seat beside him, carefully balancing the tea ring on her lap.

The family's reaction was all she'd hoped for. Leonard and Laurence demonstrated their approval by wolfing down huge portions of the tea ring. Laura commented, "Mmmm, that's good." Fred went back for seconds after dinner.

Then her parents brought out their present for her. "It sure wasn't easy to wrap," Laura joked.

The shape of the object, even wrapped, left no room for guessing. Ripping off the paper and opening the case, Esther pulled out a guitar. Her own guitar. Aside from the harmonica, this was her favorite instrument. She had learned to play years ago from her mother, who had never met an instrument she couldn't master.

Her parents stood grinning at her obvious surprise and delight. She ran her hands over the light-colored body. She fiddled with the knobs, adjusting strings till they were in tune. Settling the instrument into position, she strummed a few chords.

"Try 'Little Green Valley'," suggested Laura.

"All night long in my dreams I see a spot far away," Esther started and everyone joined in. When they finished that one, they picked from their extensive repertoire of Christmas carols, hymns and tear-jerker ballads. Before long Laura pulled out her ukulele, Fred strapped on his concertina and Leonard dusted off his violin. Laurence added his voice. The family spent one of the most enjoyable hours they had shared in years.

Later that night Fred drove Esther home. As she climbed out of the car, taking care not to bump the guitar, she said, "Thanks." Though she didn't elaborate—and would have embarrassed him if she had—she meant so much more than just the ride. Thanks for the guitar, thanks for coming back to the family, thanks for a nearly-perfect Christmas Day. Just thanks.

Times of Calamity, Times of Joy- 1942

Though life in the little cabin still had its challenges—on nights the fire went out there was often ice on the water bucket in the morning—Esther felt more able to concentrate on her studies. Lionel and Lucille showed up with a load of firewood every time he noticed her supply getting low, and she had enough food staples to last till the end of the school year.

On May 20, 1942—less than 2 months before her twenty-second birthday, Esther graduated from Palmer High School. She accepted her diploma and turned around. In the audience sat both of her parents, beaming and clapping. Nothing could have kept Fred and Laura from this moment. They knew the value of education, as both had been forced to leave school before completing the eighth grade. And of all their children it was Esther—the baby whom the medical experts had set aside to die at birth, who had overcome illness, poverty and skepticism to receive a high school diploma.

Esther's graduation picture - 1942

Once school was out, Esther went back to work for Kerwin and Ginny Frank. After last year's flood they had decided to start from scratch and replace Kroghs' elderly, dilapidated store with a new one. Esther once again split her time between babysitting the children and helping in the old store while the new building was being constructed. Aware of how short the Alaskan summer was, and never knowing when the annual flood might hit, the Franks concentrated their efforts on getting the new place built. By early summer it was ready. Esther helped box up and move all the merchandise into the new store. They worked late into the evening, until satisfied that everything was in place and they could open for business in the morning. As Esther filled her buckets at the spring at the bottom of the hill and trudged up to her cabin, she anticipated how nice it was going to be, working in the brand new establishment.

Only a few weeks later she awakened one night to a strong smell of smoke. She flew out of bed and did a quick search of her house. Nothing was burning. Then she looked out the window overlooking Matanuska. In the dusky light of what passed for night in mid-summer Alaska, she beheld a horrifying sight. A soaring blaze engulfed the Franks' new store. Esther threw on her clothes and raced the mile down the hill. By the time she got there the residents of Matanuska had formed a bucket brigade and were throwing water on the fire, but it was obvious the fire was going to win. Esther went to where Ginny stood trying to comfort her crying children. She put her arms around the woman, not knowing what to say. A neighbor woman came over and took the family to her home for the night. Esther climbed back up the hill, shaken by the realization of how suddenly and completely one's world can change.

She spent the rest of the night soul searching. Her immediate plans had been closely tied up with the Franks' store. She had figured on working there for as long as they needed her. Now the job was gone. Much as she sympathized with them for their loss, she needed to find work soon. Her best bet, she decided, was to head back to Anchorage. She knew there was a room at the creamery she could stay in until she saved up enough money to get a place of her own. It was little more than a tiny storage room, but she'd spent the night there a few times and knew it had a bed. That was all she'd need for now.

Her next decision called for a visit to the Franks. In the morning she walked back down to Matanuska and knocked on the door of the home where they were staying. When she saw them, looking dazed and shaken by the night's events, she knew she'd made the right decision.

"I'm going to move into Anchorage," she told the devastated couple. "I won't need my cabin anymore, so I'd like you to have it. It's not very big, but it'll be a place to stay until you can rebuild."

Kerwin and Ginny stared at her. "Are you sure?" asked Ginny.

"Yes, I can stay with my folks at the creamery, so I'll have a roof over my head. You don't have one, so I want you to take the cabin."

Kerwin said, "I don't know how to thank you. If you're sure you don't need it, we accept."

Esther wasted no time in packing up her belongings. She took Toby back to the farm and bade him a reluctant farewell. Laurence drove her into Anchorage and helped her unload her boxes in the cubby hole at the creamery. She stood and took stock of the room before she unpacked. A Blazo box turned on its end sat next to a narrow cot. These comprised the room's only furnishings. At some time in the past someone had tried to add a homey touch by hanging a curtain at the window. It now drooped there, an ancient scrap of cloth strung on a saggy piece of wire. The window looked—oddly enough—not to the outside, but into the upstairs hall. Esther made the bed and hung her clothes on the nails in one wall. Her cubicle began to feel like home.

Esther had only been in Anchorage a few days when an unsettling incident brought back all her mother's admonitions about the untrustworthiness of men. She lay relaxing on her bed one evening, reading. She got up to start undressing for bed when suddenly she got a creepy feeling that someone was watching her. Turning her head sharply, she saw an eye pressed to the window where the drooping curtain didn't completely cover the glass. She flew across the room and yanked the cloth in front of the eye. Thankful that there was a lock on the door, she rechecked it to make sure it was secure. There were several rooms above the creamery that single men would rent for short periods. There had been one guy around recently whom Esther suspected to be the Peeping Tom, but with no physical evidence besides an ogling eye, she had no basis to accuse anybody. She tightened the wire so the curtain hung straight, and always made sure it was completely closed and the door was locked.

Job hunting started out much like her previous attempts in the city, with employers once again looking at her petite frame and judging her unfit for employment. One morning, Esther noticed a bus stopping not far from the creamery, picking up a crowd of young women, many younger than she. She found out that they all worked on Fort Richardson Army Base. "Well," she thought, "if they can work there, I can. I know I'm at least as capable as they are." From her vast age of 22, those 19-year-old girls looked like silly children.

The next morning Esther joined the crowd at the bus stop and rode to an area of the base known as Elmendorf Field. (After the war this area was turned over to the Air Force and became Elmendorf Air Force Base.) The personnel director gave her a test to determine her abilities, and was so impressed she hired her on the spot. As an entry-level employee Esther was put to work filing. Though grateful for the job, she found the work boring. When she heard of an opening in blueprints, she applied and was given a transfer. She liked this job better because,

Esther at work on Elmendorf.

though it was still repetitious, she felt like a more productive participant in the war effort.

Several months earlier she'd gotten a letter from Gladys, announcing that she was pregnant, and the baby was due in September. Gladys begged Esther to come over for the birth and Esther made plans to be there. All the money she could save from her small paycheck she set aside to pay for airfare to Bristol Bay. Their sister Alice had had three children over the past few years down in Minnesota, but this would be the first niece or nephew that Esther would actually get to see and hold.

In early September, Esther flew to Dillingham. She was met by a very pregnant Gladys, who took her to the tent near the cannery where she and Stan lived. The sisters chattered nonstop and Stan finally said, "I don't see how either of you knows what the other one's saying, with you both talking at the same time."

Nothing could dampen their joy at being back together. Esther admired the bassinet Gladys had prepared for the baby. Not knowing the gender of the baby didn't stop Esther and their mother from making gifts. Laura had crocheted a baby blanket and Esther brought bibs she'd embroidered. Esther also brought receiving blankets, cloth diapers and baby bottles that Laura had purchased.

Since Gladys and Stan lived in Dillingham, they were just a few miles from the hospital in Kanakanak. Gladys told Esther a friend had already promised the use of his car for Stan to drive her to the hospital when the time came. Stan said, "I don't know what all the fuss is about having a baby. In Poland the women work in the fields until the baby comes, have it on the side of the field, and get right back to work."

Esther longed to punch him. "Yes, I'm sure growing up in Michigan makes you an expert on what they do in Poland," she retorted silently.

On September 11 Gladys indicated that it was time to get to the hospital. Everything worked just as she planned, with Stan driving her and Esther to Kanakanak. A nurse got Gladys settled in the labor room and Stan asked, "Where is Dr. Oleson?"

"Oh, he'll be here," the nurse replied—somewhat nervously, Esther thought. She went scouting around the hospital and eventually found the doctor coming in a side door, smelling like a brewery. She scampered off to find Stan.

"Dr. Oleson is drunk!" she told him.

"Well, he'd better get over *that* pretty quick," Stan said, heading for the door.

He and Esther located the doctor and Stan confronted him. "My wife's in labor and you're supposed to deliver this kid. You'd better lay off the booze."

"I'm fine," slurred the doctor, staring at them with bleary eyes.

"We'll see about that," said Stan.

Over the next hours, as Gladys's labor continued, Esther and Stan kept watch over the doctor. The man came up with all sorts of outlandish excuses to leave the building, but his two human watchdogs kept him from escaping to the bar. Though Esther still had reservations about Stan, she had to admit he came through for his wife that night. The next morning Gladys gave birth to a son, Joseph Stanley. In those days family members weren't invited into the delivery room, so Esther remained in the waiting room with Stan. Years later Gladys laughed as she said she was glad Esther wasn't in there, because she probably would have decided she never wanted to have kids.

Esther stayed until Gladys was back on her feet, then flew home to Anchorage and resumed her job at Fort Richardson. The meager pay never did allow Esther to rent a place of her own, so she continued to live in the cubby hole at the creamery. As winter approached, Esther discovered that the builders had skimped on insulation for her room, and mornings found her just as cold as she'd been in her cabin.

Lionel kept himself very much in the picture during the time Esther lived in Anchorage. He lived on Fort Richardson, so he could stop in to see her at work when he had free time, and managed to come around often during after-work hours. One day he dropped by her office beaming with pride, carrying a guitar. He had been around the Larson family long enough to know they all loved music, and he'd heard Esther play her guitar. He'd found a friend on base who taught him some chords, and that was enough to inspire him to get his own instrument. Now when he came over in the evening he and Esther went over to her parents' apartment (as Esther's tiny room had no space for entertaining a visitor, especially a gentleman). The four of them would sing and play for hours, giving Lionel some practice. He had a good ear for melody and could hear the chord changes, but Esther continued to despair over his lack of rhythm. He eventually developed his own strumming technique that worked for nearly any song he tried to play.

One talent he possessed that took no special practice was his gift of mimicry. He loved to tell stories about his fictional Uncle Ole back in North Dakota and Ole's sidekick, Sven. Though Lionel's English was as American-sounding as Esther's, he'd grown up in a bilingual family and could slip into a Norwegian brogue as authentic as Fred's.

One evening the conversation turned to hunting and Lionel commented, "That reminds me of when my Uncle Ole and his pal Sven went bear hunting up in Canada. They stayed at a little cabin deep in the woods, and in the morning they took their guns and went out to find a bear. They were walking along and Sven was getting tired of not finding anything. He said, 'Ay t'ink it's time to go back to da cabin. Dere's no bears around here.' Just then they came face to face with a big black bear.

Instead of aiming at the bear they both dropped their guns, turned tail and lit out for the cabin with the bear in hot pursuit. Well, Ole outran Sven and reached the cabin before him. He pulled open the door and Sven dashed in, followed by the bear. Ole slammed the door and yelled, 'Dis vun's fer yoo; Ay'll go git me anodder vun!'"

The young couple's relationship wasn't all about laughter and fun. Not long after Esther returned from Bristol Bay Lionel broached the subject of marriage. Esther was not averse to the idea, but she had some issues she wanted to clear up before they got more serious.

"I couldn't stand the way my parents argued," she told him. "When I get married, any disagreements we have will be discussed when the kids aren't around."

"I agree," said Lionel. "My dad wasn't easy to live with. If he got mad about something, he'd give us all the silent treatment. He'd mope around for days, not speaking to anybody. Most of us kids left home as soon as we could find work to support ourselves. I promised myself I'd never treat my wife or family like that."

Esther knew she'd found her Prince Charming. She

Lionel and Esther courting , 1942

couldn't wait to tell her mother. The next day she caught Laura when she was alone and said, "I'm going to marry Lionel."

Laura's head jerked around and she stared at Esther. "Not that fool!" she exclaimed.

Esther didn't take the words seriously. She knew Laura was saying, in her rough way, that no man was good enough for her little girl.

A few days later Lionel showed up at Esther's workplace, wearing a huge smile and carrying a small round plastic case. Esther's heart leapt as she accepted it from him. Inside lay an engagement ring with a tiny diamond. A wedding band with four even smaller diamonds accompanied

Esther and "Lucille," the car

it. Esther had no quarrel with Lionel's choice. She knew that, on his military pay of $21 per month, these rings were all Lionel could afford. Emotions threatened to swamp her as she slipped the engagement ring onto her finger. She was really getting married. She felt like the luckiest girl in the world.

That night when the couple visited Fred and Laura, Esther tried every trick she knew to get them to notice her latest accessory. When offered coffee, she accepted the cup with her left hand. She felt sure they'd notice when she played the guitar, with that diamond flashing and winking in the light as she changed chords. Her folks remained oblivious. Finally Lionel couldn't take any more and exclaimed, "Esther, what's that on your hand?"

Laughter and congratulations followed. Esther knew her folks were delighted for her and happy with her choice, despite Laura's previous comments. She recalled a complaint her mother had voiced during the time that Lionel had worked for them on the farm. "He can't leave my stove alone. I'll just get it a perfect temperature for baking, and in comes Lionel. He goes straight to the stove and starts poking at it and putting more wood in. It either goes out or ends up way too hot." Esther figured if the only criticism her mother could find had to do with how he stoked a fire, she had a keeper.

The family planned again to celebrate Thanksgiving on the farm. This time, Lionel would be included as an almost-

189

official member of the family. Then, just days before Thanksgiving, Lionel received his orders. He would be shipping out to Atka, a small island far out on the Aleutian Chain. These islands had become increasingly important since the war began, as two of the most remote islands— Kiska and Attu— had been captured, and the U.S. feared an air attack on the mainland. The Aleutian Islands became a first line of defense in preventing such an attack. Although Atka would not be a major base, its indigenous residents were relocated (in an unfair, and probably unnecessary, move) to Southeast Alaska for the duration of the war. Lionel and several dozen other soldiers were tasked with construction and maintenance of a communications base to facilitate interaction between the major bases, including Dutch Harbor, Shemya and Adak. Instead of enjoying Thanksgiving dinner with his future wife and in-laws, he shared the meal with fellow soldiers on an Army transport ship somewhere along the Aleutian Chain.

A Long Year with an Unexpected Ending - 1943

The months of 1943 crept by, made more bearable for Esther by Lionel's frequent letters. She understood that he couldn't say much about his job, but she enjoyed his humorous accounts of life on Atka and the eccentricities of his fellow soldiers. He had an eye for the ridiculous, and often included funny stories about his experiences on the island. He thought it was hilarious — yet so typical of the Army — how he got his job assignment. In one of his previous jobs he'd worked for the electric company, not doing anything technical, just driving the boom truck, lifting electric poles and setting them into holes. In the Army's mind this qualified him to be in charge of the electrical and communications operations on Atka. Esther was confident that, though Lionel might lack experience, he'd learn quickly and perform the job as well as anyone and better than most.

Always one to appreciate a corny joke, Lionel wrote about one of his fellow soldiers who often got stuck with KP duty. As the man stood, spoon in hand behind a gigantic serving container of canned pine-apple, he would greet each person who came through the line, "Here I stand, 'Dole'-ing out the pineapple."

Lionel, at work on Atka.

191

Left: Lionel with his guitar on Atka.

Below: Actress Olivia DeHavilland dances with one of Lionel's buddies during a visit to Atka.

Lionel also wrote about the island, the cold, wind and fog. As the weather warmed he went exploring, hiking the hills and fishing in the streams. Boredom was his biggest enemy, as much of his time was spent trying to stay prepared for an assault that never happened. One day, though, Lionel wrote that he and his comrades earned their keep. In one of those unexplained quirks of nature, on this particular day the sun shone brightly out of a clear blue sky over Atka. At the same time, the entire rest of the Aleutian Chain lay socked in by fog. All day long the fighter planes that normally landed at the larger air bases roared in and out of Atka. Lionel and the others stationed there ran themselves ragged as they fed and housed the pilots and crews and helped fuel planes for their next missions.

When they had gotten engaged, Esther and Lionel had agreed to delay their nuptials till the war ended. Reports now poured in via radio and newspaper recounting battles in Europe and Africa as well as the Pacific. Esther knew that the Aleutian Islands which had been invaded and occupied by the Japanese had been reclaimed, but the threat of more attacks remained. Every day she prayed for safety, not just for Lionel, but for Leonard, who had joined the Marines the previous year. In June, Laurence joined the Army and, after boot camp, was sent almost immediately to Germany.

In the fall came word from Lionel that he would be home for a month-long furlough in December. At once Esther began planning how to spend every possible minute with him. Her job—inconvenience that it was—would keep them apart more than she liked.

On December 19, Lionel arrived home. Esther greeted him as he stepped off the plane at Elmendorf Field. Nearly from the first moment every conversation ended with something like, "...once the war's over and we get married."

Lionel wasn't content for long with this nebulous state of affairs. The next evening he picked Esther up from work and said, "Y'know, this war could go on for years. I don't want to wait that long to get married. I'll be home for a month. Let's do it now."

"Now?" Esther was flabbergasted. "What do you mean by 'now'?"

"How about next Sunday," Lionel suggested. It was obvious to Esther this wasn't the first time he'd considered the issue.

"The day after Christmas?" Esther exclaimed.

Lionel shrugged. "Why not?"

"Where could we get married on such short notice? I don't have a dress. Where would we live?" The questions tumbled out of Esther's mouth as they raced through her mind. Terrified yet elated at the prospect, she thought of all the roadblocks to such a plan.

"I'll bet Pastor Alfsen at the church in Palmer would marry us. And we'll live in my cabin. It's been empty since Martin and I enlisted."

"Isn't that Martin's cabin, too?" Esther asked, not sure she wanted to share a house with Lionel's buddy should he come home while Lionel was off in the Aleutians.

"We made an agreement when we built the place," Lionel explained. "Whichever one of us got married first, the other one would sign his half of the house over. So the place will be mine. Ours," he amended.

"Well, I still need a dress," Esther said.

"It doesn't matter what you wear," said Lionel with the flippancy of someone who worried not a whit over his own wedding garb. As a military man during time of war, he would naturally wear his dress uniform.

From that point Esther felt she'd been pulled into a whirlpool. Her sister and family were in town for the holidays, so she and Gladys went dress shopping. Practical-minded Esther knew she didn't want a frilly gown she'd never wear again. Anchorage dress shops in the dead of winter didn't cater much to that sort of dress anyway.

After pulling out and discarding several choices, Esther zeroed in on a neat woolen skirt and jacket in a deep brown. "I think I'll try this one," she said. The suit fit her slender frame perfectly, and Esther knew she'd found her wedding dress.

"I should have some flowers," she said. "Where am I going to find flowers I can afford in the middle of winter?"

"Oh, you know our mother," Gladys laughed. "She'll 'know somebody' who can help."

Sure enough, when approached with the problem of flowers Laura said, "Don't you worry about that. I know somebody. I'll take care of it."

Esther said a prayer of gratitude for her mother's resourcefulness and seemingly endless number of "somebodies."

Lionel and Esther drove to Palmer and spoke with Victor Alfsen, the minister of the Palmer Presbyterian Church, who said he'd be delighted to perform the ceremony on Sunday afternoon. Gladys and her husband, Stan, would serve as matron of honor and best man.

Rain poured down as the small wedding party made its way to the church that Sunday. Mrs. Alfsen played the piano while the group gathered. Fred and Laura sat in the front pew with young Joe while his parents joined Lionel and Esther at the altar.

The ceremony was short and simple, just the way this bride and groom preferred. Once Pastor Alfsen pronounced them man and wife and the license was signed, the family set out over wet, icy roads for the Larson farm. There, Laura treated them to a bountiful turkey dinner.

The house was warm and the mood convivial as the group celebrated. Lionel kept glancing out the window and finally spoke his thoughts. "We'd better get on the road if we're going to get to Anchorage tonight. It's already getting dark and with this rain and ice…" He left the rest unspoken. They all knew what a long, dangerous trip lay before the newlyweds. Lionel had taken the precaution of putting chains on Lucille earlier in the day, but on a Sunday evening, the day after Christmas, they'd be on their own if they ran into trouble during the 60-mile trip.

After a flurry of hugs and good wishes, Lionel supported Esther as they slithered their way across the ice and climbed into the car. Esther waved as Lionel reached for the key. It wasn't there. "Now what," he grunted. He climbed out and looked toward the small group still clustered in the doorway.

"Alright, Stan, give them back," Esther heard him say.

Stan stood in the doorway, cackling like a demented rooster. In his upraised hand he held Lucille's keys. "Come and get 'em," he yelled.

Lionel strode over to him and put out his hand. Stan danced away, holding the keys just out of reach. Through the house, back into the yard and out to the barn the two men wrestled. At first Lionel went along good-naturedly, but as time passed and daylight diminished, Esther knew he was losing patience. Stan seemed oblivious to all but his own prank, wriggling out of Lionel's grasp again and again, always keeping up that infernal giggle. After nearly half an hour he finally relented and handed over the keys. Lionel slid back into the car. He sat in tense silence for a few moments, then relaxed. With a wry grin at Esther, as if to say, "Leave it to Stan to spoil our wedding day," he started the car. At last they were on their way.

Esther shivered as Lucille slowly rolled along the dark, icy road. The car was a convertible, and its cloth top barely stopped the raindrops, and did nothing to keep out the cold. She tucked her coat as tightly as she could around her legs, glad she'd kept the woolen wedding dress on for the trip. She thought about the inadequacy of women's overshoes. Obviously they were designed by men. Women would put a little fur or something inside to keep them warm. Her overshoes were made of the same rubber that men's were made of, but shaped to fit over a shoe with a modest heel. Despite being covered with a pair of nylon stockings, the shoes and the boots, Esther's feet still felt like blocks of ice.

"Can you turn on the heater?" she finally asked.

"It's on as high as it'll go," Lionel replied.

Esther reached down, unfastened the boots and wiggled her feet out of her shoes. She drew her feet up onto the seat, pulled her woolen skirt down as far as she could, and wrapped her arms around her knees. Their first car ride as a married couple certainly was no romantic moon-dappled drive.

Lionel peered through the wet, foggy windshield. He cranked down his window a few inches. Esther felt the draft and huddled tighter into a ball.

Lionel noticed her discomfort. "I have to keep the window open," he apologized. "Otherwise the windshield fogs up so bad I can't see to drive."

Esther nodded, but decided to put all her energy into keeping warm, rather than making conversation. Presently Lionel spoke again. ""We're coming to Eagle River. I sure hope we can make the hill okay."

The tap of raindrops on the canvas top and the chug of Lucille's chained tires were the only sounds in the car as Lionel started down the steep hill. Esther held her breath. She knew he'd have to speed up when he neared the bottom in order to have enough momentum to get up the other side. She clutched the seat on either side of her, glad it was dark. Not that she didn't trust Lionel's driving, but these road conditions were about as bad as they got. She fervently prayed that they wouldn't have to back up the hill. At least there was no traffic to get in the way if they went into a slide.

Lionel cautiously accelerated as he guided the car down the grade. Reaching the bottom, he pressed the gas harder and Lucille forged up the other side. Esther's stockinged feet were now planted firmly against the floorboards. She pushed with all her might, as if she could help. Lucille almost crested the hill, fishtailed a few times, then spun 180 degrees.

"Well," said Lionel, "since we're facing downhill now I guess that's the way we're going." He let the car roll back down the hill, then put her in reverse. "Let's try it backwards."

All cars of that era were rear-wheel drive, and sometimes it was easier to back up a slippery hill than to take it frontward. Sure enough, between Lucille's chains, Lionel's skillful driving and Esther's pushing against the back of her seat, they finally made it up the Eagle River hill.

From that point on into Anchorage the ride seemed tame. As they drew nearer to town there was some sand on the road, and other vehicles (nearly all wearing chains) had chewed up the ice somewhat, increasing traction.

It was almost 10:30 p.m. before the couple pulled up outside the Anchorage Westward Hotel. The clerk greeted them. "Good evening, Mr. and Mrs. Haakenson. Your room is all ready for you."

Esther felt a jolt of surprise when she realized "Mrs. Haakenson" meant her. She felt her icy feet and hands begin to thaw in the welcome warmth of the lobby. They were shown to their room, which was warmed by an in-room oil heater. Everything seemed so luxurious to her. Though the toilet facilities consisted of a shared bathroom down the hall, the toilet flushed and the sink offered hot and cold running water. No outhouses or hand pumps for this honeymoon.

They thanked the young man who brought their bags up to the room. Lionel shut the door and adjusted the heater while Esther removed her coat and boots. Then her new husband turned and smiled at her. Esther smiled back and walked into his arms, ready to embark on this new adventure called marriage.

Making Adjustments - 1944-1946

The newlyweds stayed at the Westward Hotel for two nights. During the day they ferried Esther's belongings from the creamery to the small frame house on East 10th Avenue. Lionel's buddy, Martin, had begun building it several years previously, and when Lionel moved in the two worked together to complete it.

As she started settling into her new home Esther realized just how much work lay before her. While Lionel and Martin were not slobs, they were men, and men just don't arrange a house the way women do. She found hammers and screwdrivers mixed in a drawer of silverware, while jars of bolts and nails jostled with cookware for space on the shelves. This place needed a woman's touch.

Only a few days after they moved in Lionel received word from the Army. His furlough was being cut short and he needed to return to Atka. He bade his bride a reluctant good-bye and boarded the plane back to his assignment.

Though Esther missed him, she had plenty to keep her busy. She continued her job on base, so five days a week she walked uptown and caught the bus to Elmendorf Field. In the evenings and on weekends, she put all her energy into making the little house into a home.

The Haakensons' house in Anchorage.

199

A well under the house fed cold water up into the kitchen. From the kitchen a hall led back to a bathroom and two small bedrooms. The front of the house was the living room, where a small oil heater had been installed. Esther didn't use it, depending on the kitchen's wood cook stove to heat the house. A door off the kitchen opened into an unheated 6 x 8-foot mud room. Out in this area Esther stored all the "man stuff" that cluttered her new home—fishing poles and tackle, snow shoes, gold panning supplies, and tools of all descriptions.

The early months of 1944 didn't seem greatly different to Esther than when she'd been single. She lived alone, with frequent letters from Lionel. She didn't see her mother as often as she had, as Laura had moved back out to the farm. With Laurence in the service, Laura took over the farm duties. These now consisted solely of Laura's flock of chickens. The horses and dairy cows had been sold off in an attempt to cut down on the expenses the farm incurred.

One bright spot was Gladys's return from Bristol Bay. She and Stan moved back to Anchorage and settled in the small house that Laura and her daughters had lived in when they first came to Anchorage. Joe was an active toddler and Gladys was now expecting her second child. Though both she and Esther had busy lives, they made time to get together as often as they could.

A change from her single days took the form of a package that arrived on the twenty-sixth day of every month. Somehow Lionel had arranged for a box of chocolate covered cherries to be delivered on the day of the month that they had been married. All Esther's family and friends soon knew about this special sign of Lionel's devotion, as Esther shared her candies with everyone. In demonstration of how love can conquer obstacles, Esther's dislike of chocolate didn't seem to extend to those special candies. A couple of times Gladys showed up, saw the chocolates and quickly checked the calendar. She shook her head. "I can't believe it," she declared.

Gladys stopped by the house one Saturday that summer. "Joe and I are going out to the farm to see Mom," she said. "Want to come along?"

Esther jumped at the chance to spend the day with Gladys and her young son. She knew that the drive could get long for 22-month-old Joe. And with Gladys's next baby due in less than two months, she'd probably appreciate help with driving as well as baby wrangling.

The threesome spent the day visiting and helping Laura with chores around the farm (or in Joe's case, getting into everything), then started home in the late afternoon. Only a few miles out of Palmer Esther spotted a fellow in uniform walking down the road. "There's Tommy," she said, recognizing a former schoolmate. "Looks like he's hitchhiking." Gladys stopped beside the young man.

"Thanks for the ride," Tommy said as he climbed in. "I came out to the Valley to visit my folks, and I'm supposed to be back at Fort Richardson in a few hours. I could have taken the bus but I thought it'd be quicker to hitchhike."

"Don't worry," Gladys told him. "We'll get you there in time."

They rumbled on over the rough, dusty road for several more miles. Then, with no warning, the car quit. Gladys pumped the gas and pushed the starter and was rewarded with nothing more than a few clicking noises from the car.

The passengers climbed out and Gladys lifted the hood. The two women and Joe stood back, waiting for Tommy to take the lead in this inspection. In the Larson family Fred, Laurence or Leonard would have dived under the hood and had the problem fixed before the women could get out of the car. Tommy stared at the car's workings with a blank look. Esther could tell that fixing cars was not this male's forte. They took turns gawking under the hood, which led to no appreciable change in the car's performance. Esther noticed

Tommy taking furtive glances at his watch and she knew that he was worrying about being AWOL.

Then, like the cavalry coming to the rescue, the bus that ran the route between Palmer and Anchorage appeared in the distance. Though he had scheduled stops along the way, the accommodating driver would pick up and drop off passengers wherever they wished. Esther thought quickly.

"Let's flag down the bus and you three go on into Anchorage. Tommy, I know the bus will drop you off at the base and, Gladys, I'll wait here till you come back with help."

Gladys, Joe and Tommy scrambled onto the bus and Esther scooted back into the car. She watched the dust settle as the bus disappeared. She had intended to wait as she'd told Gladys, but she wasn't the type to do nothing for long. Soon she said to herself, "I'll just take a look. Maybe I can find what's wrong."

She lifted up the hood and studied the unfamiliar innards that somehow worked together to make this car run. "Hmmm…This hose hooks in here, and this wire goes over here." Slowly she worked through the mechanisms of the vehicle. She might not be able to name each part, but she was learning how they fit together. Suddenly she noticed a dangling wire. "Let's see where this is supposed to be," she muttered. She grasped a similar wire and slid her fingers along it until she found its other end, securely attached to another unknown piece of this complicated machine. Keeping track of the properly placed wire, she soon located a hole in which to insert her stray wire. "I guess it can't hurt to try," she told herself, and pushed the wire in. She stood back, dusted off her hands, and climbed into the driver's seat.

"C'mon Nellie," she encouraged the car. She turned the key and pushed the starter. The engine purred like a happy cat. "Yippee!" Esther yelled. She put the car in gear, let out the clutch, and headed toward Anchorage.

Gladys and Joe had just disembarked when Esther pulled up behind the bus.

"Esther! Did someone come and help you get the car going?" asked Gladys.

"No, I just figured it out myself," Esther laughed. She felt a glow of pride in what she'd done, but didn't really consider it unusual. To her it was just one more problem to solve so she could go on about the business of her life.

One evening in late August, Esther heard a knock on her door. She opened it and there, grinning at her surprise, was Lionel.

"What on earth are you doing home?" she exclaimed, throwing her arms around him.

"We got an unexpected furlough," said Lionel. "We had a job to do up near Mount McKinley, so they let us take a few extra days to sightsee. I didn't realize it till we were up there, but I could've taken you with us. Some of the other guys' wives met us."

Esther felt a brief twinge of disappointment at missing out on a trip with Lionel, but joy over having him home soon pushed out any hurt feelings. She showed him proudly through the tidy little house, and he exclaimed appreciatively over the many changes—big and little—that she'd made. The kitchen now contained only things that belonged in a kitchen. Lionel's fishing gear and building supplies had been moved and stored neatly in the mud room. A rag rug lay in front of the couch in the living room and a white chenille spread with pink and blue pastel flowers covered the bed. "This place really looks like a home now," he said.

Lionel only had a few days before he had to return to Atka, but the two enjoyed every moment of their time together. Esther couldn't take time off from her job, but the evenings and nights were theirs. They visited Gladys and Stan, where Lionel got reacquainted with Joe and met Donald, who had been born earlier that month. Esther saw Lionel off when he had to go, feeling like they'd gotten the chance to have the rest of their honeymoon.

The next months settled back into a normal routine, though as Christmas neared, Esther began to notice a change. Many days she felt slightly nauseated, and even the chocolate covered cherries didn't tempt her anymore.

At the farm on Christmas Day, the women worked in the kitchen while Stan and Fred visited in the living room and Joe toddled around from room to room. Laura shot a series of interested glances at her daughter and finally asked quietly, "Esther, are you pregnant?" This was not the sort of conversation that men were supposed to hear.

"I think I might be," she replied. (If Esther ever suffered from true morning sickness she never would admit to it, and often claimed that women who did just wanted to be "interesting.")

Gladys, overhearing, crowed, "I thought so!"

The three chattered and laughed, bringing up every story they could think of regarding good and bad pregnancies and births. Finally, feeling rather overwhelmed with the thought of what lay in store for her, Ether decided it was time to change the subject.

"What do you hear from Laurence?" she asked Laura.

"I got a letter a few weeks ago. He just said he's somewhere in Germany," Laura replied. "I don't know if he's near the front or not, but he's in the infantry, so he's probably in the fighting."

The three stood silently for several minutes, thinking of the danger Laurence might be in. "Well, we'll just have to keep praying for him," Esther said at last.

"Amen," Gladys seconded.

The letters between Esther and Lionel took on a new focus over the next months. The doctor said the baby was due in late May, which was perfect timing, as Lionel was due to return from Atka about then. There was little debate over names. Lionel had already told Esther he'd always wanted a son named Jimmy. To make things easier, they agreed the child, depending on its gender, would take that parent's first name as its middle name. If it was a boy he would be James Lionel; a girl would be called Mary Esther. As it turned out, the feminine choice got quite dusty awaiting its turn to be used.

Shortly after the start of the new year, Gladys pulled up in front of Esther's house. As she came into the house Esther noticed her face looked white and drawn. "Gladys, what's wrong?" Esther demanded.

"I just talked to Dad. The Army sent an officer to tell them that Laurence has been captured. The Germans have taken him prisoner." Gladys's voice trembled.

Esther stared at her sister. "Oh no," she said. The response sounded weak and inadequate in her ears, but they were the only words that came. Dread wrapped around her like an icy quilt. Frantic questions jostled in her mind. "What happens to prisoners of war? Will Laurence be killed? Or tortured?" She shook so hard her legs wouldn't hold her and she dropped into a chair.

"We need to keep praying," she said, finding her voice. "Laurence is tough. He'll be okay." She knew she was trying to convince herself as well as Gladys.

In the days following this news Esther struggled with conflicting emotions. Worry for Laurence would give way to excitement about the baby, then she'd feel guilty for being happy, when Laurence might be suffering unimagined horrors over in Germany.

A few months before her due date, Esther quit her job at the base to concentrate on preparing for the new arrival. She had already scrounged scraps of wood and drawn up plans for a crib. Confidently, she started in with saw and hammer. It took several weeks to complete, but she found it kept her mind from focusing obsessively on Laurence through the short winter days and long nights. In the end she produced a crib that rivaled any she could have bought, if she'd been able to afford one. From there she turned her attention to knitting blankets, and sewing tiny clothes. Laura had taught her girls well, and Esther's innate perfectionism helped her turn out a growing stack of neatly hemmed cloth diapers as well as several white nightgowns that would be appropriate for either a boy or a girl. When possible Esther used her mother's sewing machine on the farm, but most of the clothing she stitched by hand.

Despite her petite frame, her belly didn't protrude as so many pregnant women's do. Somehow the baby positioned itself so that, up until the last few weeks, Esther wore some of her looser clothing and only had to buy a couple of maternity outfits.

Esther welcomed the warming weather as April turned to May. She was glad Gladys planned to remain in Anchorage when Stan went to Bristol Bay for the fishing season. With two children and a third on the way, Gladys stood as the veteran mommy who could advise Esther as she prepared for this new phase of her life. Esther also looked forward to Lionel's return. She wanted this child to know from the start that he or she had a loving family.

Several weeks before her due date, she woke up realizing that her water had broken. After a quick run through the house to make sure everything was neat, she asked her neighbor to take her to the hospital. Once there, things slowed down. She lay in the bed wishing she had a way to inform Lionel. Not that he'd be able to come rushing to her side. Atka was a long way from Anchorage.

Her contractions continued through the day and on into the night. Finally, at 3:40 on the morning of May 9 the baby arrived. The smiling nurse said, "Congratulations, Mrs. Haakenson, you have a son."

Esther smiled back, exhausted but happy. Lionel was going to have his Jimmy. She watched the doctors and nurses fuss over the baby in a way she thought must be normal until the doctor snapped, "Get the oxygen!"

A nurse ran down the hall and returned with a cart carrying the oxygen tank. Esther caught a glimpse of Jimmy's face. It was blue! In a daze she watched the medical staff working frantically over the tiny body.

"Please breathe," she pleaded silently as the chaos around her son continued. Precious seconds ticked by before she finally heard a faint cry, signaling that Jimmy was breathing. She relaxed and exhaled, aware that she'd been holding her breath. She accepted the squalling baby from the nurse and set about comforting him. She ran her fingers gently over his body, marveling at the miniature fingers and toes. Before long the nurse came back to whisk Jimmy away to the nursery. Though she hated to be separated from him, exhaustion overtook her and she sank into a much-needed sleep.

She awoke to the sound of voices beside her bed. Her parents and Gladys stood beaming at her. After receiving their congratulations Esther said, "I need to send a telegram to Lionel. He doesn't know about the baby yet." Though telephones were becoming more common around Anchorage, Esther didn't have one. A telegram was still the quickest form of communication for the majority of Alaska's population.

"And we have more good news," Gladys told her. "We got word that Laurence has been released from the prison camp in Germany. He'll be coming home before long."

"Oh, thank God," Esther replied fervently. "Lionel will want to know about that, too."

Esther prepared a telegram and sent it with Gladys. At that time the typical hospital stay for a maternity patient was a week, so Esther relaxed, slept and enjoyed time with her baby. One of the first things she noticed was how disinterested he was in the world around him. He had to be coaxed to nurse, then he went right back to sleep once his tummy was full. Esther talked and played with him whenever he was with her, but had trouble keeping him awake. The nurse, coming in and finding him sleeping, would scold Esther, urging her to interact with him more.

Lionel arrived a few days after Jimmy's birth. He couldn't stop smiling as he held his son. Esther knew her

husband was going to be a wonderful father.

She knew he had a second reason to be happy. He told her that just before he left Atka, some brass had arrived and mustered all the personnel that were stationed there. The captain announced which men planned to reenlist and which ones would be leaving the service at the end of their current terms of duty.

Lionel with Jim, 1945.

Lionel related the incident. "When he read my name as one who was leaving he mispronounced it, of course—called me Hackinson instead of Haakenson. Then his aide said, 'I thought Sergeant Hackinson was going to re-up.' I yelled out, 'No sir, Sergeant Hackinson is *not* going to re-up!' I was so rattled I pronounced my own name wrong."

When Esther was released from the hospital, the family returned to the little house on 10th Avenue. Lionel still had a few months left of his military service, so he continued to report to Fort Richardson each day. As soon as he got home in the evenings he'd give Esther a kiss then head directly for

Jimmy's crib. Whether the baby was asleep or awake, his father picked him up and started playing with him. Sometimes Jimmy would open his eyes and watch as Lionel talked and sang to him; at other times he slept on.

A few weeks later Jimmy still was not responding to his parents' attempts to engage his attention. Though no longer slow to nurse, he was content between feedings to lie awake quietly, or sleep. At his first check-up the doctor looked him over, pronounced him healthy, then gave Esther what seemed an odd piece of advice. "You probably shouldn't try to have any more children," he told her. "You're so small, and with the problems you had, it could be dangerous to your health."

Esther didn't think the problems had been that severe, or wouldn't have been, if they'd had the oxygen in the room like they should have. She didn't argue with the doctor, but both Lionel and she planned on having a large family. If God blessed them with more children, they would all be as welcome as Jimmy was.

In early summer Esther answered a knock on the door. Standing there was a tall young soldier, looking pale and even thinner than his usual 150 pounds, but grinning like his old self.

"Laurence!" Esther grabbed her brother. "Come and see your nephew," she said, drawing Laurence into the house. The two spent several hours catching up, taking pictures with Jimmy, and reveling in their reunion. Underneath the lighthearted joking, Esther sensed a change in Laurence. When she tried to broach the subject of his time as a prisoner of war, he cut her off. "Aaah, it was nuthin'," he growled, and turned the conversation.

Laurence, Esther, and Jim –1945.

Later Esther discussed it with her mother. "Laurence wouldn't talk about Germany," she said. "He said it wasn't bad, but…"

"It was awful for him," Laura broke in. "He finally told me about it one day. He was at the Battle of the Bulge and saw some horrible things. He was captured when he and several of his buddies got separated from the rest of their unit. They heard the Germans coming and tried to hide in a potato patch. He said that shortly after they were captured they were forced to march nearly every day. They didn't know if they were going to be shot, pushed to march till they dropped, or just end up in another prison. Fortunately, the Allies got there and freed them."

Esther had read about the carnage at the Battle of the Bulge and felt sickened to know that Laurence had to witness it. Later it came to light that his captors forced their prisoners to march because they knew the Allies were advancing, and they were trying to stay ahead of them.

After Laurence left, Esther sat rocking Jimmy and thinking about how blessed she was. She had a loving husband and a beautiful baby boy. Lionel, Laurence and Leonard were now all safely home from the war. Her sister's family and her parents lived nearby. A snug house, good friends, and an Alaskan spring in progress—who could ask for more? "Yes, Esther," she murmured, "you've got a lot to be thankful for."

In August, Gladys gave birth to her third child, Alice. Watching the little girl follow her mother with her eyes and respond to voices and other sights and sounds brought home to Esther how slowly her own son was developing. Each doctor's appointment brought the same scenarios. Esther would ask why Jimmy was so slow in reaching typical milestones. The doctor would tap Jimmy's knees with his little hammer to test his reflexes. "He's fine; babies just develop at different rates," he'd say and send her on her way.

Lionel officially separated from the Army Air Corps in mid-October of 1945, and planned to take a short break before looking for a job. The break ended up being extremely short, as he met a friend on the street just days following his release from the military. After some small talk the friend said, "Say, Lionel, have you ever done any work with sheet metal?"

Lionel said no, he hadn't, and the friend said, "I have a short job I could use some help with. You interested?"

Lionel always found it difficult to refuse a direct request for help, so he agreed to work for a few days. Thirty-seven years later he retired, one of the earliest members of the sheet metal workers union in Alaska.

In early fall Esther realized she was expecting another baby. She wished her eldest would show a little interest in moving around by himself. At Jimmy's baby shower someone had given Esther a Johnny-Jump-Up — a contraption with a seat suspended from a spring. A hook at the top of the spring could be fastened to a door frame. A baby placed in the seat would pull the spring down enough so it reached the floor. Most babies instinctively pushed up with their legs so they bounced up and down. The process strengthened their legs and prepared them to walk. Jimmy enjoyed sitting in the Jump-Up, but didn't try to bounce it.

In late March, 1946, Timothy Wayne joined the family. During the days Esther spent in the hospital, Jimmy stayed with his aunt Gladys and three cousins while Lionel worked. In the evenings his daddy picked him up and took him home where they enjoyed some wonderful times of bonding. Lionel was handy around the kitchen, cooking himself meals of "meat and spuds" and fixing Jimmy's formula. Now more than ten months old, Jimmy was sitting up for brief periods, but not yet trying to move around.

About the time of Jimmy's first birthday, Esther, feeling overwhelmed with a newborn and a one-year-old, decided to try a little potty training. Surprisingly, Jimmy took to this concept like a kitten to a litter box. Esther had noticed how he fussed when his diaper wasn't dry, so she figured he must have been waiting for her to show him how to avoid that discomfort.

Within a few months Timmy showed that he would soon pass up his older brother in many areas of development. When he demonstrated his interest in walking before he turned one, Esther decided she needed to take drastic measures. Jimmy would stand for long periods, grinning as if it were a great accomplishment, but never tried to take a step on his own. With the lightest grip on a finger or a handful of Esther's skirt he toddled around, but never under his own steam.

One day Esther decided this state of affairs had gone on long enough. She stood Jimmy up with his back against the bed and crouched down in front of him, holding out a cookie. If all else failed to attract Jimmy's attention, she knew food would do the trick.

"Look, Jimmy," she coaxed. "Do you want a cookie?"

Jimmy reached out for the cookie, and Esther pulled it back, keeping it just out of his reach. Jimmy gave her a puzzled look and stretched his hand out again. Esther let him

feel it, then pulled it back. This went on for several minutes until Jimmy forgot about everything but his desire for that cookie. He swiped his hand at the cookie and as he did he nearly lost his balance. He brought one foot forward to keep from falling, and the other followed. Jimmy could walk! Thrilled, Esther caught

Jimmy and Timmy, summer 1948.

212

him up in a big hug and surrendered the cookie to him. He'd definitely earned it. It still took practice, but now that Jimmy realized what walking was all about, he was more willing to try. Of course, once Timmy was on his feet Jimmy did his best to keep up with his favorite playmate.

Esther decided that Lionel also needed instruction; for him it was in the area of family finances. Despite all he knew of her struggles through hard times with little money, he seemed to think she needed his oversight in order to handle his paycheck frugally. While on Atka—because it was considered an overseas assignment—he'd earned the princely sum of $27 per month. In civilian life, his take-home pay was several dollars less than that. Once a week Esther took a few of those hard-earned dollars and visited the grocery store. On shopping days Lionel came home from work and headed straight for the kitchen cupboard. There he'd inspect Esther's purchases and comment: "You sure bought a lot of oleo today," or "Do we need that much cereal?"

After a few weeks of this, Esther had had enough. She pulled out the newspaper ad from the Piggly Wiggly supermarket and opened it for Lionel to see. "Look, they had margarine on sale this week. It's 2 pounds for 25 cents; usually it's 25 cents a pound. I always stock up on what's on sale, so we save a lot of money."

Lionel nodded. He didn't say anything, but he never again questioned Esther's money management skills.

Summer approached, and Esther noticed a certain restlessness in her husband. It seemed to grow worse on sunny weekends. Though he kept busy mowing grass and working on projects around the house, she would catch him staring out the window or sorting through his fishing tackle. She suspected at first, then knew beyond a doubt that he'd caught that bug that infects so many Alaskans old and young—salmon fever. He wanted to catch The Big One. He had shown her pictures of the Arctic grayling he'd caught during his gold mining days, and he often talked about the difference in fish that were available here compared to those he'd fished in North Dakota.

The couple spent several Saturdays fishing in Ship Creek just east of Anchorage and further up the road in the Knik River. The beautiful reds and silvers they brought home made the trips worthwhile, in Esther's view, because she could can them for use during the winter. Lionel loved the experience for itself. She knew he would have been content to spend all his free time fishing. Even before there was a drivable road down to the Kenai Peninsula the stories about monster salmon catches from the Kenai River and its tributaries circulated through Anchorage. Lionel drooled at the thought of all those lovely fish. Esther knew he wouldn't be content till he got his chance to soak a line in Kenai Peninsula waters.

While biding his time waiting for access to the peninsula, Lionel went off with a buddy one day for another experience new to a North Dakotan: clam digging. Since Esther had babies to care for, she stayed home. Lionel left early in the morning to catch the tide, and returned several hours later with a bucket full of sand covered clams, each clamped tightly in its shell. "Here," he said, "would you clean these? I bet they'd make a great chowder." He then disappeared on some errand.

Esther had never dealt with clams before, but set about the task in the best way she could think of. Taking a sharp knife she attempted to pry a shell open. The clam resented this intrusion and resisted her with all its might. The battle went on all day. Esther would finally get a shell open and cut the clam loose. Now—how to kill the thing. Cutting it up didn't seem to work, as all the pieces continued to wiggle. Lionel arrived in the afternoon to find his bride, knife in hand and temper at the boiling point, still trying to gain the upper hand on the still-sandy, still-wiggling clam pieces.

At this point Lionel committed a faux pas that would haunt him for the rest of his life, at least as far as clam cleaning went. He laughed. Esther threw the knife — onto the cutting board, fortunately, not at her snickering husband — and whirled to the sink to wash her hands. "Clean them yourself," she advised as she stomped out of the room. "And don't ever ask me to clean clams again. I'm done!" If either of them had known the trick of dunking clams in boiling water to kill them quickly and cause the shells to open, the family might have eaten a lot more clams.

The Family Grows - 1947-1949

As the boys grew, Esther reveled in her role as mother. Teaching Jimmy demanded much time and patience, while Timmy seemed to pick things up with little or no effort. She was reminded of her school days in Minnesota, when her teacher assigned her to supervise young Jack, the boy with developmental delays. She had wondered at the time why she was chosen to help this child. Now she reflected: was God preparing her for this special role as Jimmy's mother? He may not be as quick as Timmy, but his big smile and twinkling eyes melted hearts everywhere he went.

In January of 1948, Esther entered the hospital for the birth of her third child, Robert George. As before, her sister Gladys took care of the older boys during the day and Lionel picked them up after work. A difference this time was that Jimmy was now old enough to realize Mama was gone. Every day, no matter what Gladys did to try to entertain him, Jimmy slumped on a stool and stared listlessly at the wall. Food didn't tempt him. Timmy and the cousins tried to get him to play. He ignored them. Gladys and Lionel grew concerned he would die before Esther returned. Just in time, it seemed, Esther's week in the hospital ended and Jimmy discovered that his mother hadn't deserted him forever. His demeanor changed immediately and he became the happy, fun-loving, food-loving boy he'd been before.

With Jimmy potty-trained and Timmy well on the way, Esther had fewer diapers to wash; however, three small boys can generate a fair-sized pile of dirty clothes each week. Esther looked forward to nap time when she could work on the laundry and other household chores undisturbed. Some days, she finally got them down for their afternoon naps just in time to start supper. As she raced around, trying to get everything finished before the kids woke up, Lionel came home. He continued the habit he'd developed when Jimmy was a baby. A quick kiss for Esther was followed by a beeline to the bedroom. There he picked up the sleeping Bobby, which woke up the other two boys. This effectively ended Esther's chance to work on chores as end of nap time meant beginning of mealtime for the baby. Lionel had no problem changing diapers, but when Bobby wanted to eat, that was a task only Esther could fulfill.

Shortly after Bobby's birth, Lionel contracted a severe infection. He lay in bed for several days, too sick to do more than eat a little food and get himself to the bathroom. Finally, Esther loaded kids and husband into Lucille and hauled him to the doctor. There Lionel was diagnosed with erysipelas — a skin infection that causes blisters and fever — and put on medication. By Bobby's six-week checkup he was feeling much better, but needed the doctor's clearance before returning to work. Once again the whole family showed up at the doctor's office.

Dr. Hall pronounced Lionel out of danger. Relieved, he and Esther took all three boys into the office of Dr. Edmond for Bobby's check-up. He assured them their baby was healthy; the family was about to leave when in walked Dr. Hall. He started to smile at Jimmy and Timmy sitting quietly on chairs as they'd been taught to do. His smile faded slightly as he eyed Jimmy. He turned to Dr. Edmond.

"Is he a Cretin?" he asked.

"No, probably a mongoloid," replied Dr. Edmond.

Too shocked to question the doctors about these unfamiliar terms, Lionel and Esther returned home. There they looked up the words "Cretin" and "mongoloid" in the dictionary and medical encyclopedia. Their recently-published medical encyclopedia defined Jimmy's condition:

Mongolism is a peculiar condition of unknown cause. It is not hereditary. It shows itself soon after birth and is characterized by slanting eyes, broad nose, small head, loose joints, large hands

217

and feet, protruding abdomen, idiocy, and often congenital heart disease and other physical defects. Such infants, fortunately, usually die soon after birth, but occasionally one lives to become an adult. There is no cure for the condition, and no useful treatment. They looked at their oldest son, playing happily with Timmy. Questions jumbled together in their minds. The books seemed to agree with the doctor. Jimmy was a "mongoloid." What did that mean? How did it happen? The encyclopedia said most people with the condition didn't live past their teens. Were they going to lose Jimmy? Was this why he was so slow to learn things? If the doctor knew this, why on earth hadn't he told them? Esther had certainly asked him often enough.

The routine of the day proceeded — lunch, naps, supper. Always, no matter what path the parents' conversation took, it always came back to the bombshell the doctor had dropped on them.

"Well," Esther said when they finally crawled into bed, "we'll just give him the best life we can. He's not that much behind Timmy. We'll just work a little harder to help him."

Lionel agreed, and the two stuck to this course. Very shortly thereafter, Dr. Edmond died in a plane crash, so Esther never got to ask him why he'd never shared information about Jimmy's condition with them.

During the winter, letters arrived from various members of Lionel's family talking up a reunion they were planning for the summer. Lionel hadn't been home to North Dakota for nearly eleven years, and was eager to see his parents and eight siblings and meet the various nieces and nephews that had been born during his absence, and introduce them to his own wife and three sons.

July found them at Elmendorf Air Force base, ready for the first leg of their adventure Outside. They flew to Seattle, where they were met by Lionel's brother Earl. From there they hopped on a train for the long trip to North Dakota. This trip seemed even longer traveling with three small boys.

Jimmy never was much of a problem, only fussing when he was hungry or needed the restroom. Five-month-old Bobby demanded all the care required of any infant, but toddler Timmy taxed his parents' imaginations in their efforts to keep him contained.

His dad soon learned that Timmy found the sight of a body of water — which he, in his two-year-old way called "vonny" — moving past the train entrancing. Lionel kept a sharp eye out for any lake, river or puddle that might appear outside the window. When Timmy became frustrated from lack of movement, Lionel lifted him up and pointed out the window. "See, Timmy? There's vonny!"

"Where vonny? Where vonny?" Timmy demanded. If no water was immediately visible, he dissolved into tears. "I don't see no vonny!" he wailed.

Five weary travelers disembarked in North Dakota. Lionel's brother, George met the train and took them to the Haakenson parents' farm. Hugging her eldest son tight his mother, Caroline, exclaimed, "Oh, Lionel, you're not going back to that dreadful place, are you?"

Lionel, who had spent most of the "dirty Thirties" in North Dakota dealing with drought and grasshopper plagues, clearly thought he'd left the "dreadful place" when he'd headed north. He replied, "Alaska? It's full of great opportunities. It's my home now."

Caroline shook her head and muttered something in Norwegian. Esther didn't know what she said, but from Lionel's shrug she assumed it was less than complimentary of their northern abode.

George's wife, Evelyn, made a beeline for the baby in Esther's arms. "Oh," she gushed, "George's little namesake." Esther had never considered Bobby's middle name as a family heirloom, but she smiled good-naturedly. After all, Lionel had been the one to suggest it, so perhaps he'd been thinking of his younger brother at the time.

When Lionel introduced his family to his sister Cora—whom the family all called Corky—she stared openmouthed at her tow-headed nephews and declared, "They don't look like Eskimos at all!" Esther chuckled to herself. One thing she'd quickly learned about living in Alaska was that people from the Outside needed a good deal of education about what the Great Land was actually like. Once she became more familiar with Corky's sense of humor, she realized her sister-in-law had been joking.

For Esther, the next two weeks were a time of getting acquainted with Lionel's large family—parents Pete and Caroline, older sisters Dagmar and Lillian, younger sisters Hulda, Cora and Norma, and brothers George, Herman, and Earl, all of their offspring—and keeping track of her own boys. Timmy loved playing with his newly-met cousins and the aunts and Grandma Haakenson all doted on Bobby. If Esther wanted to find Jimmy, she usually didn't have to look any farther than wherever Lionel's sister Lillian was. Lil had no children of her own, but seemed to have an extra-soft spot for Jimmy. Whether they were out for a walk, looking at books, or just snuggled on a chair watching the family, the two were rarely apart.

When the time came to leave North Dakota, Lionel and Esther rounded up their brood, boarded the train and headed west back to Seattle. At that time, nearly all flights bound for Alaska were routed through Seattle. Besides, they had an important appointment there.

After Dr. Edmond died, Esther had begun taking the boys to another doctor. This one was more open to talking about Jimmy's condition. As a general practitioner, he told her he didn't feel qualified to give her any information about Jimmy's potential, and recommended that she visit a specialist in Seattle. Since resources were so scarce, she and Lionel considered this their best shot at getting up-to-date information.

In Seattle, Lionel stayed at Earl's house with Bobby and Timmy while Earl's wife, Elinor, dropped Esther and Jimmy off at the doctor's office. The doctor asked Esther a barrage of questions regarding Jimmy's abilities. He seemed impressed that, at age 3, Jimmy was toilet-trained and able to feed and dress himself with very little assistance. He complimented Esther on Jimmy's manners then said, "I have to make my rounds now. I'd like Jimmy to come with me. We'll spend some time together so I can get to know him a little better."

Esther was surprised, but agreed. She spent a long day waiting for the pair to return. When they did, the doctor had nothing but praise for Jimmy's behavior and skills. Esther felt a thrill of pride in her firstborn, relieved that he'd remembered his manners as she and Lionel had worked so hard to teach him. She sat expectantly, waiting for the doctor to give a glowing forecast of Jimmy's future.

She was caught completely off-guard when the man said, "Unfortunately, having Jimmy in your family will only cause unnecessary hardship. Nothing can be done for his condition, and if you look for cures you'll just be wasting money. My advice is to put him in an institution with others of his kind. Do your best to forget about him. That way any other children you might have won't have to suffer from having him around."

Esther sat rigid with shock as this "expert" went on to offer to get her a list of local facilities that housed "children like Jimmy." Finally she interrupted him. "I don't need a list of institutions," she said. "I already have two other kids, and they're not suffering a bit because of Jimmy. He's part of our family, and we're *not* putting him in an institution!"

She was still steaming when Elinor picked her up. She poured out the story of her day to her sister-in-law. "Jimmy's got better manners than a lot of 'normal' kids I know. How can that guy say to just put him away and forget him? What's wrong with the man?"

Lionel echoed her sentiments when she arrived back at Earl's place. They agreed on one thing: if this was the best the medical community could provide, they'd be better off making their own path. Though Esther had never faced institutionalization, she recalled hearing of families during the Depression who'd been forced by poverty to put their children in orphanages or adopt them out. She remembered her brush with that issue when Eula, her friend from Rainy Lake asked Laura if she could adopt Esther. Of course her parents wouldn't hear of it, but it had caused Esther to wonder what it would be like to leave her family forever. Jimmy had practically died of grief during the few days Esther spent in the hospital when Bobby was born. He wouldn't last a month in an institution.

The family returned to Anchorage and life resumed its normal rhythm. Many years would pass, and the term "mongoloid" would be replaced by "Down Syndrome," before they received any new information about Jimmy's condition. Meanwhile, Esther continued to treat Jimmy as much like the other boys as she could, and slowly but surely he acquired more skills and appropriate behaviors.

When Christmas of 1948 arrived, Lionel and Esther decided to splurge. With Jimmy and Timmy both well on their feet and Bobby almost on his, the couple agreed it was

time to buy them some wheels. Jimmy and Timmy each received a pedal car built to look like a real car. Though there was little room in the house for moving around, during the warmer months of the

Christmas 1948. L-R: Lionel, Timmy, Jimmy, Esther and Bobby.

next few years those cars were kept very busy on the sidewalk that stretched from the front yard to the back.

Early in the winter Esther realized she was expecting another baby. She began wondering where all these little ones were going to sleep. Right now the older two boys shared a bedroom across the hall from their parents' room, where Bobby slept in the crib Esther had built. She and Lionel made plans for another bedroom off the living room. Lionel did as much of the work as he could through the winter, and had it almost finished when son #4, John Roger, arrived in mid-May, 1949.

Esther marveled at how four boys raised in the same house could display such distinct personalities. Jimmy, though he tried to keep up with his brothers, was the quiet one who loved to snuggle. Timmy usually took the role of leader, employing typical big brother tactics to direct their play. Bobby showed an independent streak, often challenging Timmy's authority as ruler. Young Johnny displayed a fear of heights, objecting even to being hoisted to the altitude of his mother's arms unless wrapped in a blanket.

Until recently the boys had enjoyed play times with their cousins Joe, Don and Alice. Unfortunately, Gladys discovered Stan had set up housekeeping with a woman in Bristol Bay. As Gladys told Esther, "He left me behind like a dirty shirt. I knew there was something more than fishing that was keeping him over there."

With three young children and no way to support herself in Anchorage, Gladys returned to International Falls and moved in with Alice, who was now widowed. Alice's step-children, Claude and Margaret, were grown and living away from home, while the children she'd had with her late husband Ed—Travis, Curt and Trudy—were just slightly older than Gladys's three. Though it wasn't easy, Alice and Gladys strove to blend the two families into one household. Gladys enrolled her children in school, found a job, and after a time began dating.

The Joys of Travel -1950 and 1951

The year 1950 found Esther and Lionel struggling to make ends meet. Lionel's work in the sheet metal shop kept him away every day, yet barely paid the bills. To add to the family coffers, Lionel took on a project building a house for the Walkers, a middle-aged couple. The construction site was only a few blocks from home, so he was able to spend most evenings and weekends working on it.

Esther missed Gladys, but had some friends with whom she enjoyed the occasional visit. The family attended the

Church of the Open Door, and Esther struck up friendships with several other young mothers. She taught Sunday School classes, helped out with Vacation Bible School each summer, and did her best to keep herself and the boys available to participate in all church activities. There was even a woman who came to the neighborhood each week and conducted a mini-class at Esther's house for any of the local children who wanted to come.

John and Esther, 1950.

Sometimes friends from past years showed up unexpectedly. One chilly day Esther and her sons stood on the platform of the train station, preparing to ride out to see her mother on the farm at Matanuska. Carrying one-year-old Johnny, she attempted to herd the other three onto the train. Timmy clambered up the stairs, with Jimmy close behind.

Bobby's legs were still too short for him to easily navigate the steps. Just as she reached to guide him with one hand while clutching Johnny with the other, she heard a familiar voice. "Hello, Esther; need a hand?"

She looked around. "Reverend Bingle!" she greeted the preacher from the Valley. "If you could just help Bobby up the stairs…"

"Sure. Come on, young fella." Reverend Bingle caught Bobby under the arms and attempted to swing him up onto the train. Bobby, having no idea who this stranger was, pedaled his legs furiously in an attempt to escape.

"Whoa! You almost kicked me," Bingle laughed as he deposited his protesting burden on the train. He reached back for Esther's arm and assisted her up the steps.

"Thank you," Esther said. "You sure have a knack for finding people who need help. I remember how much you helped everyone when we first came to Palmer."

"I guess I'm just lucky."

The two adults caught up with each other's lives as the train clacked along. At the depot in Matanuska, Bingle helped her guide the boys down the steps. Esther waved to him as the train pulled away, thinking again how almost providential it was the way the man always showed up when he was needed. She gathered her boys and headed down the road toward the farm. As she'd expected, it wasn't long before a neighbor stopped his vehicle and gave the family a lift.

Early in the summer, Lionel walked in one evening after work with a familiar look in his eye. "I hear the road is open now down to the Kenai Peninsula," he began. "Some of the guys are talking about the salmon fishing on the Kenai River. There's a town called Cooper Landing where they say you can't help but catch fish. How'd you like to go down there some weekend?"

"Well, I guess we could," Esther began.

"Good, let's head out this Friday," Lionel said. "They say the road's still real rough, so we'd better take a couple of spare tires."

That Friday evening they loaded the car's trunk with enough food, diapers and tires to make the long trip. Lionel threw in his fishing gear and the family set out. The three older boys shared the back seat with blankets and sleeping bags, while 1-year-old Johnny sat up front on the bench seat between his parents.

"Calling this road 'rough' is an understatement," Esther said to herself as the car bumped along. The rock cliffs lining Turnagain Arm had been blasted to carve out a narrow, winding road. With those looming cliffs on one side and the waters of the Arm on the other, Esther fervently prayed that no disaster would strike them. After more than an hour of crawling around the Arm, the road rounded the end of the Arm. The next adventure began with a climb into the mountains. About the time they reached Turnagain Pass Lionel said, "Well, we have a flat."

At the nearest turnout Lionel pulled over and got out a spare tire. Though sightseeing was not the reason for the stop, Esther gazed around, appreciating the beauty surrounding them. Alder bushes were just beginning to show their leaves, patches of leftover snow lay here and there in shady spots, and a tiny waterfall tumbled down the rock wall. She took each of the boys to the bushes for a potty break, then dug into the box of food she'd packed. The boys had been getting cranky for the past hour or so and she knew it was at least partly because they were hungry. She found the peanut butter and jelly sandwiches she'd made earlier in the day, and produced plastic cups for the older boys. "Go hold your cup in the waterfall," she directed them. The boys giggled as the water splashed into their cups. The icy cold water tasted good after hours of dusty driving, and the family continued on their way refreshed by the brief stop.

By the time they arrived in Cooper Landing the boys were asleep. Though it was nearing midnight, daylight was just beginning to fade. Lionel pulled the car into a campground where tiny Cooper Creek drained into the Kenai River. He grinned at Esther, obviously excited to begin fishing in the morning. His practical wife had a more immediate problem. "What are we gonna sleep in?" she asked. "We brought sleeping bags, but no tent."

Lionel shrugged. "It's a warm night. The boys are all comfortable where they are in the car. We can just sleep next to the car on the ground."

Though this was far from Esther's idea of an ideal campsite, she was exhausted and not inclined to argue. Without a word she unrolled her sleeping bag and wriggled around till she found the least uncomfortable spot on the lumpy ground. She had always been blessed with the ability to fall asleep quickly, and even in this situation she soon dozed off. During the night she was aware of an odd sensation, but didn't awaken entirely. About 6 o'clock she heard Lionel stirring. Before long he grabbed his fishing pole and headed down toward Cooper Creek.

Esther lay with eyes closed, savoring the warmth of the sleeping bag and pondering the strange feeling she'd had during the night. When the memory cleared, it shot a bolt of adrenaline through her that shook away all thoughts of repose. While she lay sleeping, something with a wet nose and tickly whiskers had explored her face. Was it a bear? A moose? A stray dog? What it was she never found out, but she let Lionel know when he returned: this was the last time she'd sleep on the ground without so much as a tent for protection. The pair of plump salmon he had caught drove Lionel to promise to bring a tent next time—whatever his bride needed to agree to another weekend like this one.

About this time Esther realized she was pregnant again. When her friends threw a shower for her, the women who attended apparently assumed that she was incapable of producing a girl. All the clothes she received either were blatantly blue, or had a distinctly masculine look to them. Imagine everyone's shock when, in mid-February, 1951, Esther gave birth to a girl. The name Mary Esther finally came off the shelf.

If Esther had hopes that her daughter's sunny disposition would lend a sweet, feminine presence to the house full of boys, they were quickly dashed. Mary arrived yanking at the thick black hair that rayed out from her head like quills on an enraged porcupine, face contorted from the strength of her angry howls. Lionel, gazing at Mary in bewilderment, commented, "If she'd quit pulling her own hair maybe she'd be happier." (Mary's habit of pulling her hair whenever she was mad continued until she was 3, at which time Esther set her up on the kitchen counter and gave her daughter a Tonette—a home permanent specially formulated for children. To Esther's astonishment, Mary sat like an angel through the process, and never pulled her hair again.)

Mary frustrated her dad further by not welcoming his regular after-work routine of snuggling with the baby. He'd come out of the bedroom, the baby's elbows braced against his chest, her back arched as she screamed. "She won't let me cuddle her," he told Esther, hurt evident in his voice.

Johnny (on Lionel's lap), Jimmy, Timmy, Bobby, Esther and Mary.

"I know," Esther replied. "She only wants to be held when I nurse her. She's sure a different one."

About this time faithful old "Lucille" died, leaving the family in need of a new car. In one of those beautiful moments that can only be attributed to God's providence, a new car appeared. When Lionel finished the house he was building for the Walkers, in lieu of a cash down payment they gave him a 1950 Pontiac sedan.

As Jimmy neared the age of six, Lionel and Esther had many discussions about schooling. They knew his skills weren't yet at a level that would allow him to hold his own in public school, and the few private schools were well out of reach financially. Esther did her best to teach him along with his brothers, and wondered if this was the way it would always be for him.

While they puzzled over the issue, Lionel's sister Lillian wrote a letter referencing an article she'd read in a recent *Reader's Digest*. The article told of a school close to Lil's home in Los Angeles. Many children with learning problems were being helped by the excellent teaching methods used there. In addition, the school administered a substance called glutamic acid, which was supposed to increase the brain power of the children. While Lionel and Esther were reluctant to send Jimmy so far away, they realized finding a school for Jimmy nearby would be difficult if not impossible. Lil's letters overflowed with enthusiasm for her idea. She lived near enough that she could pick Jimmy up on Friday evenings, keep him through the weekend, and return him to school on Monday. The reassurance that Jimmy would spend 3 of every 7 nights with his beloved Auntie Lil was the deciding factor. Tuition at the school was expensive, but the monthly payments made by the couple who'd bought the house Lionel built would cover it. Everything seemed to be working out for Jimmy to go to California. The only challenge remaining: how to get him there from Alaska.

In 1942 the U.S. and Canadian governments had joined forces to build a road that would connect Alaska and northern parts of Canada to the Lower 48 states. With the war providing incentive, the workers punched the road through in about nine months, finishing up in November of 1942. The road was named the Alaska-Canada, or Al-Can Highway, with the spelling soon shortened to "Alcan."

The Alcan Highway quickly developed a reputation for not being a road for the timid or easily discouraged. Lionel and Esther knew that ongoing improvements over the nine years since its inception had made it more passable. And no matter what the hardships, they figured it had to be a cheaper way to go than flying a family of seven Outside. With the new Pontiac they could be fairly confident that the worst vehicle problems they'd encounter would be flat tires, and having lived in Alaska for over 15 years, flat tires held no terrors for them.

The family set off in July. The first portion of the trip would take them north and east for several hundred miles on the Glenn Highway. The weather had been drizzly for several days. None of the roads were paved at the time, so, as Lionel commented, "At least the rain keeps the dust down."

With evening approaching and the rain still falling, they planned to spend the night in the town of Glennallen at the

junction of the Glenn and Richardson Highways. The road in this area contained more dirt than gravel, and the unrelenting rain turned the road into a long stretch of slippery goo. Lionel guided the car through one mud hole after

Heading for the States, 1951

another. Several times he nearly got stuck, but managed to escape. Finally, his luck ran out. Still a couple of miles from Glennallen, he was confronted by a huge mud hole that covered the whole road. He tried to skirt it, but the car slid sideways and sank to the axles in thick slop.

"Great," thought Esther, "here we are in the middle of nowhere, stuck in a loblolly, with 5 little kids and no one around for miles. What are we gonna do now?"

"Hey folks, need some help?" The shout came clearly across the mud hole. Lionel and Esther swiveled their heads to see who could possibly be out here. On the edge of the mud hole next to a large, competent-looking truck stood their old friend from the Valley, Reverend Bingle.

Lionel shook his head. "I can't believe it," he said to Esther. "That guy really *is* anywhere he's needed." He rolled down his window and raised his voice. "We sure could use a hand," he yelled.

"I think I have a chain in the truck that'll do the trick," said Bingle.

Esther and the kids stayed inside the car while the two men slithered and slipped in the muck. When they got the chain attached to the car, Lionel climbed in, mud and all, to steer the car. A few mighty lurches brought them out of the hole and back onto firm ground.

"Thanks," Lionel began. "I don't know how long we'd have been stuck in that hole. What can I give you for your trouble?" He reached for his wallet.

"No, you're not gonna pay me. I was up this way anyway, and I'm glad I could help." Reverend Bingle brushed aside the offer. "I know you'll help the next person you see in trouble, and that's payment enough for me."

Lionel and Esther never knew what brought Bingle to that lonely stretch of highway, but they remembered his kindness. They made it a lifelong practice to offer help to those in need just as the good preacher had done. They made it to Glennallen with no further delays, and found a motel where they collapsed into bed, worn out from a journey that had just begun.

The next morning the family pushed on. A few hours' driving brought them to Tok (pronounced Toke), which had begun as a camp for highway construction workers. As this was the junction of the Glenn and Alcan highways, some folks saw the potential to make a living off of travelers, and the beginnings of a town had appeared. Turning right onto the Alcan, the Haakensons continued on their way. A long, slow trip over 1,500 miles of rough gravel and mud lay between their present location and the highway's southern terminus in Dawson Creek, British Columbia.

Once the rain quit, dust became almost as big an issue as the mud had been. Long days passed as Lionel fought road conditions outside the car and the boys fought each other inside. As a six-month-old, Mary added her part to the misery of the trip by being carsick. Sometimes Esther felt she just had to get everyone out of the car.

"Stop at the next pull-off," she'd tell Lionel. He pulled over and the boys spilled out of the car, running off their bottled-up energy. They ran for another reason, as well. Hordes of mosquitoes lurked everywhere, waiting to attack any warm-blooded creature that entered their domain. Esther spread a blanket and set the baby down, fanning her to keep the bugs at bay. Mary sat and beamed until anyone took a step toward the car. That was all it took to turn her smiles to howls of protest. Back in the car, Esther tried all the usual tricks to calm her down—a bottle, positioning her to look out the window or at her brothers making faces at her from the back seat. When nothing worked, Esther simply plunked her down on the seat between herself and Lionel, and left her to bellow till she wore herself out and fell asleep.

This was only the second time Lionel and Esther had been out of Alaska since they'd moved there, so they planned to see some relatives as they traveled. Lionel wanted to take advantage of the trip to again visit his relatives in North Dakota, so once he reached Dawson Creek, he turned eastward. The roads from that point, being vastly improved, allowed the family to make much better time than had been possible on the Alcan Highway.

On the way across Canada, the family stopped in Alberta to visit Pete Larson, Esther's uncle who had brought her father Fred to America back in 1909. Pete and his wife welcomed the family, until they noticed the baby was covered in spots. On top of all the other disruption she'd contributed to this trip, now Mary had broken out with chicken pox. This made for a most uncomfortable visit, with Esther feeling guilty for bringing a communicable disease into someone's home.

Leaving Pete's place, the family continued on to North Dakota, where they spent a week or so with Lionel's parents and the few siblings who still lived in the area. From there they headed to California. After several decades in Alaska, a drive across the midsection of America in the middle of the summer was an extremely uncomfortable experience. The only air conditioning in the car came from rolling down the windows. Esther spent most of her time—when she wasn't reading maps for Lionel—refereeing the hot, bored, cranky boys in the back seat and trying to keep Mary pacified. Lionel's idea of a good day's travel started well before daylight and lasted till darkness had fallen. Though Esther had vowed before she married never to be disagreeable in front of the children, on a couple of occasions she spoke up and insisted, "Stop in the next town. I don't care where it is. We all need to rest." Lionel always obliged, though he seemed to Esther to be oblivious to the discomforts of his family.

Lillian's house in Los Angeles was a welcome sight, despite the fact that it meant the family would soon be parting from Jimmy. Esther's heart ached at the thought of leaving one of her children behind, but she saw no alternative if Jimmy was to receive an education. Lillian could scarcely contain her joy at the prospect of having Jimmy with her every weekend, and this attitude provided some comfort to Jimmy's parents. They visited the school he would attend, and there, too, found an open and welcoming attitude. Jimmy quickly bonded with his school mates and the house mother. Once they were sure he was going to be happy and well cared for, Lionel and Esther headed north, already missing Jimmy's cheerful presence, but hoping they'd made the right decision.

Baby Mary enlivened the return trip by becoming ill again, this time with German (or 3-day) measles. The lights of Anchorage welcomed them when, nearly two months after they left, the dusty car and its weary occupants finally reached the little white house on East 10th Avenue.

In November, Esther received an early Christmas present in the form of Gladys. Her sister moved back from International Falls with her new husband, Maurice Dixson, whom she'd married in Minnesota, her 3 kids, and a bun in the oven. Later that month her fourth child, William, was born.

Welcoming Another Baby - 1952

As spring of 1952 approached, Jimmy's school year in California neared its close and Lionel and Esther took stock of their finances. The payments made by the couple who had bought the house that Lionel built were about to end, which meant there would be no extra money to cover another year's tuition. Unexpected charges from the school for such things as speech therapy and dental appointments created more strain on the family budget. The knowledge that a new baby would be arriving in August added another dimension to the discussion.

"I don't see how we can possibly afford to send Jimmy back to that school next year," said Lionel. "It's gonna stretch us just to fly him home for the summer."

"Well, I'm glad he's coming home," Esther replied. "It's been lonely around here since he's been gone. Are you sure you've got all the arrangements made for him?"

"Yes, Lil will get him on the plane in LA, and Earl will meet him in Seattle and make sure he gets on the flight to Anchorage. He'll be fine. It'll sure be good to see him again."

It was still several weeks before Jimmy was due to come home, and the warming temperatures got Lionel's fishing juices flowing. "How about we head down to the Kenai this weekend and see if we can catch a few fish? I'll bet we could get your mother to stay here with Mary so we wouldn't have to take her." (He probably deliberately dangled this like an extremely tempting carrot. The thought of her 18-month-old daughter on a weekend camp-out in the boonies had to strike terror into even Esther's stalwart heart.)

The request was made, and on Friday evening Grandma Laura saw the family off. She probably figured that she was in for a quiet couple of days with only the baby to deal with. Little did she know.

When Esther walked into the house late Sunday evening the first thing she noticed was a pile of unfamiliar luggage inside the door. Laura jumped up from the couch and came to greet the family.

"You have company," she informed them quietly. "Lionel, your mother and father showed up this evening from North Dakota. They're sleeping in the front bedroom. I didn't know exactly what to do with them, since I didn't know they were coming."

"I didn't know, either," replied Lionel. He didn't seem particularly put out by his parents showing up with no warning. Perhaps it was genetic—he had a lifelong penchant for landing in on friends and relatives unannounced.

"Thanks for getting them settled, Grandma," said Esther. (Once grandkids started arriving, Laura and Fred became Grandma and Grandpa to everyone in the family, including their own offspring.) Esther felt a moment of panic familiar to most hostesses—what was she going to feed these people? How was she supposed to entertain them? How long were they staying?

By the next morning she had calmed down a bit. The boys charmed their grandparents for much of the time just by being themselves. Lionel proudly showed his adopted state to his parents, who had rarely left the prairies of North Dakota. The weather cooperated, so the group was able to enjoy picnics and other outings, and Lionel took his dad— also an avid fisherman—to some of the nearby streams to try their luck. Grandma Haakenson was handy around the house, and helped take care of the kids and even learned a little about canning salmon when the men came home from a successful day of fishing.

When the grandparents realized they were scheduled to fly home just a few days before Jimmy was due to arrive from California, they rearranged their plans so they could stay until he got home. On the day of his arrival, the group assembled at Elmendorf Air Force Base to meet Jimmy's plane.

He was the last passenger off the plane, and came off holding the stewardess's hand. Everyone strained to see his face when he disembarked. And what a face it was. When Jimmy was sad, his whole body drooped with the weight of his woe. All this time with strangers, shuttling from plane to plane and flying for hours, had taken its toll. His expression clearly said, "I'm behaving because I'm supposed to, but I'm not liking it." Esther struggled with conflicting emotions. Her heart ached as she thought of what her poor little boy had gone through these past hours, not understanding where he was or why he wasn't with anyone he knew. At the same time, joy at the sight of him surged through her. She started toward him, calling his name.

She saw his head snap around at the sound of her voice. A smile broke out on his face, like sunlight beaming through dark clouds. He dropped the stewardess's hand and ran to her. The family surrounded him with hugs and laughter. Lionel swung him up in his arms. Jimmy's joyful giggle put the seal on this reunion. The family was back together, and all was right in the world.

As the summer rolled on, Esther grew more uncomfortable not only from her pregnancy, but from a nasty bronchial infection that sent her into spasms of coughing. Another fishing trip to the Kenai in late July proved to be an ordeal for Esther as she coughed so hard she was sure she cracked a rib.

A few weeks later, her rib was feeling only slightly better when Esther went into labor. As usual, the baby was more than a week ahead of its predicted arrival time. Something more was wrong this time, though.

When the doctor examined Esther he quickly discovered the problem. "The baby's breach," he informed her. "I'll have to turn it around."

"Oh no," thought Esther, "I'm in enough pain without him adding to it." She knew she had no options, though, so she submitted to the procedure. To her surprise, the doctor was both gentle and efficient. Within a short time he said, "There—things will go easier now."

Sure enough, her labor began to progress more normally, and soon her sixth child—and fifth son—Kenneth Peter entered the world. His middle name was a salute to several generations from both sides of the family. Lionel's father was Peder—the Norwegian form of the name—and Esther's paternal grandfather was also Peter. Her dad, Fred, had both a grandfather and a brother with that name.

After his wife's requisite week in the hospital, Lionel took the boys and Mary to bring their mother and new brother home. On the way, Johnny sat in the car more quietly than usual. As the car pulled up outside the hospital, he voiced his thoughts. "Daddy," he began, "now that we have a new baby, what are we gonna do with Mary? Are we gonna give her away?" (Did he perhaps say this with a hopeful tinge to his voice? It was probably the secret wish of all Mary's older brothers.) Fortunately, their parents knew there was room for more than one baby in a family, and they welcomed the new little one into their midst.

Over the next weeks Esther found herself unable to bounce back physically as well as she had with her previous pregnancies. She knew she was running a fever, but with six children needing attention, there was no time to collapse into bed, which was all she wanted to do.

In September, Timmy started first grade. Esther knew she should look for a school for Jimmy, but she didn't have the energy. Since the family had just one car, she had to bundle all the kids up every morning to drive Lionel to work and Timmy to school. In the afternoon she repeated the process to fetch them home. Just making it through each day took all the stamina she could muster. Her body ached, and pain in her hands and arms made even lifting baby Kenny an ordeal.

One Sunday she kept her bathrobe and nightgown on as she got her five older children ready for church. When they'd finished breakfast and the dishes were done she said to Lionel, "You take the kids. Kenny and I are staying home today."

Lionel was surprised, but went on with the older boys and Mary. Esther closed the door behind them and sighed. Kenny, with a full tummy and clean diaper, was already asleep in his crib. He was such a sweet-tempered baby; even if he woke up earlier than expected, she knew he'd tumble around in the crib and entertain himself until he got hungry again. Esther dragged her aching body to the bedroom, slipped out of her robe and slid under the covers. In minutes she was deep in sleep. She didn't stir till the noise of her family's return awakened her. She lay quietly in the darkened room, assessing how she felt. Though her joints still ached, she felt more rested and ready to face the coming week. This had definitely been a worthwhile way to spend a Sunday morning. She swung her legs out of the bed and saw several small faces peering around the door at her. Rest time was over; it was time to resume her life.

After several weeks of this routine, Lionel informed her, "The ladies asked about you again today. One even made a comment about it not setting a good example for the kids when you don't come."

"What they don't know," Esther replied, "is that if I do go, I'm knocked out for the rest of the week. I need a few hours to rest or I'll end up in the hospital. I think God knows my main job is taking care of these kids every day, and I can't do it when I'm too weak to stand up."

"Then you'd better see a doctor," Lionel said.

"Why—so he can tell me to get more rest?" Esther retorted. "I'll be okay if I keep doing what I'm doing."

About this time Fred, after years of working for the Matanuska Maid dairy, took a civilian job on Fort Richardson. Though their farming years were now behind them, Esther's parents knew there was still the little issue of the 30-year loan given to them by the government back in 1935 when they'd moved up with the colonists. The job on base offered a better salary—which would help them pay off their debt—and a pension they could depend on once Fred retired. Since Laurence's return from the service, he had moved back to the farm, gotten married and changed the focus of the place from livestock to growing potatoes. He'd started a well-drilling business to supplement his income. Relieved to leave the farm in his capable hands, Fred and Laura moved into Anchorage and settled on 10th Avenue, just one house away from Esther's home.

This turned out to be a blessing for Esther, as Grandma could usually be counted on to help when Esther felt too weak to carry on. Although Laura would not drive, she occasionally stayed with the younger kids while Esther ferried Timmy and Lionel to school and work. With this bit of respite, Esther's health slowly improved.

When she finally was able to return to church, she had an interesting conversation with Mrs. Thomas, a friend who had recently opened a private preschool. The lady had taught Esther's boys in Sunday School and she knew Jimmy quite well. "I think Jimmy would fit right in with the students in my preschool," she said. "It's a small group, so I can give him extra help if he needs it."

The charge for attending was reasonable, so Esther enrolled Jimmy. Now she felt like she spent the entire day in the car as she bundled the kids up, took Lionel to work in the morning then delivered Timmy to his school. At noon, Esther again hit the streets with her carload of kids to drop Jimmy off at school. With lunch and naps the afternoon flew by, then she raced out to collect Timmy and Jimmy. A few hours later, she picked up Lionel from work.

In the middle of the school year, Timmy got sick. His symptoms of high fever, aching body and swollen joints closely mimicked Esther's recent illness. The doctor diagnosed rheumatic fever, and ordered Timmy to stay in bed for at least six weeks. Esther put two and two together and concluded she, too, had been suffering from rheumatic fever. Unlike the way she treated herself, she followed the doctor's orders and insisted that her normally-active little boy remain in bed. Timmy tolerated this state of affairs for the first few weeks, but as he began feeling better, he chafed at not being able to get up and play with his siblings.

Esther decided if he was well enough to want to be up, he was well enough to do some schoolwork. Six weeks is a lot of school for anyone to miss, especially a youngster just learning to read. She visited Timmy's teacher who gave her a stack of activities to work on. Timmy sailed through the list of sight words, and Esther felt quite proud of his accomplishments. Then she tried changing a few letters to make "look" into "book" or "and" into "hand." She was appalled to discover that Timmy had no clue how to figure out the new words. His teacher was a disciple of a theory of teaching popular during that era that bypassed phonics, focusing solely on learning words by sight. As Esther told her mother, "He doesn't know how to sound out words. He knows his ABCs, but doesn't know what to do with them. That's gonna change if I have anything to say about it."

Of course she had plenty to say about it, and by the time Timmy returned to school he had word attack skills that kept him up with his classmates, and ahead of most of them. The teacher was less than pleased. She tried to reason with Esther. "The latest research shows that learning sight words is the best way," she said. "They can pick up phonics later. It's too slow to start with."

"I want my son to be able to read anything, not just a list of words he's been taught," Esther replied. "Just look at how well he's able to read now."

The teacher shook her head, unhappy with this mom's stand on the subject, but not having a good answer. She broached a different topic. "He's left-handed."

"I've noticed that," said Esther.

"Left-handed kids have a harder time with writing. I wish he'd try to use his right hand. Or at least he should quit curling his hand all the way over the line he's writing on. It's not good penmanship."

"My mother is left-handed," Esther commented. "She gets along fine. I think you should let him write however it works best for him."

The conference ended with neither participant completely happy with the other's viewpoint. Timmy, unaware of the tension he'd caused, continued to read phonetically, and continued to be left-handed.

Eruptions and Fallout - 1953

On July 9, 1953, Esther prepared a lunch of sandwiches for her hungry brood. "Huh," she thought, "it's sure looks dark out there. I wonder what happened to the sun."

She opened the door to summon her boys just as they came running from the back yard.

"Mama!" yelled Timmy. "Why is it gettin' so dark?"

"And something stinks," added Bobby.

Esther had already noticed the odor of sulfur in the air. She held out her hand. Tiny grayish flakes landed on her palm. She knew it was too warm for snow, and somehow these flakes seemed different. She rubbed one between her thumb and forefinger. It felt like a grain of sand. "C'mon in," she directed the boys. "I think a volcano must be erupting."

Inside, she turned on the radio. "Don't be alarmed, folks," the announcer's voice sounded reassuring. "We're getting reports that one or more of our local volcanoes has erupted. The stuff you see falling is just ash."

Over the next hour the sky continued to darken. Esther and the kids watched cars going by with their headlights on — a highly unusual sight in the middle of an Alaskan summer.

"I think you'd better play inside today," she told her disappointed boys. She went outside and shooed the neighbor kids out of the yard. So many of them congregated in the Haakenson yard on a normal day, she suspected the mothers sent their children over so they could get their work done, knowing the kids would be safe.

Mt Spurr, which sits about 80 miles west of Anchorage, took everyone by surprise that day. Though it was known to be a volcano, its last eruption had taken place long before records were kept. At first the local papers reported three or four volcanoes had blown simultaneously, but that was soon discovered to be erroneous. As it turned out, the kids spent more time playing in the house than they wished, though their mother-turned-referee probably did not consider many of their behaviors "play." Anchorage received about ½ inch of ash. Spurr's eruptive phase lasted for about a week, bringing air travel to a near standstill and doing much damage to car engines from driving through the highly corrosive silt.

An Alaskan summer slips by too quickly to let a blanket of ash bring activities to a halt for long. Once the sky cleared and the debris was swept aside, the family returned to their normal activities. As often as he could manage, Lionel took the family fishing on the Kenai Peninsula. On weekends when they stayed in Anchorage, a picnic after church on Sunday got everyone out of the house and the yard, which to Esther seemed to be shrinking by the day.

One Sunday at church Mrs. Thomas approached Esther. "Jimmy did so well this past year, I think he's ready for public school."

"But he's 8 years old now," said Esther. "That's a little old for first grade."

"Give it a try," Mrs. Thomas urged.

That fall Esther took Jimmy to the school for a visit with the teacher, who ran some tests to determine his readiness. Jimmy confidently demonstrated his skills, naming colors, numbers and letters. Impressed, the teacher encouraged Esther to enroll him. "I'll give him extra help if he needs it," the teacher assured her.

On the first day of school Esther dropped Timmy off at his second grade class, then accompanied a proud Jimmy to first grade. The teacher welcomed him, and Esther left believing he was in good hands. That afternoon when she returned to pick him up, the principal accosted her.

"Your son can't be in this school," he informed her abruptly.

"Why not?" Esther asked.

"Because kids like him can't learn and he'll just slow down the other students," he growled.

"I'd like him to have the chance anyway," Esther said. She walked down to Jimmy's classroom, where he greeted her happily. "Did he do okay?" she asked the teacher.

"Yes, he's a joy," replied the teacher. "He doesn't always catch on as fast as the other kids, but he's so willing…"

"The principal says he has to leave."

The teacher made a face. "I know. Why don't we ask if we can try it for six weeks and see how he does?"

Esther agreed. That evening she told Lionel, "That old grump doesn't care if Jimmy can handle the work or not. He just wants him out. He sounds just like that Seattle doctor. To people like them he's just a bother to get out of sight as soon as possible."

Over the next two weeks Jimmy attended school each day, falling more and more in love with his teacher and class. At the same time, his parents were becoming less enthralled with the school's head man. Despite the teacher's best efforts, the principal ordered her not to spend any extra time helping Jimmy. Finally, Esther and Lionel could take no more of his unrelenting animosity. They knew it wouldn't be long before Jimmy began to be affected by the negative atmosphere. They pulled him out of the school, and Esther, as she had previously, included him in whatever his younger siblings were learning.

Growing Pains - 1954

On a cold winter Saturday in early 1954, Esther stood at the window and watched the chaos outside. As usual, it seemed like every kid in the neighborhood had congregated in the Haakensons' yard. Snow forts protected the combatants as they stocked up on ammunition for the next onslaught. Esther fervently hoped no stray snowball would come through a window. The four older boys enjoyed these battles, but Esther wanted Kenny and Mary to have a chance to be outside, too. At about 18 months and 3 years, respectively, they would be vulnerable targets for these fierce skirmishes. The fenced-in yard, which had seemed large enough when there were fewer kids, no longer sufficed.

When summer came, Esther gazed out at the yard, thinking again how small it looked. She told Lionel, "With another baby on the way, I think we're going to have to think about finding a bigger place. Seven kids on a city lot…it's just not gonna work."

Lionel agreed. "Maybe we should think about a place out in the Campbell Creek area. There's lots of open space there."

Esther nodded. They often picnicked along Campbell Creek. The area was beautiful and near enough so that downtown Anchorage was less than a half-hour's drive away, yet the place had the feel of being out in the country.

That summer Lionel added a new destination to his fishing itinerary. "Let's take a trip down to the Anchor River," he suggested. "A buddy from work spent a week there recently. The road's still pretty rough, but he told me about a place on the river called the Silver King Lodge. They rent cabins so we can take the whole family. You can take the pressure cooker along and do the canning right there. I hear the king fishing is terrific."

"The fishing had better be good, if we're gonna take the whole crew down there," commented Esther.

A small but well-built cabin greeted the family at the end of the long, dusty trip. Inside, Esther supervised dispersal of sleeping bags on all available floor space for the older boys. Kenny and Mary shared a small cot, and Esther and Lionel took the double bed. Early the next morning Lionel set out to try his luck on the river. By mid-day he was back, toting several kings. Esther, who had spent the morning feeding her brood and making sure the stove was reliable enough to handle the canning process, stepped out to greet him, with Mary following close behind.

"Mary!" Lionel exclaimed, "You're covered with spots!"

Kenny came outside to see what all the fuss was about. "So is Kenny!" Mary said, observing her younger brother's speckled face.

"Red measles!" pronounced Esther. "Since Mary had the 3-day measles on the Alcan these must be the other kind." In a short time the two youngsters were tucked back into bed. Esther hung a blanket to darken their corner, since red measles caused sensitivity to light, and could lead to eye damage. The two stayed in bed for the rest of the weekend while Esther filleted, skinned and canned salmon as her husband brought them in.

In those days, having both types of measles was practically a rite of childhood. Since no vaccines existed, catching measles at a young age was considered a good thing, as it ensured kids wouldn't have to worry about contracting the disease in later life. Fortunately, Kenny and Mary had mild cases, and the family took it in stride, considering the timing of the outbreak more inconvenient than the disease itself.

As the year and her pregnancy progressed, Esther chafed anew at the restrictions caused by living on a small city lot. Timmy, Bobby and Johnny, feeling the need for more room, frequently ran off with their friends. Usually she didn't mind, as long as they told her where they were going and came back by the required time. One day, though, shortly after the boys left, Esther realized that Mary had also disappeared.

She did a quick search of the house and yard, then grabbed Kenny and ran over to her parents' house. "Mary's gone," she told them. "I can't find her anywhere."

"Did you look in the playhouse?" asked Grandma.

"Yes, that was the first place I looked." The playhouse was Mary's favorite play space. Lionel had built it a year earlier and the kids used it daily as a fort, castle, or simply as a hideaway from annoying siblings.

"We'd better call the police," Fred put in.

Just then the radio, which had been supplying background music, caught everyone's attention. "The police tell me they've found a little girl in the Eastchester area..."

"That's Mary!" Esther exclaimed.

Fred was already on the phone. "Yep, we'll be right there. T'ank you, officer." He hung up. "C'mon, I'll drive you down."

When Esther and Grandpa walked into the station, Mary looked up from the fascinating instrument covered with buttons the nice policeman was letting her play with. "Hi, Mama. How come you got your apron on?" It struck the little girl as odd that Grandpa, who hardly ever went anywhere with the family, had driven down in his car to pick her up. It seemed funny to see him and her mother coming to the police station. But strangest of all was the apron. Mary knew, from living her entire 3½ years with Mama, that aprons belonged at home. You wore them when you worked around the house, but always, *always* took them off before going out in public. Many years passed before Mary appreciated the state of mind Esther was in that caused her to forget to take off that apron.

In the fall, Esther found herself doing more driving than ever. She had found a half-day program for Jimmy at the Alaska Crippled Children's School. While not a perfect fit for his needs, the teacher, Mrs. Marsh, welcomed him and did her best to adapt the curriculum for him. The local grade school, which was filled to overflowing, had morning and afternoon shifts. Timmy, now in third grade, attended the morning shift and first grader Bobby went in the afternoon. Fortunately, Lionel had found a good deal on a Model A Ford, so Esther no longer needed to drive him to and from work.

One afternoon that fall, Esther worked in the bathroom, washing clothes with her new wringer washing machine. This marvel of technology had an agitator in its tub that sloshed the clothes in water and detergent, saving Esther the trouble of scrubbing each piece on a washboard. However, it didn't remove the water. Once Esther determined that the clothes were clean, she fed each garment through the wringer perched atop the washer's tub. The wringer consisted of two rubber cylinders which pressed together and squeezed the water out of the clothes, then released them into a pan on the other side. From there it was a simple matter for Esther to drain the water out of the machine, refill it with clean water, dump the wrung-out clothing in for a rinse, then run every piece through the wringer one more time. Then all the clothes were loaded into a pan for a trip to the clotheslines stretched across the strawberry patch behind the house.

Esther leaned over the machine, fishing small shirts and tiny socks out of the water. Suddenly she heard an ominous thump followed by a loud howl from her youngest. The wash forgotten, she dashed into the living room. Kenny lay on the floor, clutching his foot and screaming in pain. "What happened?" she demanded of the rest of her owl-eyed offspring.

"I don't know," came the unhelpful answer.

Feeling she didn't have time for an extensive inquisition, Esther raced down the street to Grandma's house. "Can you stay with the kids? I have to get Kenny to the doctor."

Grandma came right over; Esther wrapped a jacket around Kenny and headed out the door. When she returned with him a few hours later, he was sporting a huge, snowy-white cast. "He broke his foot," Esther told the rest of her brood. "He's not supposed to walk on it, so you kids don't try to make him move around. And no rough-housing," she warned them sternly.

After a few weeks Kenny was given the okay to walk with his cast. Esther, nearing the end of her pregnancy, hailed this progress with a thankful heart. Carrying a two-year-old wearing a bulky cast was an armload for anyone, especially for someone as petite as she. She wasn't sure who was happier — herself or Kenny — when the cast came off for good.

On Thanksgiving, the family of eight gathered around the table. Esther thought back to the doctor who'd told her to stop having children after Jim's birth. Of course there had been some rough patches, but she felt blessed by God, and wouldn't ask for life to be any other way.

Anchor Point

In January 1955, Esther went into labor nearly a month before her due date. She remembered her mother telling about her own birth. Now she worried about the fate of this new baby. Would its early arrival cause health problems? Her fears were allayed when Ronald Mark was born, weighing 5 pounds—the smallest of all her children at birth—but perfectly healthy. As she told anyone who expressed concern about his size, "He's a whole pound more than I was. He'll be fine."

Her life had been busy enough before, but now Esther felt stretched to her limit. Every school morning she bundled up Ronny, helped Kenny and Mary into their outdoor gear, and supervised the rest of the boys as they donned coats, boots, mittens and hats. All that to drop Tim off for his early shift at the grade school. At noon she did it again, picking up Tim and dropping off Robert for the afternoon shift. Into the few inches of room left in the car, she squeezed one or two students who attended the Alaska Crippled Childrens' School with Jim. Once they were dropped off and the remaining passengers could breathe normally again, she headed home, only to reverse the process a few hours later when it was time to pick up Jim and Robert.

This routine continued through the winter. As May neared, Esther looked forward to the end of school. Summer in Alaska was always busy, but at least, with school out, she should be able to cut down on the number of car trips she made each day. One morning in early May, she'd just returned from the morning run when in walked Lionel. "What on earth would bring him home at this time of day?" she wondered.

She didn't remain in suspense for long. "How'd you like to move to Anchor Point?" Lionel asked.

"What's in Anchor Point?" Esther questioned.

"Well, we've been talking about needing to get out of town and get a bigger place to raise the family," Lionel began. "A guy I work with told me about a buddy of his who has a 40-acre homestead in Anchor Point he wants to get rid of. His wife and little girl hate it down there, and he can't really make a living."

"And how would *we* make a living?" Esther interrupted. "I didn't see much of a town when we were down there fishing. Is there a school? Or a post office? How much does he want for the place?"

"The guy is asking $350 for the cabin that's on the land." Lionel answered the last question first." I'm sure we couldn't get that kind of deal if we tried to buy land around Tudor Road or Sand Lake. And you can't buy a homestead; you have to live on it and meet certain requirements to prove up on it."

"What about work for you?" Esther persisted. "And what kind of town is there?"

"I can keep my job here. This house'll be empty, so I'll live here during the week and come home on the weekends. I remember seeing a little store and a post office sign when we drove through last time. And I'll be home every weekend, so I can bring anything we need from Anchorage."

"What's the cabin like? Does it have an indoor bathroom? I'm not going to potty train all these babies in an icy outhouse."

"If there's not one there, I'll have you one by winter," promised Lionel.

Esther could tell that in his mind Lionel was already halfway to Anchor Point. She had one last question: "Do we have $350 to spend on a homestead?"

That slowed Lionel down just a mite. "We have a little more than that in the bank," he admitted. "But if I keep this job, we'll have money coming in every week. We can do it. We want to move anyway; this will be the best deal around, I bet."

"Well, all right," Esther capitulated. "Forty acres will definitely give the kids more room than this little yard."

As if afraid his wife might change her mind if he stayed, Lionel shot out of the house, revved up the Model A, and headed out to strike the deal. When he got home that evening, his smile told Esther he'd been successful. "I'm gonna go down this weekend and take a look at the place," he told her.

This sounded like an adventure too good to pass up. "I wanna go!" Tim and Robert exclaimed, nearly in unison. Friday evening, as soon as he got off work Lionel, accompanied by 9-year-old Tim and 7-year-old Robert, climbed into the trusty Pontiac for the 220-mile trip to Anchor Point. The rest of the family carried on with their normal routines, playing in the yard on Saturday and attending church on Sunday.

Grandma and Grandpa expressed shock at the news that Esther's family was moving over 200 miles away. "What's down there that makes you want to move?"

"Room," Esther said simply. Whatever doubts she harbored as to the wisdom of such a move she kept to herself. The thought of living on a homestead certainly held no terrors for her. She'd lived without electricity or indoor plumbing for most of her life. She'd also lived in her share of tents and split plenty of firewood. At least this place had a cabin.

A tired trio of scouts returned late Sunday night. The boys went straight to bed, since they had to be up for school the next day. Lionel and Esther stayed up talking, planning, figuring out how to make this work.

"What was the place like?" Esther asked.

"Well," Lionel hesitated. "There's a lot more snow there than we have here. The place is about a mile down a side

253

road. They're still in the middle of spring break-up down there, and the road was real bad. We kept getting stuck; it took us almost 4 hours to go that one mile. The cabin is about a quarter-mile back in the trees, so we need to hike in. There's a well with a hand pump inside the cabin; I drained the water out before we came home. There were dead mice down in the well. There's a good water table, so we'll never have to worry about running out of water. And I'll close in the well so the mice can't get in again."

Esther grimaced. Mice in the well. Wonderful. "What else is there?"

Lionel correctly interpreted her question. "I don't think you'll approve of the outhouse. It's just a piece of canvas stretched around some trees with a log inside to hang your hind end over. It'd be hard for the little ones to use. Don't worry, though, I'll get a good outhouse made right away."

"I want an inside toilet," Esther reminded him.

"Yeah, I'll get that done by the end of the summer."

A week later Lionel showed up with another surprise: a brand new Pontiac station wagon. "We can't get all the stuff we're gonna need in the old car, and I'll need a good car to drive back and forth to Anchorage every week."

"How can we afford this?" Esther was astounded. "I thought we spent all our money on the place in Anchor Point."

"I sold the Model A, and got a good deal on this one."

Esther felt a twinge of hurt that Lionel had made these decisions without consulting her. She hated to lose the Model A. Sure, it was old, but there was something comforting about riding around in a car similar to the one her parents had owned back in Minnesota. She was sensible, though, and knew the station wagon was a more practical choice for their life going forward.

The family decided to make the move over Memorial Day weekend at the end of May. The boys' school would be out for the summer, and the holiday would give Lionel an extra day to help Esther get settled in.

Early (as in 4 a.m. early) on Saturday morning, May 28, the new Pontiac headed out of Anchorage, its rear cargo area stuffed with food, blankets, clothing, dishes and anything else Esther felt she'd need before Lionel returned to their new home in another week. Lionel drove, and on the other side of the front seat Esther held 5-month-old Ronny. Kenny and Mary curled up on the seat between their parents. Jim, Tim, Robert and Johnny shared the back seat. This scenario worked fine for the first few miles, until the kids came fully awake. Restlessness led to squabbling and even some pokes at each other. The parents, anxious to keep the peace, scanned the rock cliffs along Turnagain Arm for something to entertain their youngsters.

"See how many waterfalls you can count," suggested Esther.

This proved to be the perfect pastime, as water gushed down the bluff every mile or so. "There's one!" the boys would yell. Keeping track of the number of waterfalls, who saw each one first, and who had seen the biggest one kept them busy until the car left the cliffs behind and headed around the end of the Arm. As they started into the mountains a waterfall appeared occasionally, but not often enough to keep the kids occupied. A few stops to fix flat tires and one for a picnic breakfast gave them opportunity to get out and run off a little excess energy.

Nearly eight hours later they arrived in Anchor Point. Lionel eased the car onto the North Fork Road. "Good," he commented, "it's dried up a lot since we were down here before." The road still had numerous soft muddy spots, but Esther was relieved there was nothing worse as the car jounced its way along, nearly sending kids and other cargo airborne on some of the deeper ruts.

About noon, Lionel pulled the car into the yard of Bert Paraday. Bert wasn't home, but his sled dogs—each tied to its dog house — welcomed the newcomers with a chorus of howls. Lionel found the least muddy-looking spot as far across the yard as he could get from the fierce-sounding dogs and parked the car. "This is where we get out," he informed the family.

A snow-covered path ran past the outhouse and into the woods behind Bert's log cabin. This was the access to the Haakensons' new home. Lionel, Tim and Robert loaded pack boards with supplies and hefted them onto their backs. Jim and John each had a small parcel to carry, since they needed to concentrate on navigating the snow.

Forward the group marched — Tim and Robert in the lead, then Lionel carrying Kenny and using his free hand to assist John or Jim as needed. Esther brought up the rear, with Ronny in one arm and Mary clinging to her other hand. The winter's record snowfall may have melted somewhat since Lionel's previous trip, but enough remained in the forest to provide a memorable tramp in to the cabin. Esther struggled to keep Mary moving, as every few steps she sank into the snow up to her hips.

The cabin at the end of the trail was small — only 12 x 16 feet — and nearly bare inside. The moss the former owner had stuffed between the logs for insulation had dried, and now large gaps revealed daylight from nearly every angle. Lionel, Tim and Robert stopped just long enough to unload their back packs, then set off to ferry in another load. Esther surveyed the outhouse. "Well, if any of you kids have to go potty, it'd be best to just use the bushes."

A stack of firewood lay beside a small cook stove and Esther soon had a fire going. After a peek into the well to assure herself that no more mice had gone swimming there, she primed the hand pump, drew a bucket of water, and filled a tea kettle and coffee pot. By the time the guys had all the supplies carried in from the car, the rough, homemade table had been scrubbed, and coffee steamed in the pot. Esther gathered everyone for a quick lunch of sandwiches, supplemented with coffee for the adults and Kool-Aid for the kids.

While Lionel and the older boys explored the surrounding acreage, Esther conducted a more thorough survey of the main floor of the cabin. In addition to a narrow table, the previous owner had built a bed frame and

The original cabin, 1955.

topped it with an ancient mattress. Esther spread sheets and blankets over it. "Now Lionel and I have place to sleep; what about all the kids?" she asked herself. Not finding answers on the main floor, she tackled the ladder of sapling logs that clung to one wall. In the attic, she came across a few dusty boxes of items the erstwhile occupants had either forgotten or didn't want to pack. Most of the contents were rags and unusable clothing, but one find that thrilled her daughter was a large doll. Someone had apparently left the doll too close to the stove at some point in her life, as she had a melted flat spot on one side of her head. Mary couldn't believe that anyone who had a little girl would dream of leaving such a treasure behind. She named her Marcella after the girl in the *Raggedy Ann* stories, and cared for her devotedly for many years.

Back in the attic, Esther checked out the space while Mary tended to Marcella. "Well, it looks like you kids will fit up here," she remarked. Climbing down the ladder, she took stock. Everyone now had a place to sleep but Ronny. At five months, he was too young to be thrown in amongst the rest of the kids in the attic, and the parents' bed was too small for him to share. Esther solved the problem by unpacking the biggest box she'd brought down—one that had originally held her sister Gladys's new rinse tub. With a folded blanket for a mattress and another blanket for a cover, Ronny's bed was made.

Though it was still May, the mosquitoes had already arrived; Esther could almost hear their gleeful cackles as they surveyed the newly-arrived smorgasbord of warm-blooded victims. She foiled their plans for baby Ronny by attaching cheese cloth netting over his new bed. Many times that summer, the other kids envied Ronny his bug-free domain as they dodged, swatted and occasionally swallowed mosquitoes.

True to his word, Lionel immediately started throwing together a more user-friendly outhouse. The result—built from old pieces of wood found lying around the yard—wasn't up to Lionel's usual standards, but he promised to build a sturdier one soon.

By the time their dad left the next Monday afternoon, Tim and Robert had learned to split wood, and John, Jim, Kenny and Mary knew where to stack it on the porch so it was handy for Esther. Knowing the house needed to be expanded before winter set in, Lionel also had felled some trees with his new chain saw and left them whole, to be used when he started building the new addition.

A tree with a trunk about 3 inches in diameter stood just behind the cabin in the space where the added room would sit. Tim, anxious to demonstrate his newly-acquired axe skills, volunteered to chop it down. It took hours, but the tree finally toppled. Esther had to chuckle at the sight of her second son, axe slung over his shoulder, strutting around like Paul Bunyan.

The morning after Lionel left for Anchorage, Esther awakened early. She sat on the bed while Ronny nursed, mentally prioritizing the chores that lay before her. "Take 'em one at a time, Esther," she told herself. A bucket of bleach water sat in one corner, a growing pile of diapers in it. She heard rustling sounds in the attic, then Tim's sleepy face peered down at her. She knew the rest of the kids would follow shortly, so when Ronny finished nursing, she checked to see if he needed a clean diaper, then set him back in his box-crib. She stepped outside to get some kindling for the stove and stood for a few moments, listening. Bird songs filled the air. No roar of motors, no shouts of humans—just the birds. The sun shone on the small clearing around the cabin and filtered through the branches of the spruce trees that framed the yard on all sides. "What a peaceful place," she thought.

"Mama! Help!" she heard the squawk from inside the cabin. Hurrying in she discovered Mary, Kenny and Jim trying to figure out how to navigate the ladder. With encouragement and some physical assistance she got them all down the ladder and pointed toward the outhouse.

After a breakfast of cold cereal and powdered milk, the kids were anxious to explore, and Esther was just as anxious to get them out from underfoot. "You can go into the woods a little ways, but make sure you can see the cabin," she told the older boys. "And stay where you can see and hear each other." The younger kids were given strict orders to stay in the yard.

While her offspring acquainted themselves with their new home, Esther pumped a bucket of water and set it on the stove. While it heated she set out ingredients for a batch of bread. Every so often she ran to the door to keep track of what her little ones were doing. Mary and Kenny were busy getting dirty digging for treasures in the yard, and she could hear the voices of the older boys.

By noon the bread was baked and the kids were hungry. Sandwiches and Kool-Aid made a quick lunch. Afterwards, Esther put Tim and Robert to work splitting more stove wood. John helped his mother roll out some fluffy yellow insulation which she cut into long, narrow strips. "You see these places where the light comes in between the logs? Poke this in to chink up those spots."

Esther poured the now-heated bucket of water into a galvanized tub and set the scrub board in it. What she wouldn't give for that wringer washer sitting in the house in Anchorage. Though it wouldn't do much good without electricity. She pulled the soiled diapers out of their bleach water bath and tossed them into the wash tub. Each diaper got its turn being scrubbed up and down over the corrugated surface of the washboard, then dropped into another pan for a rinse. Her hands and back ached as she wrung the rinse water out of each piece of cloth. Glad the former owners had strung a clothesline, she carried the diapers out and hung them to flap in the breeze.

When she finally called the kids in for supper, she eyed their clothing. Only a few days ago those pants and shirts had been pristine. She foresaw another wash day in the very near future. For now, though, they'd just have to be a little grubby.

Esther was glad the first work week for Lionel was a short one. He had taken the station wagon when he went back to Anchorage, leaving her with no transportation. Halfway through the week she told the older boys to watch their younger siblings and hiked down the trail to talk to Bert. Most of the snow had melted off the path, giving her a clearer view of the family's only avenue in or out of the property. From the yard the trail led into the woods and wound through the forest. Soggy moss and dead grass lay across the path, and tree roots jutted up in unexpected places. Emerging from the woods, the trail took a sharp turn and ran atop a raised area of grass hummocks, flanked on both sides by muskeg—one side fairly dry and the other containing a shallow pond. A few steps past the hummocks brought her into Bert's yard. She walked to the front of his cabin and knocked on the door.

"Bert, I wonder if I could hitch a ride to the store with you."

"Sure," Bert responded, "I'll fire up ol' Gutless Gert and get you there in a jiffy." Bert named all his vehicles. Gutless Gert was his rattletrap truck, and his John Deere tractor was Poppin' Priscilla.

As Bert approached the town, Esther gazed with interest at the few buildings that comprised Anchor Point. The North Fork Road ended in a T at its intersection with the Sterling Highway. Across the highway sat a small building with a sign, "Homestead Supply Company and U.S. Post Office". Fifty yards or so to the north, another sign proclaimed that "Modern Builders Supply" offered lumber, building materials and army surplus furniture for sale. Esther predicted that place would receive a lot of business from the Haakensons over the next months.

Inside Homestead Supply, Esther observed a wall of post office boxes. To the right was the store. A man smiled from behind the counter. He stuck out his hand. "Hi," he said, "I'm Ken Rickley. I suppose you'll be wanting a post office box." Mr. Rickley disappeared into a back room and came out with a scrap of paper. "You'll have box number 42," he said. "Here's the combination for opening it. The mail truck comes on Mondays and Thursdays, unless the roads are closed because of avalanches or floods or something."

Esther accepted the paper, then turned to explore the small store. A few heads of lettuce lay in a bin alongside some carrots and potatoes. The rest of the space was taken up by shelves holding canned and other nonperishable goods. A strategically placed shelf of candy bars stood at kids' eye level directly in front of the counter. Esther picked out a few items she had forgotten to bring down from Anchorage, and returned home.

Lionel arrived in the wee hours of Saturday morning, exhausted from the drive. Esther had a lot to tell him, but she restrained herself until he'd had a good night's sleep. He expressed appreciation as he looked around the cabin the next morning. "You've got this place looking real homey," he commented. He took another swig of coffee as he surveyed the shelves beside the stove. Dishes, along with boxed and canned goods, filled them to capacity. A shallow box on the countertop contained silverware and cooking utensils.

"I need some place to put the sugar and flour," Esther said. "They're just sitting under the counter, and I've seen at least one mouse already. I don't want mice and shrews in my flour. Bring that dresser that I made with the two big drawers down with you next week. I think I can use it for flour and sugar bins."

Esther's carpentry talents were not limited to the crib she'd built before Jim's birth. Sometime in the past she had seen a need for a 3-drawer dresser, and had proceeded to build one. The finished product stood about 36" high and 30" wide. It had a shallow top drawer and two deeper ones, each about 15" high.

"I need a couple of other things, too," Esther continued. "There's no way to keep anything cold except to put it in the shade on the north side of the house, and we don't have a bathtub. I've been sponging the kids off in the wash basin, but they're eventually gonna need a bath. And I could use one, too."

Lionel nodded, but said little about her requests. He spent most of the next two days, chainsaw in hand, felling trees. Some he sawed up for firewood and some he limbed and left whole to be used as walls for the cabin extension. He taught Tim and Robert how to skin the bark off these logs. Esther had already been busy calculating the dimensions and placement of the new room.

Before Lionel left, she told him, "We need to figure out how to get the old Pontiac down here. I can't be stuck here in the woods with no transportation. What if there's some kind of emergency?"

"Well, I'm going to ask for a few weeks off pretty soon so we can get rolling on this building project. Then we'll have the station wagon down here." It was clear Lionel didn't understand her concern over not having transportation, but she resolved to find a way to get that other car to Anchor Point as soon as possible.

Lionel showed up the following weekend with evidence that his wife's requests had been duly noted and his sheet metal talents had been employed during his after-work hours. In addition to the requested dresser, he deposited a galvanized metal tub and a smaller metal box on the cabin floor. "Here's your bathtub," he said.

Esther admired the tub then asked, "What's this other one?"

"You'll see," he replied.

With the chain saw Lionel cut a hole in the wall on the shadiest side of the cabin and inserted the metal box. He installed an insulated door over the opening. "This is your 'Homestead-aire'," he announced with a grin. "It won't be as cold as a refrigerator, but it'll at least keep things cool."

That evening as she heated water for the first real baths any of them (except Lionel, who could bathe in Anchorage) had had in several weeks, Esther reflected on her blessings. With the large dresser drawers lined in tin foil, her flour and sugar now had a home safe from hungry little beasties. The Homestead-aire was already proving its usefulness as Esther could tell it was noticeably cooler than the air inside the cabin. And now she had a bathtub. Of course, she'd have to wait until the kids were in bed and then bathe in the same water they'd used, but she was in no mood to be picky. A bath was a bath, after all.

When Lionel got several weeks of leave from his job, he hit the cabin addition project full force. The pile of skinned logs shrank as he, Esther, Tim and Robert lugged them one by one to the northeast side of the cabin and stacked them up to make walls. Before long the endeavor showed promise of becoming a 12 x 20-foot room that would more than double the current living area.

In addition to sawing logs and working on the cabin extension, Lionel constructed items to make his family's lives more comfortable. Esther had mentioned the need for a bigger dining table that would accommodate nine people. He solved the problem by sawing a sheet of plywood in half, making a 4 x 4-foot table. He rounded the corners and assigned the older boys the job of sanding it smooth. Some sturdy legs finished it off. For chairs, he picked firewood rounds of various heights and nailed 1" x 6" boards to the tops. These made chairs of custom heights for the kids, but Esther found them heavy and ungainly to work around in her kitchen. Also, they were ugly, and not an efficient use of space.

A few days later she stood outside the cabin, surrounded by lumber and gripping a saw with confidence. Once she'd cut her boards to the proper lengths, she swapped the saw for a hammer and began nailing the pieces together. Within hours, a bench took shape. Then another one. When placed along the sides of the table, the two benches comfortably held the 6 older kids. Mail-order catalogs set on the benches provided booster seats for the smaller children.

When Lionel's working vacation was over, Esther put her foot down. "We're riding to Anchorage with you," she told him, "and I'm going to get my car." Everyone piled into the station wagon and returned temporarily to the house on 10th Avenue, giving the kids a chance to catch up with their cousins and grandparents, whom they hadn't seen for several months.

They couldn't leave the homestead for long, though, as the summer was short and the to-do list long. After only a few days, Esther loaded the seven kids into the old Pontiac and hauled them back to their new home in the woods.

Just knowing the car was there in Bert's yard, a mere quarter-mile from the cabin, provided peace of mind for

Esther. It was nice to be able to go to the post office on mail days, or pick something up at the store. The homestead lay a little over a mile from town, which Esther would have walked without a second thought in her younger, carefree days. She couldn't leave seven youngsters alone, though, while she hiked to town.

In late August, Esther and the kids watched as workers from Homer Electric Association set poles and strung wires, hooking the house up to

Building the first cabin addition, 1955.

one of the most marvelous of modern conveniences — electricity. A single bulb hung from the ceiling a few feet inside the front door and another lit the corner near the stove. A third bulb, up in the attic, illuminated the kids' sleeping area. Esther had to shoo the younger children away from the cords dangling from each fixture, as they found the thrill of turning the lights on and off by pulling the strings irresistible.

A few days before Labor Day, Esther drove her crew into town to register the older boys for school — Tim in the 4th grade, Robert in 2nd, and John beginning his first year. Esther hoped, given the small numbers in each grade, that Jim would be able to attend.

"Mary and Kenny, stay in the car," she ordered. Scooping young Ronny up in her arms, she led the other four boys into the schoolhouse. Inside the front door they entered a small cloak room. To their right were hangers for coats and room for the boots and other snow gear that would be needed later in the year. On the left, a bucket of water with a dipper floating in it sat on a small stand. Esther opened the door into the main classroom. She was greeted by a young woman seated at the teacher's desk. "Hello, I'm Mrs. Dalton," the woman said.

Esther introduced herself and the four boys. Mrs. Dalton explained that she taught grades 1-4 then pointed to several double tables, each with two chairs, placed near the front of the room. "These tables are for the first graders. John, would you like to choose your seat?" She addressed Tim and Robert. "You can each pick a desk over here." Mrs. Dalton indicated the correct rows of desks.

Esther gave a brief outline of Jim's challenges then said, "He's been attending the Alaska Crippled Children's School in Anchorage. I know he can't keep up with his age group, but if you could let him come and learn what he can..."

Mrs. Dalton shook her head. "I don't have any training in teaching kids like him, and with almost twenty students in four grades, I just don't have extra time to give him. I'm sorry."

A man came through the door of the adjoining room. "This is my husband," said Mrs. Dalton. "He's the head teacher, and teaches 5th through 8th grades in the back room."

Everyone stuck their heads into the small back room with its neat rows of desks. "Wow," thought Esther, "this room is smaller than our cabin. He must have 15 desks in here. That's gonna really be tight."

Out back of the school sat an outhouse. As with almost every home in Anchor Point, the school had no indoor plumbing.

Esther returned home, disappointed but not surprised that Jim was refused admission to school. She had known it was a long shot, but she had to try. Jim loved school so much. "Well, we'll just have to figure out how to teach him at home," she thought. It seemed like a daunting task, with no materials and no guidance.

266

On the first day of school, she loaded everyone back into the car and drove the boys to school. Given the logistics of plodding out the trail with her four remaining kids, she was thankful she wouldn't have to do this twice every day. She had discovered that tiny Anchor Point had a school bus. Bob Williams—owner of Modern Builders Supply—had a Jeep he used to run a bus route. The Williamses lived about a mile past the Haakensons up the North Fork, near the point at which the road ended.

Just weeks after school started, Esther, as usual, was spending the day working on the cabin addition. She knew how crucial it was to have it closed in and livable by winter. The sun had come out after several days of rain, and 8-month-old Ronny amused himself with toys on a blanket in the yard while Jim, Kenny and Mary played nearby. Suddenly Mary spied an unusual sight. "Mama, there's a man coming in the trail."

"Who would be coming here?" Esther wondered aloud. They all watched as the figure drew closer. "It's Mr. Dalton," she said, recognizing the head teacher. "Something must be wrong at school."

Mr. Dalton wasted no time with small talk. "We think your son Robert broke his arm. He slipped on a log and fell."

"Where's the nearest doctor?" Esther asked, her mind racing through all the tasks that lay ahead of her.

"Seldovia," replied Mr. Dalton.

Esther wasn't familiar with Seldovia. "How far away is that?" she asked.

"It's across Kachemak Bay from Homer. You'll have to drive into Homer and catch a plane from there."

Esther was aware the gravel road continued past Anchor Point for nearly 20 miles to the town of Homer, but she'd not yet had occasion to drive it. Wrapping Ronny in a blanket, she called to the other children. "Mary! Kenny! Jim! We need to go down to the school." She strode as quickly as she could down the bumpy trail, the three youngsters trotting behind.

At the school, Robert, his face pale and tear-stained, slid clumsily into the front seat of the car, hugging his right arm against his body. Esther drove as fast as she dared, knowing if she hit the bumps in the gravel road too hard the jarring would cause unnecessary pain for him.

"How on earth did you break your arm?" she asked as she drove.

"Well, I was goin' to the outhouse and there was a pile of slabs in the way. They were wet 'cause of the rain and I slipped and fell."

"Couldn't you walk around the slabs? Did you have to climb over them?"

"Yeah, there's a path, but…" Robert's voice trailed off.

Esther could picture the scenario. Given the choices of going around or over a pile of slabs, what's an 8-year-old boy to do? Climb the slabs, of course.

Esther entered Homer and stopped at the first business she saw—a small café called Dari DeLite. "Where's the airport?" she asked the lady behind the counter. "I have a boy in the car with a broken arm and I need to get him to Seldovia."

She drove to the airport ,where she was met by the pilot of a small plane. "I'll get him to the doc," the man promised. "Don't worry—I'll take good care of him."

Esther watched the plane taxi and lift off. Poor Robert. He must be scared to death. She looked at the other kids' solemn faces. "We'd better go pick up Tim and John," she told them.

She headed the car back toward Anchor Point and managed to catch up with the bus. Tim and John joined the rest of the crew and once again Esther drove to Homer. "At least," she thought, "I'll never say I'm not familiar with the road to Homer."

The family sat in the car at the airport, scanning the sky for the small plane that would return Robert to them. The sun was setting by the time it appeared. They watched it circle, land and taxi up to the car. Out hopped Robert, his right arm encased in a bright white cast, and a book his new pilot friend had given him clutched in his other hand. "He did good," the pilot told Esther. "He filled a couple of airsick bags on the way over, but after that he was alright."

Esther thanked the pilot, who refused any pay for his services. Robert, now that his arm was tended to and aspirin was dulling the pain, looked on the experience as a grand adventure. He was much more interested in telling about the flight than the visit to the doctor. It made the other kids almost envious to hear what a great time he'd had. He did have a concern, though. Later that evening he sidled up to Esther. "Is Daddy gonna be mad at me for breaking my arm?"

"No, he'll know it was an accident," Esther assured him. "Just don't go climbing on any more piles of wet slabs."

It was a joyous day in October when Lionel fired up the chain saw and cut a doorway between the original cabin and the new addition. He opened up the space even more by sawing off the logs on one side of the doorway to a height of about 3 feet. He attached a piece of plywood, making a countertop. This gave Esther a place to set things as well as a way to keep track of the goings-on in the new room. Lionel and the boys moved the bed to the other side of the short wall, which gave Esther much-needed space in her kitchen. She sent Lionel down to Modern Builders Supply, where he picked up an Army-surplus kitchen sink. When set between the stove and the pump stand, it provided Esther with a real sink, rather than a metal pan set on the kitchen table. Now she had easy access to cold water from the pump on one side, and heated water from the stove's reservoir on the other. A 5-gallon bucket in the sink's lower cabinet caught the used dish water.

The opening of the addition to the cabin brought small luxuries the family hadn't had room for previously. Lionel made good on his word to give Esther an indoor toilet. A space about 2 x 2 feet, tucked into the northeast corner behind the barrel stove, contained a toilet, offering a warm place to "go." The toilet was flushed with buckets of water poured directly into its bowl; from there, a pipe carried the contents out to the cesspool Lionel and the boys had dug behind the house. The bucket under the kitchen sink furnished some of this water. Esther also saved her laundry water to use in the toilet. Lionel had constructed a sturdy log outhouse with two holes—one of standard height and one several inches lower. Even with the indoor toilet, with 9 people needing the facilities, the outhouse got a fair share of use.

On one of his trips home Lionel had brought down a couch from the Anchorage house. It, plus the parents' bed, a 50-gallon drum made into a barrel stove and the tiny bathroom, largely filled the new room. Just past the doorway between the old and new rooms a trap door in the middle of the floor provided access to a root cellar. Here, potatoes and other vegetables were within easy reach when Esther needed them for meals.

The upstairs of the addition became bedroom space for all the kids except Ronny, who still slept in the large cardboard box. When he built the addition, Lionel had constructed a dormer on the south side. A set of bunk beds now sat on either side of this dormer—sleeping space for the four older boys. Kenny and Mary each slept in a cot along the sloping wall across the room.

In a rush to finish the project and get his family moved in, Lionel nailed a log ladder to the wall beside the doorway opposite the bed. He cut a hole in the ceiling, and left it at that, intending—when he had time—to install some proper stairs. This task ended up on Esther's plate, due to an incident shortly afterwards.

Esther, being a firm believer that jobs were good training for kids, made sure all of her children had responsibilities suitable to their ages and abilities. One task she gave her 4-year-old daughter was rounding up lunch boxes. Every day, she sent her sons off to school with sandwiches, maybe a cookie or two, a small jar of canned peaches or pears and a Thermos bottle filled with reconstituted powdered milk or Kool-Aid (the staple drinks of homestead children). When they got home after school, sometimes the boys would remember to drop their lunch boxes off in the kitchen. Usually, however, already intent on their chores or a game, they carried the lunch buckets until they proved a nuisance, then left them wherever they happened to be at the time. Mary's job was to search outdoors and in, round up all three buckets and set the Thermoses where they would get washed with the supper dishes. A Thermos of milk that has spent the night souring inside a lunch box is a nasty surprise to open in the morning.

One evening as Mary made the rounds, she'd exhausted all the usual hiding places downstairs and outside. As Esther busied herself in the kitchen she heard Mary start up the ladder to the kids' new bedroom. Suddenly she heard a thud. Esther whirled around; Mary's body lay sprawled on the floor, her legs sticking out from under the bed.

"Mary!" Esther cried. She grabbed up her daughter and, plopping herself onto the bed, rocked the still body frantically. Through the fog of panic she forced her brain to function. How would she get to the doctor this time of night? What should she do with the rest of the kids if she had to go into Homer? What if Mary died? In that moment she hated Anchor Point, its harshness and isolation. What seemed like an eternity passed before Mary finally recovered enough to cry. Relief flooded through Esther at the sound. She laid Mary on the bed and climbed the ladder herself to retrieve the lunch bucket, scolding the boys the whole way. "Mary just about killed herself looking for your lunch boxes. From now on, you leave them in the kitchen when you get home. No throwing them any old place."

The day after that episode, Esther sat down with paper and pencil and drew up plans for a staircase. When the boys arrived home from school, she was ready. "Tim," she said, "we need to cut some logs." Together they used the crosscut saw to cut logs of various lengths: two 6-inch ones for the first step, two 12-inchers for the next, and so on, until she had risers for each step of the staircase. She and Tim stripped the bark from the pieces and nailed them into place.

By the time Lionel got home that weekend, a rough but sturdy stairway replaced the treacherous ladder. The bottom half marched up the back wall, then a left turn at a landing fed onto the upper part, ending at the same access hole used for the ladder.

Esther poured the story of Mary's fall and her ensuing panic into Lionel's sympathetic ears. She concluded, "It's not enough just to have the car down at Bert's. We need a driveway so I can drive up to the house. What if I'd had to carry Mary out the trail? I couldn't do it."

Lionel nodded. "Yeah, we need a driveway. It's too late to start it this fall, but I'll get going on it as soon as the frost is out in the spring."

Esther felt her anger at Anchor Point begin to dissipate. Everything seemed easier to face when Lionel was around. She remembered her main complaint about living in Anchorage—lack of room for the kids to move and grow. Anchor Point certainly had plenty of room. As for its drawbacks, she'd just have to deal with them.

Homesteading

Esther stepped out the front door onto the porch. She peered at the thermometer hanging on a post: -10 degrees. Back in northern Minnesota this would have been considered fairly mild, but it was cold enough for here and now. No wonder she needed more wood. Tim and Robert had filled the wood box that sat next to the cook stove before they left for school,

Winter, 1955-56.

but she'd already used most of it. The roar of chain saws drifted through the frigid air. "There they go again," she thought. "We can't see our neighbors, but, boy, do we hear 'em on these icy mornings. You'd think we're the only ones who plan ahead and have our wood cut before it gets so cold." She quickly loaded her arms from the stack on the porch and scuttled back inside. The barrel stove in the new addition was great for heating the room, but it consumed a lot of wood.

She chuckled as her actions triggered a memory. Tim had remarked just the other night about how much easier the wood split with these low temperatures. He said, "It only takes one swing and a big chunk breaks right in two." Later on, during a family devotional (which the kids called a "meeting") everyone had contributed ideas of things they were thankful for. Three-year-old Kenny spoke up. "I'm thankful for the cold trees." He had heard Tim's comment and wanted God to know that he appreciated the fact that the cold weather had made Tim's life a little easier.

Another sound had become familiar to Esther since the move from Anchorage. Instead of the roar of vehicles, the howl of sled dogs filled the air. The family had acquired two puppies—King and Queenie—from an elderly man who'd walked in the trail with the pups in his backpack, but at least half of their fellow Anchor Point residents kept teams of sled dogs. Many remote homes were accessible only by foot path in summer and, in winter, by dog sled. The former owners of the Haakensons' homestead must have had a team, since the kids had found an old sled and a well-used harness on the premises. Once the snow fell the kids dabbled with training King and Queenie to pull a sled—after all they were supposed to be part Husky—but they never advanced to the stage of heeding repeated commands to "Mush." The only time they'd pull the sled was when one of the kids ran ahead, coaxing them. This struck the kids as being an inefficient use of energy, so King and Queenie remained just pets.

The family's nearest neighbor and friend, Bert, kept a small team of dogs tied among the stumps next to his house. Esther shuddered as she thought of the terrifying lesson Mary had learned about the difference between sled dogs and family pets.

Lionel had related the incident. "I walked down to Bert's to talk to him about borrowing his tractor, and Mary went with me. While Bert and I were talking, she wandered around the yard. All of a sudden Bert yelled, 'Watch out for Ari!' I looked around and saw Mary face to face with that German Shepherd, Ari, who used to be a police dog during the war. I yelled, 'Mary! Get away from that dog!' She must've been frozen with fright, because she didn't move, just stood staring at his fangs snarling about 6 inches from her face. Bert and I ran over ,and I grabbed Mary and Bert shoved Ari back. I hate to think what would've happened if Bert hadn't noticed her when he did."

Bert had two dogs that he treated more as house pets, though they pulled a sled when called upon to do so. They both were named after Alaskan places. Chena, a female Husky mix, welcomed all human attention. The other, Chitina, was less tolerant, and Bert recommended that the kids stay away from her.

In the fall, Chena gave birth to a litter of puppies, which Bert's new neighbors found thrilling. For several days afterward, Tim, Robert and John made a habit when they got off the bus of stopping to visit Chena and her pups. Then one day as they disembarked, they observed Bert crouched beside the box that held the puppies. Curious, they walked over to see what he was doing. It turned out to be a harsh lesson in the realities of life on the homestead. Bert was culling the litter. With a hammer in one hand, he reached into the box with his other hand, glanced at the pup, gave it a quick knock on the head, and threw its lifeless body into the surrounding bushes. Several puppies escaped the culling, but the boys didn't wait around or ask what his criteria for sparing a pup's life might be. They arrived home shaken and sober-faced. How kind, jovial Bert could so coldly dispose of Chena's adorable offspring puzzled them.

Esther tried to explain. "Well, if you don't get rid of some of the puppies there'll just be more and more, and eventually Bert won't be able to feed them all. Isn't it better to get rid of them now, rather than let them starve to death?" From the looks on the boys' faces she was pretty sure she hadn't convinced them, but she understood what Bert had done. A year later, when Queenie produced a litter, Lionel dealt with a similar issue. Though he was unable to do the deed himself, he found a local man who took care of the problem by shooting Queenie and all her pups. This remained the community's accepted method of disposing of any animals that a family didn't want to keep and couldn't give away until, decades later, access to veterinary services enabled people to spay or neuter their pets.

The kids line up in front of the cabin, the first winter on the homestead. L-R: Mary, John, Robert, Tim, Jim.

Winter set in with cold temperatures and snow that didn't seem to want to stop. A letter from Gladys in early November caused a jolt of excitement for Esther. Her sister wrote that they planned to come down for Thanksgiving.

On Thanksgiving eve Esther peered out through swirling snowflakes. Darkness settled over Alaska early this time of year, and now another snowstorm threatened. Gladys's family was driving down in tandem with Lionel, so they shouldn't get lost, but Esther didn't like to think about them out on the roads in this weather. Near midnight, flashlight beams bounced along the trail, heralding the arrival of the travelers. Into the cabin tumbled Lionel and the Dixsons—Gladys, her husband, Maurice, and their six kids—Joe, Don, Alice, Billy, Ruthie and three-month-old Ricky.

At that time of night, the first order of business was figuring out sleeping arrangements. Gladys and Maurice crawled onto a mattress in the attic of the old cabin, while baby Ricky slept nearby in a blanket-filled box. Most of the upstairs beds became double-enders to accommodate the visitors, with pillows at both ends. By pairing up a smaller kid with a larger one, everybody got a relatively good night's sleep.

They woke up to a foot of new snow. Tim had already scoped out a possible skating rink on the muskeg pond at the end of the foot trail, near Bert's place. After breakfast, he, Robert and John grabbed shovels and led Joe, Don and Alice down to the pond for a few hours of shoveling and skating. Jim never showed much interest in skating so he stayed in the yard with Mary, Billy, Ruthie and Kenny. The youngsters rolled snowballs, made snowmen and generally did everything they could to get soaking wet and cold. Meanwhile, the babies—Ronny and Ricky—played in the cabin while Esther and Gladys worked on Thanksgiving dinner.

When everyone came in to eat, Esther hung all the gloves, mittens, socks and other snow gear on a couple of clotheslines she'd strung behind the cook stove. They dripped and steamed while the two families enjoyed turkey and all the trimmings. Half of the group had to sit in the living room with plates on their laps but nobody cared. As Esther said, "We're together, and that's what matters."

The Dixsons left with Lionel on Sunday. The house seemed quiet and empty with only eight people left in it. The boys returned to school the next day, but all that snow couldn't be ignored, and a few days later they came home bubbling over with excitement.

"We're gonna have a sledding party," Tim informed Esther. "Just about everybody in school is going."

Esther hesitated. "Where will this party be?" she asked.

"On the North Fork hill."

Since the North Fork Road was the only access to Anchor Point, Esther was well-acquainted with the hill. About a half-mile out of town a sharp turn in the road led to a steep grade down to the bridge across the north fork of the Anchor River. On the other side of the bridge the road rose steeply up to another sharp turn. This design caused numerous headaches for motorists when the road was snowy or icy, but it was great for sledding. The only drawback was that it was a public road, though evening traffic was rare.

The boys continued their campaign for permission to go to the sledding party. "Mr. Rabich and Mr. Williams will be there," Robert said.

Reassured that there would be chaperones, Esther rather reluctantly gave her permission, and Friday evening the younger kids watched enviously as Tim, Robert and John set off, pulling the family's two Flexible Flyer sleds.

The boys got home well after their normal bedtime, but couldn't wait to tell about the fun they'd had. "That hill is so fun. You can run with the sled and belly-flop at the top. We just flew down the hill. Mr. Williams was our lookout in case any cars came, but only one did. When we got to the bottom, Mr. Rabich hooked our sleds to his truck and towed us back up the hill. That way we didn't have to waste time walking up. And when we were done sledding, they took us over to Williamses'. Mrs. Williams made us cocoa and cookies."

"How'd you get that big scrape on your face?" Esther asked Tim.

"Oh, some of the big kids were trying to go down the hill standing up. They wrapped the rope around the steering sticks. So I tried it. I fell off before I got very far, but it sure was fun."

Several more times throughout the next couple of winters the boys went to similar sledding parties. One evening everyone came to the Haakensons' place afterwards, where Esther had cocoa and freshly-made cookies waiting.

When the traffic increased to the point that the lookout had to stop a half-dozen cars, the hill was deemed too risky, and the sledding parties were discontinued.

One evening Tim, Robert and John showed up from school accompanied by Bert. He couldn't stop giggling as he told Esther about the boys' latest adventure. The trail from Bert's place to the Haakensons' house led past a section of muskeg, then took a hard left as it entered the woods. Tim, as usual, had been in the lead as the boys trudged through the snow. As he made the turn into the woods, he almost ran smack into a large moose.

Bert enjoyed telling the story. "They came runnin' back to my place with their eyes as big as saucers. I could tell they didn't want to walk back in by themselves, so I said I'd come with 'em. 'Course the moose was gone by then, but I could sure tell where they saw 'im. There were their lunch boxes layin' in the snow, 1-2-3, all in a row."

With very few neighbors, no television, and mail delivery only twice a week, the radio provided the family's link to the outside world. One of the Anchorage stations had a signal powerful enough to reach Anchor Point. Esther often kept it on during the day as she worked around the house. On weekday afternoons she tuned in for the broadcast of a program for preschool kids hosted by a woman who went by the moniker "Jelly Bean." Saturday mornings everyone listened to the *Big John and Sparky* show, who always assured their listeners that there was "…n-o-o-o school today!" *Dragnet* and *The Lone Ranger* also contributed to the kids' entertainment.

The Sears, Roebuck and Montgomery Ward catalogs provided hours of amusement for Esther's youngsters, as they daydreamed over the toy sections containing dolls, toy guns and vehicles of every description. Esther put the catalogs to more practical use as she shopped for necessities that weren't available locally. Realizing she needed a sewing machine to keep her offspring clothed, she ordered one from

Sears. Over the years, dresses, shirts, pajamas—nearly everything except pants—were assembled on that machine.

Each year, a few days before Christmas, Lionel donned snowshoes, shouldered an axe and, accompanied by the older boys, tramped out into the forest to find the perfect Christmas tree. Alas, the woods near the cabin grew no perfect trees. The ones the guys brought home invariably were a little too tall, usually skimpy on branches, with a definite bald side. As the only evergreens that grew in the Anchor Point area were spruce, the short needles did little to hide any imperfections.

It took most of a day to get the tree ready to come into the house. After whacking a foot or so off the bottom, Lionel fashioned a base out of crisscrossed boards. Inside these boards he left a hole just the right size for a can of water. If the trunk was too fat to fit the can, he whittled it down and forced it in.

The family devoted an evening to decorating the tree. Each year, Esther bought a box of glass balls, hoping this was the year they'd all survive the holiday season. Each year, the kids managed to drop and break several, leaving a number of mismatched balls. Other more durable ornaments made their annual appearance—a plastic snowman, and a red plastic star that always topped the tree. A string of lights and a package of tinsel helped to cover any defects, and, with the bad side turned toward the wall, the tree always managed to look properly festive.

Long before the tree was up—usually right after Thanksgiving—the kids began Christmas shopping. With nine members in the family, Esther and Lionel took a practical approach to gift giving. Santa could visit other homes. The Haakensons drew names. Once the kids knew which sibling they were buying for, they pored over those Sears and Montgomery Ward catalogs. Esther encouraged everyone to write a list of their wants and needs. That made shopping much easier. They all brought their selections to her, and she made out the orders. Then the waiting began. Since mail service only happened twice a week during those first years on the homestead, the family sometimes was holding its collective breath by Christmas Eve, wondering if the packages would arrive. Amazingly, they usually did. Esther, double-checking her master list, distributed the gifts to each kid for wrapping and placing under the tree. Occasionally, an unexpected item showed up, with an explanation to this effect: "We have substituted your selection for an item of equal or better quality. We are sure you will be satisfied with it." Well, what choice did they have? As long as they didn't substitute a boy's gift for a girl's, the family had to accept what they sent.

In the weeks leading up to Christmas, Esther grabbed every quiet moment to work on her own set of presents for the kids. The sewing machine rarely had a chance to cool off as she turned out shirts for the boys and a dress for Mary. She took advantage of days when the older boys were in school, though she had to order the younger kids to go play in another part of the house or yard so they wouldn't get too nosy. She whipped up batches of fudge and mint candies and tucked them into drawers she knew the kids wouldn't look in.

Lionel was like a little kid at Christmas. The morning always started with him bawling, "HO HO HO! Merry Christmas!" at the top of his lungs. The kids scrambled down the stairs and sat around the lit-up Christmas tree, which somehow had more gifts under it than it had when they'd gone to bed the night before.

After breakfast, Esther made sure she had enough firewood available, then sent the kids outside. If snow was abundant they took sleds down to the woodlot behind the house and careened off the berm into the muskeg. In years when the temperatures could guarantee a well-frozen pond, they went skating on the small pond along the trail down by Bert's place. In later years, they skated with friends on larger ponds along the road to Homer. A day of skating included snow shovels, as the older boys and Lionel always spent at least an hour clearing the pond of snow.

While her children and husband played, Esther remained at home, fixing a special turkey dinner with everything from mashed potatoes to apple and mince pies. Though she loved to skate, she forewent the pleasure to create an enjoyable feast for her family. Frosted sugar cookies cut in festive shapes and her special date-filled pinwheel cookies added to the Christmas feeling.

Only days after Christmas, the tree had to come down. Somehow the can of water never really helped much to extend the life of the tree, and Esther quickly got sick of sweeping up spruce needles. After stripping it of all decorations, the kids hauled the badly-shedding twig out to the woods and dumped it back from whence it came.

Keeping enough wood on hand to feed the stoves through the winter was a constant chore. Fortunately, trees were readily available, as a spruce forest covered nearly the entire forty acres of the homestead. Most of the wood was harvested from the woodlot, which encompassed most of the northern half of the property, and which Lionel knew he needed to clear in order to fulfill the requirements of proving up on the homestead. Lionel motivated the older boys to haul wood by paying them 10 cents an hour, or 2½ cents per armload. When they were feeling particularly energetic, the boys got out an old sled—a legacy from the homestead's former owners. Into this they deposited their axes and a cross cut saw, then pulled the sled down to the woodlot, across the muskeg and over to the bluff that led down to the river. Along the bluff they found a plentiful supply of fallen trees which they limbed, sawed up and dragged back home. By the time they arrived with a fully laden sled, they felt they'd more than earned their hourly wage.

Shortly after the move to Anchor Point, Lionel negotiated purchase of 60 acres of land adjoining the homestead. This piece of property lay between the homestead and the North Fork Road, giving the family the means to build a driveway without crossing someone else's land. Once the snow melted that first spring, Lionel went looking for a man with a bulldozer who could doze out a new driveway. He found Ed, an old-timer who had worked on driveways for many folks in the area. Lionel spent several hours with Ed one Saturday, tramping through the quarter-mile of woods that lay between the cabin and the North Fork Road.

This project seemed to spark Lionel's romantic side. "I don't want just a straight driveway," he told Ed. "I want the road to wind through the trees." Perhaps having been raised in North Dakota where trees were scarce inspired him to squeeze every moment's pleasure he could on the drive through the pristine forest. Through hand motions and verbal descriptions he gave Ed what he considered a full picture of his vision for the driveway. Perhaps he should have drawn it on paper.

"I got him lined out. He'll bring his Cat in this week and get a road started. It'll be a beautiful drive," he told Esther, then left for work in Anchorage.

A few days into the following week, Esther heard the distant growl of Ed's Caterpillar. "Good," she thought, "he's getting started."

It was late in the afternoon by the time Ed's Cat appeared through the trees. From the cabin window Esther studied the mud track that lay behind the machine. Though she couldn't see the North Fork Road, it looked like at least the last half of the trail made a beeline into the yard. "That's not the way Lionel described it to me," she muttered. "I think he did it wrong."

Once Ed reached the clearing near the house, he didn't stop to chat. He swung the Cat around and rumbled back out the path he'd hewn through the woods. Esther shook her head. "Lionel's not gonna be happy," she thought.

Lionel's face when he surveyed the new trail on Saturday morning showed just how dissatisfied he was. "I told him what I wanted," he said. "This isn't right at all." He and Ed had agreed that Ed would come on Saturday to get paid for dozing out the trail. When Ed appeared, tromping up the muddy track, Lionel went out to meet him. Ed approached with a huge grin on his face.

"Ed! You put it in the wrong place." Lionel knew it would be best to get the bad news out of the way immediately. If he'd been in a mood to be entertained, he'd have laughed at the change in Ed's expression. His smile disappeared to be replaced by a look of open-mouthed chagrin.

Lionel continued, "I told you I wanted a curving driveway. Look how straight this is."

"But," Ed protested, "I put some curves in it." He indicated the point about two-thirds of the way down the cleared path where it made a slight turn into the trees. "There's a curve there, and there's another one down at the end."

Lionel shook his head in resignation. "What's done's done," he said. He paid Ed, shook his hand and the two parted amicably. In the long run, Ed's experience with Anchor Point's terrain and weather probably saved Lionel countless hours of work. Over the years, tons of gravel had to be dumped into that road, and tons of snow removed in winter. More curves would have complicated the process, so the straighter driveway turned out to be the better option.

Early in the summer, Lionel again took several weeks off from his job in Anchorage to concentrate on the many tasks that awaited his attention on the homestead. Spending between twelve and sixteen hours out of each weekend on the road left little time for productive work. Esther was glad he was home for a while; she was doing all she could, but much of her time had to go to caring for her brood and keeping up with cooking and cleaning. Tim, Robert and John

Right: The Haakenson kids at the side of the cabin, 1956.

Below: Cousins' visit, 1956.

worked on the jobs Lionel left them, but sometimes needed more on-the-spot supervision.

One of the first tasks Lionel tackled was to build a 10 x 10-foot storeroom onto the far end of last year's addition. Esther had discovered shortly after the move to Anchor Point that most folks did the bulk of their grocery shopping through orders placed at Homestead Supply. In this way a family could order all the non-perishable items they'd need for several months — flour, sugar, canned goods, noodles, etc. — much cheaper than what they would pay for the same items at the store. A supply boat came into the Homer dock twice a year — in spring and fall. Esther had placed an order several months back, and now the stuff had arrived. Once Lionel had the storeroom built, Esther installed shelves along two walls to accommodate the foodstuffs. She found there was enough space left to house her wringer washer, which had made the trip down from Anchorage once they'd gotten electricity and was presently taking up space in her kitchen. The small attic area of this new room provided more storage.

285

Lionel built a porch onto the storeroom and brought in a small chest freezer, giving Esther a place to keep meats and other perishable goods. With nearby rivers teeming with salmon and trout, and plentiful moose in the surrounding forest, Esther looked forward to filling the freezer with local meat to help stretch the family's budget.

The "driveway" at this point was still little more than a slash of mud and sticks between berms of stumps pushed up by Ed's dozer. Before it could be packed down to make it drivable, all those stumps and roots had to be eliminated. Here Lionel's inner firebug surfaced. He loved few things more than a good bonfire. With the older boys in tow, he headed out the newly-stirred-up mud trail, all of them picking up debris as they went. Every 100 feet or so, they made a pile of tree roots and branches. Once these were deemed to be of sufficient size—meaning several feet higher than the top of Lionel's head—he poured a little gasoline onto the pile, tossed in a match, and stood back to watch the fire grow. Sometimes the blazes burned their allotted material and expired without any undue excitement, but other times Smokey the Bear would have been less than pleased.

In one such instance, Esther and the younger children worked around the yard while Lionel and the four older boys toiled at the far end of the new trail. Suddenly, Jim's voice could be heard yelling something indistinguishable. Jim often played games in which he sang or hollered at the top of his lungs, so Esther thought little of it at first. When the yells continued, Esther looked up from the clothes she was hanging on the line to pay closer attention to him. She saw him round the single distant curve of the driveway, running as fast as he could over the rough jumble of dirt, moss and roots. As he drew nearer, she finally understood the word he kept repeating: "Fire!"

She looked past Jim and saw a cloud of smoke rising into the sky. It was too large to be one of Lionel's simple bonfires. "You kids stay here," she ordered, and grabbing the full bucket from the pump stand, set off at a staggering run over the nearly-impassable trail. She ran almost the entire quarter-mile before she reached the fire. The path of flames ran from a slash pile to several nearby spruce trees. As she watched, flame sprinted up a tree's trunk and exploded in a shower of hot embers among the needled branches. Lionel, Tim, Robert and John, gunny sacks in hand, dashed back and forth from the small pond behind Bert's house. With the wet sacks they beat any flames that crept away from the main pile. Esther tossed what water was left in her bucket onto a pile of dry grass that was starting to smolder, and joined her men in the frantic race to ferry water to the fire.

At least half an hour passed before they were sure the fire was under control. The tired group looked around at the blackened trees and grass, thinking how easily this could have been a full-blown catastrophe. "Man, that was close," said Lionel. "I thought we'd lost it there for a while. I guess I started that pile too close to the trees. I'm glad you got here when you did."

"I heard Jim yelling," Esther replied.

"That's what I told him to do. It was the only way I could think of to get your attention."

"You always start the fires too close to the trees!" Esther wanted to say, but would not criticize him in front of the boys. With axes and rakes they cleaned up all the debris, then poured more water on everything, making sure there were no hot spots. This scenario repeated itself over the years any time the family cleared away brush and stumps. Lionel never started a major conflagration, but his example showed his offspring how *not* to handle a bonfire.

Once enough roots were picked from the driveway, Lionel ordered a couple of truckloads of gravel brought in, had the boys rake it smooth, and called it good for that year.

Though barely passable, at least it allowed the cars to be driven into the yard.

Now Lionel turned his attention to another pressing task. A critical requirement for proving up on the homestead was clearing a certain percentage of land and putting it under cultivation. Lionel targeted the woodlot—the area which had supplied logs for building the additions as well as firewood. Now that the trees were cleared off, he planned to use the acreage for the family's garden. But first, as he playfully told his offspring, they got to play "Pick-up Sticks".

He had hired a contractor (not Ed) from Homer to doze out the stumps that were left from the logging he'd done throughout the previous year. Now the woodlot lay more or less flat, with high stump-berms all around. Of course, a bulldozer is not a machine meant for finesse. The soil and moss left behind contained thousands of roots and wood chips of various sizes. Lionel borrowed Bert's tractor, Poppin' Priscilla, and tied a disc harrow to her back end with a chain. As he dragged it across the ground, the discs turned up dirt and all those pieces of wood. The kids' job was to walk behind the tractor, pick up the roots, branches and other debris, and toss them into the berms. It was a slow, tiring job. On top of that, it seemed like no matter how many times they covered a patch of ground, the next round turned up just as many roots as before.

Seven-year-old John decided he'd had enough of that game. As the family finished up breakfast one morning, he made himself as useful as he could to Esther, fetching firewood, helping with dishes and pumping water. He could tell Esther appreciated his help, and he decided to confide in her. "I want to stay here at the house and work with you so I don't have to pick roots."

Esther chuckled inwardly, but controlled her expression. When the guys returned from the field for lunch she couldn't resist sharing the comment with Lionel. John stared at her. How could she double-cross him like that? His dad's response was inevitable: "Well, since you had the morning off, how about you come down to the woodlot and help me all by yourself this afternoon?" So John got in a few hours of root picking without the aid of his brothers.

A knock on the cabin door surprised Esther one day early in the summer. "Is this the Lionel Hackenson place?" asked the stranger who stood on the porch.

"Haakenson,"she corrected him automatically, and added, "Lionel's down in the woodlot." She pointed him in the right direction then turned back to her task of washing clothes.

She was hanging clothes on the lines strung between trees in the front yard when the stranger passed by again on his way out the trail. Lionel showed up in his wake. "I can't believe someone tracked me down out here," he said. "That was a guy from the union; they have a job for a sheet metal worker on one of the White Alice sites and they want me."

Though Lionel downplayed it, Esther knew her husband must have an excellent reputation at the union hall, or they wouldn't take the time and effort to come to Anchor Point looking for him. She had heard a little about the White Alice sites. She knew they were connected with the Distant Early Warning system—known as the DEW line. During the Cold War, the DEW line monitored Alaskan airspace to guard against encroachment by foreign aircraft.

"There's only one problem," continued Lionel. "The job is down near Sitka in southeastern Alaska. I'd have to stay down there till the job is done."

"How long would that be?" asked Esther.

Lionel shrugged. "Could be a month, maybe more. The pay is better than what I'm getting in Anchorage and all this driving every week is wearing me out. I hate to be gone so long, but when I get home I could stay for a while and really get some things accomplished."

So began Lionel's stint as an itinerant sheet metal worker. For the next several years he worked on White Alice

sites from southeastern Alaska to the northwest part of the
state. Some jobs lasted a few weeks; others went on for
several months. Once the White Alice sites were finished, a
string of other projects took him to various points around the
state, leaving Esther to fill the roles of mother and father for
large portions of the year.

Before Lionel left for Sitka he and the older boys cleared
and prepared the land in the woodlot for planting. He again
borrowed Poppin' Priscilla, this time using a plow to turn up
the dirt and ready it for planting. (The kids tried to turn a
blind eye to the new crop of roots that sprang forth at this
time, but their dad soon had them playing Pick-up Sticks all
over again.)The spruce trees that had grown there had left
the ground extremely acidic, so Lionel spread lime liberally
over the prospective garden areas.

With these preliminary steps completed, gardening
started in earnest. Esther's brother, Laurence, now planted
and sold potatoes on the family farm in the Valley, since
potatoes were a crop that grew well in the Alaskan climate
and always had a ready market. Lionel bought a hundred
pounds of "spuds" from Laurence, which Esther stored in
the root cellar under the living room floor. The family ate
most of them, but the smallest ones she cut up for use as
seed.

Tim, Robert and John had joined the local 4H group,
which was run by Vern and Bernadine Mutch, with help
from Lloyd and Pat Onstott and several other volunteers
from the community. The main 4H focus was on gardening,
so the three boys each measured out a 12 x 12-foot plot and
strung twine around to mark their areas. With Lionel gone,
Esther took charge of gardening. For days she, along with
Tim, Robert and John, raked, fertilized, then raked some
more. Following that, they drew shallow trenches and
dropped in seeds. They chose fast-growing plants that other
folks in the area had had success with: radishes, turnips,
peas and carrots. Of course, a large plot was dedicated to

potatoes. As Esther planted, she demonstrated to the younger kids how to cover the seeds without burying them so deeply in dirt that they couldn't find their way out.

Tending the garden turned out to be nearly a full-time job for the family. Some of the seeds they planted didn't seem overly enthusiastic about breaking through the ground, but the weeds—especially chickweed—loved that soft, fertilized soil. Any child who seemed bored or ready to pick a fight was sent down to the field to battle mosquitoes while working out his or her aggressions on the never-ending supply of uninvited vegetation.

While Esther rarely got a break from her chores, she sometimes relented when it came to her kids. Beyond the woodlot, across the muskeg and down the bluff, the north fork of the Anchor River beckoned Tim, Robert and John.

On a pretty summer morning Tim approached Esther. "Can we go down to the river and fish? We got all the wood in and the garden's weeded." He knew they didn't stand a chance of going if the chores weren't finished.

"I guess you can go for a while," Esther gave permission. The three boys buzzed around, fixing sandwiches and collecting their fishing gear. Jim was not a fan of long tramps across muskegs and up and down steep bluffs, so he chose to stay home with the younger kids. "Don't be gone too long, and look out for bears," Esther admonished as they left.

With promises to be careful, and with King at their heels, the boys headed out. They fully enjoyed their day of freedom from chores. They caught some fish and explored the woods. They even went "swimming," which consisted of wading into the icy water and seeing who could stand the cold the longest.

Esther and the rest of the children carried on their day, fully expecting the boys to show up before many hours passed. At suppertime they gathered around the table, feeling incomplete with three of the seven kids missing. Esther was distracted, jumping up from the table to peer out the back window, or opening the door and scanning the woods.

By bedtime she was nearly frantic. Were they lost? Had they encountered a bear? Had they drowned? Her first instinct was to head down to the river and find out what had become of her boys, but with Jim and the three youngest children in the house she couldn't do that. She settled for walking partway down the woodlot trail. She called as loudly as she could, "Tim! Robert! John!" The silent trees gave no response. She was just about to run down to Bert's and ask for help when she finally heard a faint yell. A few minutes later the three boys trudged into the yard, a string of trout in hand, tired but full of their wonderful day.

Esther's fear gave way to relief, which soon became anger, now that she knew they were safe. "What were you doing all that time?" she scolded, "Don't you ever stay away that long again!"

She knew the boys didn't understand her fears, but she'd learned a lesson that day. Any future expeditions would have a more specific time frame that the boys knew they'd better stick to.

Thanks to the long Alaskan summer days, the first crop of radishes reached maturity quickly. There was even time to plant a second crop. The turnips, too, produced a bountiful harvest, though root worms found their way to some of them before they could be picked. Undeterred, Esther trimmed off the worm holes and had plenty of edible parts left over. The peas and carrots were a disappointment. By fall there were only a few puny fingerling carrots, and some pea pods that never filled out. Harvesting the potatoes turned into a family project. Once the plants began to blossom, Esther sent one of the kids down each day to dig up some potatoes for dinner. In late August the plants began to show signs of frostbite as temperatures dipped below the freezing mark. At that point Esther took the whole crew down to the garden where they spent the entire day digging spuds. The older boys pulled the vines and shook them to remove dirt and any potatoes that might cling to them. The younger kids followed behind, rooting through the dirt, collecting potatoes and depositing them into gunny sacks. Once the pulling and digging were finished, Esther and her tired, grubby crew lugged the sacks to the house. Though the work had been exhausting, the result was worth it—a stock of potatoes that would last through the winter, and maybe enough in seed to do it all again next year.

Kenny and Ronny, winter '57-'58

An Extra Son for a Year

Esther looked up from the letter in her hand and gazed thoughtfully into space. Gladys had written that her son Don, who had always struggled in school, needed some sort of incentive. Though two and a half years older than Tim, Don had been held back several times and this fall would be entering the 5th grade — the same grade as his younger cousin. Would Esther be willing to take Don in for the school year? "I'm pretty sure," wrote Gladys, "that he'd work harder if he had Tim with him as an example. And they get along so well."

Esther and Lionel talked it over and agreed to allow Don to come to Anchor Point for the school year. The upstairs of the storeroom was cleared out and Mary's bed was moved into it, making room for another occupant in the main upstairs bedroom. An open doorway between the two spaces allowed five-year-old Mary to feel that she was still a part of the nightly bedtime scene. This scene caused Esther many moments of despair, as thumps and giggles from the upper regions continued long after the kids' appointed bedtime. At times, knowing the boys had to be up for school in a few hours, Esther mounted the stairs and administered a swat to the bottoms of everybody who was still awake. Usually that quieted the group, but based on their reluctance to get up the next morning, she doubted they'd gone right to sleep.

Though only a few years old, Anchor Point's little red schoolhouse could no longer contain all the students who registered for classes in the fall of 1956. Shortly before school was due to commence, concerned community members met and came up with a creative solution. Dale Doner had recently erected a building a hundred yards or so up the road from the school. He planned eventually to use it for a service station, but he now offered it as a temporary classroom for as many students as it would hold. The fifth and sixth grades moved into it, while the first through fourth grades stayed in the large room of the school building and the seventh and eighth grades occupied the back room. Fifth-graders Don and Tim attended school at Doner's service station. A third teacher, Mr. Boyer, was hired to teach the students at the service station, while Mr. and Mrs. Dalton remained in the two rooms in the schoolhouse.

Having her nephew Don in the house reminded Esther of life with Gladys, as he had inherited his mother's carefree outlook on life. Though Don would much rather play than tackle an academic task, Tim's example seemed to help him focus on his school work. Not that he had a lot of choice. Each night, once the dishes were done, Esther said, "Okay, let's see what you've got for homework." All four boys brought their books and papers to the kitchen table and remained until they completed the work to Esther's satisfaction. With Tim in the same class, with the same homework, Don couldn't get by with claiming he didn't have any.

A unit of study that seemed to fire Don's imagination was the legend of Robin Hood. After listening to the stories in school, all he could talk about was the adventures of his new hero. Esther laughed as she saw him acting out scenes in the front yard. Don, of course, took the part of Robin Hood, while Tim and Robert were his Merry Men. His younger cousins, seated on rounds of firewood, served as audience.

One day Don approached Esther. "Auntie, Mr. Boyer wants us to put on a Robin Hood puppet show. I told him you'd make some puppets for us. Will you do it? Please?"

Esther, anxious to do anything that would encourage Don's interest in school, spent days creating Robin Hood and the sheriff of Nottingham. Out of a plain flour sack, she sewed arms, legs and bodies and stuffed them with cotton. For Robin Hood, she made an outfit of dark green, belted with a strip of black cloth and buckled with a piece of tin foil. The sheriff was clad in brown, to appear as if he was wearing leather garments. Esther embroidered features onto their faces, even giving the sheriff a moustache to make him look sinister. The puppets were a hit at the show put on by the class, and Don's enthusiasm for the project reassured Esther that her time had been well spent. In the spring, Don passed his classes and returned to Anchorage with a stronger educational foundation, ready to take on 6th grade.

Esther enjoyed Don's year with the family not only for his own quirky personality, but because he provided her and the children a link to her extended family. The move to the homestead had especially curtailed Esther's interactions with her two brothers. Leonard worked for the Alaska Railroad, so was rarely in town on Esther's infrequent visits to Anchorage. Usually her Anchorage trips left little time for side jaunts, but, feeling it was important for her kids to be acquainted with their cousins, when possible she made the effort of driving the long dusty road to the farm near Palmer to visit Laurence, his wife, Pat, and their ten children

In December of 1957, Esther was surprised to hear that Leonard had married again. He'd gotten married shortly after the war, but at the time he'd been drinking heavily and the marriage soon fell apart. Now Esther heard—through Gladys—that Leonard had met his new bride, Kay, through a lonely hearts club. Kay hailed from Minnesota, and had 3 children from a previous marriage. Esther hoped having a wife and family would bring Leonard the happiness that so far had seemed to elude him. The new couple settled in Anchorage and over the next several years had two daughters—Laura and Brenda.

Finding a Church Home

When Esther and Lionel arrived in Anchor Point there were two churches in town. They had attended a non-denominational church in Anchorage, and had no particular attachment to either of the local choices. They visited both congregations, and for some time bounced back and forth between the two.

Early in the summer of 1957, Edna, the wife of Bob Williams, the owner of Modern Builders Supply, invited Esther to bring the kids to a Vacation Bible School that was being sponsored by the Church of Christ. Her kids memorized scriptures and sang songs at the family's "meetings," but Esther wanted them to have every opportunity to learn more about the Bible, so she enrolled them. Many of the children from the community attended, and her kids came home each day, enthusiastic about their teachers and the lessons.

Later that summer, Esther saw Edna at Modern Builders Supply, and commented on how much the children had enjoyed attending VBS. "Would you like to study the Bible with me?" Edna invited.

Esther jumped at the opportunity. Not only did she love to read and discuss the Bible, but she was hungry for interaction with other women. With Lionel so often working away from home, many days passed when she saw no one but her children. Much as she loved them, she longed for conversation with an adult. She had joined the local Homemakers' Club, but they only met once or twice a month, and many times she couldn't go, if Lionel wasn't home to watch the kids.

As she studied with Edna, the subject of baptism arose. She had been baptized as a baby, in accordance with the beliefs of her parents. The more she read about it now, though, the stronger grew the conviction that her previous understanding had been incomplete.

Lionel was due to fly into Anchorage from the remote site where he'd been working. Esther farmed out the kids amongst several neighbors and drove up to meet him, ready to share her decision with him.

"I've been reading about baptism," she told him. "I think I need to be baptized."

Lionel looked surprised. "I've been studying baptism, too," he said. "It sure sounds different than the way I grew up thinking about it."

Well, this seemed more than coincidence. "Let's find the Church of Christ here in Anchorage," said Lionel. "It's Wednesday evening; I'm sure they have a service tonight. Let's go and ask them to baptize us. The Church of Christ in Anchor Point always has an invitation where they ask people to come forward if they want to be baptized. I'll bet they do the same thing up here."

They found the Church of Christ. They were a few minutes late but they slipped into some empty seats and enjoyed the Bible study that was in progress. When the study ended, to their surprise the congregation sang a closing song, someone said a prayer, and the service ended. Lionel looked at Esther. "They didn't have an invitation," he whispered.

The group was small, and being strangers, Lionel and Esther attracted attention. The man who had led the Bible study approached them with his hand out.

"I'm Pat McMahan," he introduced himself. "Welcome."

"We're Lionel and Esther Haakenson from Anchor Point," Lionel replied.

He must have looked somewhat perplexed, because Pat asked, "Can I answer any questions for you?"

"Well, we're just wondering how to go about getting baptized," Lionel said.

"Let's sit down and have a talk," Pat suggested. Within a few minutes he realized that this couple had studied the subject quite thoroughly and knew what they wanted. Before the evening ended he welcomed first Lionel, then Esther into the baptistery to be immersed into Christ.

From that point on, the family attended the Church of Christ in Anchor Point. In those first years, the family of nine doubled the size of the congregation. The church appreciated Lionel's willingness to lead singing, since most of the other men either couldn't carry a tune or weren't comfortable singing in front of the group. Once Lionel quit working away from home, he led singing nearly all the time.

School Woes - 1957-58

In the fall of 1957, Esther saw her next chick, Mary, off to first grade. The school's space issue hadn't resolved itself, and with even more students enrolled, all classes had to be configured once again. Doner's garage was no longer available, so Bob Williams, who ran the Jeep-bus and Modern Builders Supply, stepped forward. He owned a good-sized storage shed a short distance down the North Fork Road. The building was currently being used by Red Mumey, who ran a sawmill next to it. Bob installed a blackboard on one wall of the shed. With a few dozen desks lined up in rows, some coat hooks and bookshelves, the shed became a classroom. The third, fourth and fifth graders, which included John and Robert, were assigned to this space. First and second grades remained in the larger room of the red schoolhouse, while sixth through eighth squeezed into the back.

A pleasant surprise for Esther was the appearance of Catherine Lemmon among the teaching staff in Anchor Point. She hadn't seen much of Catherine since those early days in the Valley. She recalled that the newly wed Lemmons had been the first colonists the Larson family had met, as they'd ridden the train from International Falls together. Catherine had expected to land a teaching job easily, only to learn that Alaska didn't allow married women to be teachers. She and her husband left Alaska for a while, returning when the laws changed. She had taught in various places throughout the state, and had recently been hired to teach in Anchor Point.

Catherine's first year in Anchor Point was spent teaching at the sawmill, so two of her students were third-grader John and fourth-grader Robert. One evening John came home with a note stating that he'd been sassy. This surprised Esther, as all her offspring were well aware that trouble at school meant double trouble at home.

She confronted John with the note. "What's this about? Mrs. Lemmon says you were sassing."

"No, I wasn't," John protested. "I just answered her question. Me and Paul Mutch were playin' swordfights with our pencils and Mrs. Lemmon got after us. She made us go up in front of the class and have a swordfight. When we got done she said, 'Now what do you want to do—pay attention in class or act like monkeys?' I thought it sounded like fun to act like monkeys, so that's what I told her."

Esther had to take herself sternly in hand to keep from laughing, but she knew John couldn't get by with such behavior. "When you're in school, you're there to learn. You have plenty of time to act like a monkey at home."

Mary seemed to enjoy school, coming home with new songs she'd learned and talking non-stop about the friends she'd made. Esther was surprised when she went to a parent/teacher conference and learned that all was not quite as rosy as it seemed.

"She's doing well with her classwork," Mrs. Jackson told Esther. "She just can't seem to keep out of trouble."

Esther came home and confronted her daughter. "I thought Christy Rabich was your good friend."

"She is," replied Mary. "We sit together in class, and me 'n' her and Joanne Sonnichsen play together every recess."

"Mrs. Jackson says she's had to send you and Christy to the corner for arguing during class."

"Yeah, well, we fight sometimes, but..."

"Mrs. Jackson is going to separate you if you keep acting like that. And I don't want to hear any more about you being put in the corner! Do you understand?"

Mary understood. She knew better than to tempt Esther to bring out the airplane wing. The previous summer, John and Robert had built a model airplane out of scrap wood. The plane disintegrated after a few flights, but its wings—an

18-inch-long piece of thin but flexible lumber, now hung above the doorway between the original cabin and the new addition. While the kids generally just called the stick "the airplane wing," Lionel referred to it as "The Board of Education" and usually added, in case they didn't quite get it: "To be applied to your seat of learning." Esther knew where and how to apply it, and her kids respected that board.

Family in front of cabin, 1958. Back Lionel and Esther. Middle: Robert, Jim, John, Tim. Front: Mary, Ronny, Kenny.

The year of 1957 saw strong feelings amongst the residents of Alaska, including the community of Anchor Point. The issue of statehood was fiercely debated anywhere Alaskans gathered. A bill granting statehood had been kicked around Congress for several years, while many folks in the far north had very little confidence that politicians on the other side of the country could have any clue about what was going on in their lives. As with any subject, opinions on what was best for Alaska ran the gamut from horrified rejection to wholehearted support. For years, Alaskans had felt the unfairness of taxation without representation. Then again, could the three people they'd be allowed to send to Washington adequately represent such a vast area with its small but varied population?

The matter was decided on June 30, 1958, when the statehood bill was finally passed by both houses of Congress. Without the president's signature, though, Alaska's position was not official. For the next six months the residents of Alaska lived in a sort of limbo, no longer just a territory, but not yet a full-fledged state.

Grandpa's Visit

Despite the arguments over statehood, life on the homestead, with its ups and downs, continued. One evening in January of 1958, a knock sounded on the cabin door. Lionel opened it to see the new postmaster, Dick Rutt, standing there. His normally smiling face was solemn. "I'm sorry to have to give you this, Lionel," he said.

Esther immediately recognized the small yellow paper. It was a telegram. Since the post office was the only place in Anchor Point that had a telephone, all messages that came into town by phone had to be hand-carried to their intended recipients.

"What's wrong?" Esther asked sharply. No one sent telegrams just to pass the time of day. Lionel's face tightened and he replied, "Mother died."

Esther felt a stab of sympathy. For several years now the letters from North Dakota had kept them informed on Caroline's fight with cancer. Though expected, the news still came as a shock.

"Can I do anything?" asked Dick.

"Thanks, no," replied Lionel. "I'll have to figure out how to get a flight to North Dakota." He rubbed his hand over his face.

"I can phone the airport in Homer," Dick persisted. "Maybe we can get you on tomorrow's flight. Come on down to the post office with me and we'll make arrangements."

Esther closed the door behind the two men and turned to her children. "Grandma Haakenson died. Daddy's going to go out for the funeral." The younger kids had either never met Grandma Haakenson, or were too young to remember her. The older boys had some hazy memories of her, but it had been years since any of them had seen her. Esther's thoughts flew to her own parents, who were nearly the same age as Lionel's mother. Surely they weren't teetering on the brink of death, were they? They were only in their 60s.

Lionel returned home with a reservation. "I'll fly out from Homer in the morning. Dick said he'd take me to the airport."

Esther felt grateful for the neighborly spirit that filled this community. Homes may be separated by distance, but people were always ready to pull together when someone needed them.

Lionel was gone for a week. He returned saddened by his mother's death, but glad he'd been able to be with his father and siblings during that time.

Several months later a letter arrived from Lionel's father, Pete. He wrote that life without Caroline was lonely. What would the family think about his coming up for a visit?

Lionel's thoughts immediately focused on the obsession he and his father shared. "Let's have him come in August when the silvers are running." Silvers, or coho salmon, were a favorite among fishermen, whether they fished mainly for sport or for subsistence. Lionel continued, "A silver always puts up a good fight, so by the time you land it, you feel like you've earned the right to eat it. I remember, when Dad was up here before, he was thrilled at the size and fight of the salmon he caught. "

Lionel immediately set about constructing an 8 x 12-foot shed at the edge of the clearing in front of the cabin. His seven kids filled up almost all the available sleeping space in the house, and perhaps Lionel knew his dad might like a space of his own. He fashioned a small stove from sheet metal so Grandpa would be able to heat the place. He was coming in August, which meant cool nights, possibly even frost. Since the shed was not insulated, the stove could prove very useful. A cot, table and chair completed the room's furnishings. He pounded some nails into the walls so the shed's occupant could hang his clothing.

"This'll come in handy after Dad leaves," said Lionel. "I've needed a tool shed, and this'll be perfect."

In mid-August Lionel drove to Anchorage and picked up his father at the airport. Esther could tell the two men couldn't think of anything but fishing. Lionel dropped his dad's luggage off in the new shed and immediately led him to the back porch where the fishing gear was stored. The two practiced casting, obviously already dreaming of the big ones they were going to catch.

The next morning Lionel was up by 4 a.m. He poked Esther. "We'd better get the kids up." Correctly translating this as, "*you'd* better get the kids up," she moved from bed to bed, shaking each child awake while Lionel trod over to his dad's cabin. "Time to go fishing," she said.

The night before she'd made sure everyone set out sweatshirts and warm pants, socks, coats, boots and hats. Now she supervised as the kids slid sleepily into their clothes.

Everyone piled into the station wagon, with Kenny and Ronny sitting up front with Esther and Lionel. The other five and Grandpa squeezed into the back seat. Most of the kids eked out another half-hour or so of sleep as Lionel drove north over the rough gravel road. Reaching the outskirts of Ninilchik, he parked the car in a pull-off at Deep Creek. Esther, Lionel, Grandpa and the older boys pulled the fishing gear out of the back of the car and donned hip boots. Single-file, the small army tramped down a slick mud trail through alders that blocked sight of anything but leaves. Lionel and Grandpa led the way, next were Tim, Jim, Robert and John. Esther held Ronny's hand while she herded Kenny and Mary in front of her. In this way they eventually reached the fishing hole. There weren't enough fishing poles to go around, so the adults and older boys fished while the younger ones explored the river and studied the minnows and other tiny creatures that inhabited it. Every once in a while a splash and a whoop signaled that someone had hooked a salmon. This brought everyone running to watch until the fish was safely landed.

Several hours later, with their day's limit of salmon, they headed down the alder path and tramped back to the car. Now everyone was wide awake, and the activity had made them all hungry. As soon as they reached the cabin Esther got to work. She added wood to the cook stove and mixed up a huge bowl of pancake batter. For the next hour she made pancakes until everyone but she had eaten their fill. She made sure the water reservoir on the end of the stove was full, as well as a tea kettle. While the water heated she scraped the last of the batter onto the griddle and made two small pancakes for herself. She ate quickly, knowing her day's work awaited her just outside the door.

She poured the hot water from the tea kettle into a metal pan in the sink. Using a ladle, she dipped cold water from the pail sitting on the pump stand. When the water was just barely cool enough to stick her hands in, she dumped a load of cups and glasses into it, and quickly washed them. She rinsed them in a second pan of scalding water and set them on the end of the sink. At that point, Mary ran a dish towel over each item and set it in its appointed spot in the cupboard.

While Esther and her daughter did the "women's work" in the house, the guys toiled outside, cleaning their morning's catch. Esther barely had the dishes finished when Tim brought in the first salmon wrapped in newspaper to keep from dripping blood and water all over the floor. Meanwhile, Lionel had sharpened up Esther's kitchen knives.

Esther dumped the dish water in the flush-bucket that stood just outside the bathroom and refilled the pan with a fresh batch of hot water and detergent. Into this she put 3 cases' worth of canning jars. These had been cleaned previously, but they still went through a hot wash and rinse process. She placed them upside down on a towel to dry, set her large pressure cooker on the stove and, once again, stoked the fire.

She turned to the headless, tailless salmon lying on the table, picked up one of the newly-sharpened knives and set to work. For the rest of the morning she filleted, skinned and cut up fish, measuring the pieces against the pint-size canning jars. By noon the first batch of fish was processing in the pressure cooker, and the remaining pieces filled several cake pans and a large mixing bowl.

Knowing mealtimes still came around even on fish canning days, Esther moved the fish onto the counter, scrubbed the table, and pulled out three loaves of bread she'd made the previous day. Her crew would have to get by on a lunch of sandwiches on this day. Once the simple meal was over, she kicked everyone out of the house so she could finish canning the fish without interruptions.

The last jars came out of the canner just in time for her to start supper. At least she didn't have to think too hard about what to have. A portion of that freshly-caught salmon lay awaiting its trip to the frying pan. She'd round out the meal with fried potatoes and a few cans of corn. The only thing needed was dessert. Esther was glad she had some boxed cake mixes. She always felt like she was cheating when she used them, but they came in handy for times like this. She measured water and broke eggs into a bowl, and dumped in the cake mix. Thanks to the canning she'd done all day, the oven was already hot and ready for baking. All that remained was the beating. With a serving spoon she started beating the batter: one, two, three... The directions said beat four minutes with an electric mixer or 400 strokes by hand. Her arm felt ready to fall off by the time she finished, but she completed the whole 400 strokes.

Into the oven went the cake. Esther grabbed the sack of potatoes and began peeling. Figuring about two potatoes per person, she stacked up 20 potatoes. A simple coating of flour, salt and pepper went into a paper bag and Esther shook chunks of fish until they were coated. She pulled out two large frying pans and scooped generous amounts of Crisco into each. Into one she cut up as many potatoes as the pan would hold. When the first batch was done, she dumped it into a large pot and set it on the back of the stove to keep warm while the rest of the spuds cooked. The fish received similar treatment in the other pan. Esther shook her head. All that work, and once she called the family in for supper, everything she'd cooked would disappear within minutes.

This remained the pattern for most of the days of Grandpa's visit. Some days they caught fewer fish, so Esther didn't have to spend quite the whole day processing salmon. She was thankful for these short breaks, because they gave her time to do other chores, like cleaning and laundry, which piled up whether or not she had fish to can.

When Grandpa's visit ended, he left with several rolls of film of pictures he'd taken, and several cases of canned salmon. Everyone said good-by, looking forward to more visits from this grandfather they'd hardly known. Unfortunately, it turned out to be the last time any of the Lionel's family would see him. Less than two years later, while visiting his daughters Lil and Hulda in California, he contracted pneumonia and died at the age of 74.

Grandpa (Pete) Haakenson standing in the potato patch with Kenny and Ronny, August 1958.

A New State, a New School, and a Library

That fall Kenny started school along with more than 100 other students. Mrs. Lemmon had moved over to the schoolhouse as the 1st and 2nd grade teacher, so both Mary and Kenny were her students. The head teacher, Mr. Taylor, taught 6th, 7th and 8th grades in the tiny back room. A new teacher, Mr. Stokes, took on John, Robert and all their cohorts with 3rd through 5th grades over at the sawmill. Both educational facilities were bursting at their seams. The community petitioned the territorial government and won support to erect a new, larger school building. The kids watched as the edifice grew on the lot next-door to the old schoolhouse. To them, this was much more important than the brouhaha over statehood. The new building would contain four large classrooms, a separate office area, drinking fountains, and, for the first time in Anchor Point, indoor bathrooms. The last days before Christmas vacation, the entire student body was pressed into service — under the supervision of their teachers — to lug everything from the sawmill-school and the red schoolhouse into the new school. The first event held in the new building was the 1958 Christmas program. On January 5, 1959 — just two days after Alaska officially became a state — the students of Anchor Point met for classes under one roof for the first time in four years.

Even before the move, teacher Catherine Lemmon had plans for the old schoolhouse, but knew she needed to recruit support from as many of the local women as she could. With that in mind, in mid-1958 she attended the monthly meeting of the Anchor Point Homemakers' Club, where she was sure to see the majority of the town's women.

"We need a library in Anchor Point," she told the group. "I've been looking into it, and I know we can do it. The old schoolhouse is going to be empty and would be the perfect place to set up a library. It's right next to the new school, so the kids would have easy access to books. It's important for kids to have all the opportunities to read that they can get."

Esther felt a surge of excitement as she looked around at the group. She saw heads nodding agreement. She had loved books ever since she first learned to read, and wanted that joy to be passed on to her own children. Over the years the family had accumulated a large number of books for babies and toddlers but her kids were quickly moving beyond that stage. They needed lots of books—more than any one family could provide.

"Where would we get these books?" asked one of the ladies.

"We'll have to raise funds to buy some," replied Catherine, "and we can put out the word around the community that we'll take any books people want to donate. We might be able to get some money from the state for some new books, and we can take books that other libraries want to get rid of. We'll be small to start with, but over time I know we can grow into a really fine library."

Suggestions for fund-raising were tossed around; finally the ladies decided to raffle a doll. Most of these women, like Esther, sewed the majority of their family's clothes, so had more than a passing acquaintance with sewing machines. They all agreed to participate by making one or more articles of clothing for the doll. The winner of the raffle would get not only the doll, but a full wardrobe of handmade clothing. Esther went home with several patterns, and over the next weeks created a wool winter coat with flannel lining and a sparkly blue dress with starched ruffles. Somewhat to the surprise of everyone, this little raffle raised over $100 toward the establishment of the library. When the idea of turning the old building into a library was presented to the school board, there was some resistance. Finally, a compromise was reached: the small back room of the old school was given for use as a library.

Over the next months the stack of boxes of donated books grew in Mrs. Lemmon's living room. Letters flew back and forth between Juneau and Anchor Point as the new library board worked out the details to become an official entity, complete with constitution and articles of incorporation. The library opened in 1959, just a week after classes commenced in the new school. Each Wednesday — the one day the library was open — every child in school had the opportunity to check out books. Esther was soon elected as treasurer. For nearly a decade, on top of keeping home and homestead running smoothly and — during Lionel's absences — fulfilling the roles of both mother and father to her seven kids, she kept neat and accurate records of the flow of money in and out of the library accounts.

The new school building with its four large classrooms had only been open for a year when the student population required additional space. Another teacher was hired, and the larger room of the old school again became a classroom.

Bossy

By the following summer, Lionel realized that readying the gardens for planting was taking up more time than the family could afford to spend, so he bought a rototiller to speed up the process. Taking Tim, Robert and John down to the woodlot, he demonstrated its use. "You can tilt the blades up to move the tiller to where you want it, but make sure you have the blades in the dirt before you squeeze the lever to start them turning." He watched each boy as they took turns practicing until he felt sure they'd mastered the technique.

Busy with her own work in the cabin, Esther missed out on these lessons, though she'd seen Lionel "walking" the tiller through the yard. It looked easy enough. With Lionel off on another job, Esther supervised the kids. The boys were busy with their 4-H gardens when Esther decided that one particular area of the potato patch needed a little more tilling. Not feeling it necessary to call one of her sons to help, she examined the machine, found the starter cord and gave it a yank. The motor roared to life and Esther grasped the tiller's handles. She positioned the blades over the area she wanted to till, but neglected to set them firmly into the soil. She squeezed the lever and suddenly felt like she'd grabbed the reins of a runaway horse. The rototiller's blades, freed from the toil of grinding chunks of humus into garden soil, galloped gaily over the top of the dirt, dragging Esther behind at a dead run. After several large leaps she realized the tiller would stop if she released the lever, and did so immediately. Her composure badly damaged, she risked a glance at the boys, hard at work in their garden plots. None of them looked at her, which told her that they'd seen the whole thing, and now couldn't meet her gaze for fear they'd laugh out loud. Esther decided right then that rototilling was a job she'd leave to the guys.

Once the gardens were established, Lionel and Esther knew there was more land that needed to be under cultivation in order to meet the requirements of homesteading. Being a farm boy from North Dakota, Lionel's thoughts went immediately to grain crops. He realized the amount of oats and timothy he could raise on a few acres of Alaskan soil wouldn't produce enough for him to sell. So how could he use the crop? Why, buy a cow, of course. This scheme would solve several problems: Lionel's grain crop wouldn't go to waste, the family would have fresh milk, and the chores involved with having a cow would keep his kids from the boredom of not having enough work to do. It certainly wasn't done as a money-making scheme.

The Muth family, who lived several miles farther up the North Fork Road, owned a herd of dairy cows, and Lionel struck a deal with Albert Muth to buy one of his cows. Several years previously, one of Albert's best milkers had given birth to twins. The smaller twin—a pretty black cow with a white star on her forehead—now produced milk, but not in the quantities that made for a good dairy cow. She would be better suited to providing milk for a large family— a perfect fit for the Haakensons.

Bossy in front of the silo.

313

The Muths had named the little cow Mary, a marvelous coincidence in the view of Esther's only daughter. Esther, foreseeing non-stop teasing from her male offspring, objected to her daughter sharing a name with the family's new bovine member and called for a name change. Mary-the-daughter protested: "How come we have to change her name? Daddy planted timothy, and we didn't change its name, just 'cause it's the same as Tim's." She was outvoted, though, and the cow became known simply as Bossy.

Tim, Robert and John were the main caretakers of Bossy at first, making sure she had water in the large tub in the barnyard, and milking her twice a day. A bucket of milk does not arrive from the barn ready for consumption, especially if its consumer objects to a few floating cow hairs or specks of barn dirt. It needs to be strained. For a few days, Esther fashioned a strainer by pinning cheesecloth to the top of a gallon jug with clothespins and pouring the milk through the cloth. It didn't take many tries before she told her husband, "I need a better strainer. The clothespins pop off the top of the jar, the cheesecloth falls down inside and I end up with dirt in my milk."

A store-bought strainer is usually a large, metal funnel-shaped object into which one inserts a ready-made filter. Lionel, with typical ingenuity, fashioned one from materials he found around the house. He took a two-quart can that had held some sort of food product and had the kind reusable lid that is pressed down into the can's mouth to close it. Of course, it takes strong fingernails or a screwdriver to pry the top off the next time the user needs to access the ingredients, but at least they're kept clean and somewhat sealed from the outside world. This type of can was readily available, since Esther rarely threw away a container that might come in handy for something. Lionel turned the lid upside down, drilled numerous ¼-inch holes in it, then trimmed it so it would slide fairly snugly down inside the can. Cutting a 2-inch hole in the bottom of the can, he soldered a smaller can over the hole, so the unit looked roughly like the manufactured version of a strainer. Esther spread a square of cheesecloth over the top of the larger can, inserted the repurposed lid, pushed the cheesecloth to the bottom and the milk strainer was complete. She set the strainer on a gallon jar (also one of a large stash saved from destruction by her certainty that one day she'd need them), poured milk into the larger can, and from the bottom came fresh, warm, dirt- and hair-free milk. Once it cooled and sat for a few hours, several inches of thick cream rose to the top. For daily use Esther stirred the cream back into the milk, but for special occasions she skimmed the top layer of cream off and beat it into delicious whipped cream. Church potlucks weren't considered complete without a gallon of Bossy's milk and usually a bowl of whipped cream as well.

The small chest freezer on the back porch became the family's refrigerator in the absence of a real one. Keeping things at proper temperatures with several jars of warm milk going in twice a day, took more vigilance than a regular fridge would, as Esther needed to set a timer, and remove the milk to the "Homestead-aire" cooler once it was sufficiently chilled.

Lionel built a snug barn with room for the tons of hay and oats needed to sustain one small cow through the long winter. To supplement these expensive foodstuffs—and to get the needed percentage of the homestead under cultivation—he sowed oats and timothy in the 20 acres surrounding the gardens. While the crop grew, he took Tim and Robert to a spot next to the barn. "I want you to dig a hole here," he told them. Together they measured a 12 x 12-foot square and the boys set to work with shovels. They dug to a depth of about 8 feet before their dad called it good.

Lionel again called on the older boys, this time to help him build a tall, square wooden structure over the hole. This edifice was completely foreign to his Alaskan-born children. When John asked what it was supposed to be, Lionel replied,

"This is a silo." Though this information enlightened most of his kids not at all, they accepted it, knowing in time it would become clear.

The oat and timothy crops looked just like grass as they grew, until they reached maturity and began to produce their heads of grain. The kids were especially intrigued by the oats, as they studied the small, green, pointy things and wondered how they ever turned into the oatmeal they were familiar with that came out of a round cardboard carton.

One characteristic of Bossy that became evident within days of her arrival was her lack of understanding of boundaries. She needed a fence to keep her from roaming. Lionel rigged up an electric wire that enclosed the area around the barn and some of the surrounding woods. A few touches of the fence with her inquisitive nose taught Bossy to stay within the electric fence's confines. Over the years her area was expanded till the wire stretched to the near edge of the grain field in back of the house, and halfway down the driveway in the front.

Moose didn't have the same reaction to an electric fence, though. Where Bossy would feel the mild electric jolt and back off, when a moose felt the shock it forged ahead, breaking through the wire. A break stopped the pulse of current through the fence, necessitating repair. This was a tedious task, and one Esther found perfect for any of her offspring who demonstrated aggressiveness toward their siblings, thereby signaling need of a job. A complaint of boredom was answered in the same manner: "Go walk the fence." This attitude taught Esther's kids that boredom wasn't worth the price they'd have to pay, so they learned to amuse themselves.

One day in late summer while Lionel was away on a job, Bossy found a break in the fence and made good her escape. Esther's first inkling of impending disaster was Jim's panicked voice coming from the direction of the field. "Mama! Bossy's in the oats!" Esther looked out the window to see Jim hastening up the path that led to the gardens and grain field.

"Kenny! Mary!" she called the two kids who were nearest at hand. "Go down and help Jim get the cow out of the field." She watched as the kids scurried down the trail through the trees. She tried to carry on with her work, but she found herself repeatedly drawn to the window, watching for the prodigal cow to come home. Finally, she could stand it no longer, and she trotted down to the field.

An appalling sight greeted her. The kids were doing their best, but their inexperience as cattle wranglers was obvious. Bossy, having discovered an herbivore's heaven, was extremely loath to leave it. As Esther watched, Kenny ran toward the cow through the waist-high grain, waving his arms. Bossy, with surprising agility, dodged around him and galloped just beyond his reach. There she stopped, unfurled her long, rough tongue and snatched a mouthful of the lush greens. Next Mary charged her, with similar results.

Esther could see nothing was being accomplished by this except the trampling of Lionel's grain crop. She knew from experience with her dad's dairy cows that the kids were going about it all wrong. "Come out of there," she called. "You can't chase her like that. Kenny, go get a rope."

Kenny jogged up to the barn and returned with a stout length of cord. With this in hand, Esther approached the now-skittish cow. "It's okay, Bossy," she soothed. She put out her hand and stroked the cow's nose. Bossy tossed her head and eyed her warily, but didn't flee. Esther continued to speak softly as she slid the rope around Bossy's neck and knotted it. "Come on, Bossy, time to go home." She turned and made her way out of the field, Bossy following without protest.

Back in the barnyard, Esther eyed Bossy's rounded sides with concern. It certainly looked like she'd gorged herself on the forbidden greens. Though the cow had been eating wild grass all summer, the amount of rich oats she'd ingested could be enough to cause her to bloat. "Lionel, why do these things always happen when you're gone?" she groused silently to her absent husband. Aloud she said, "You kids keep an eye on Bossy today. I don't want her getting sick from eating so much oats."

As evening approached, Bossy seemed sluggish. She usually spent an hour or two each day lying down, chewing her cud. Today, she lay down, but seemed uncomfortable. Esther thought about the story her friend, Edna, had told of their experience with a bloating cow back in Colorado. "We couldn't get her to stand up, and her belly kept swelling," Edna had related. Esther imagined the cow, flat on her side, inflating like a large, hairy balloon. "Bob took a garden hose and ran it down her throat," Edna continued. "He had me sit on top of the cow and bounce on her. We were sure relieved when all that gas finally came out the hose, even though it was awfully stinky."

Esther wouldn't let the situation get that critical if she could help it. After watching Bossy lying down for some time without chewing her cud, she told the older boys, "Make her stand up. We're gonna walk her. She needs to burp up that extra gas." For the next several hours, the kids took turns walking the cow up and down the driveway. Every so often they'd check in with Esther. "I heard a few little burps." "She tooted a couple of times." Finally Esther felt enough time—and gas—had passed that Bossy would survive. Until the crop was harvested, though, everyone remained vigilant about keeping the fence mended and the cow out of the field.

In the fall, Lionel again borrowed Poppin' Priscilla from Bert and a harvester from another neighbor, Lloyd Onstott. The harvester chopped the still-green stalks into short pieces; these were loaded onto a wagon and brought from the field and pulled up in front of the new silo. Lionel called his younger kids: "Mary, Kenny, Ronny—hop down in the hole." That sounded almost like a little adventure, and the three willingly allowed themselves to be assisted into the pit. "Now, stamp down the oats as we pitch them in," Lionel directed. "They need to be packed tight."

The three youngsters spent the rest of the day in the silo, stomping on the stalks as their dad and older brothers used pitchforks to throw the stuff in. Hours passed as the silo slowly filled. Finally, when the younger kids' heads were nearly bumping the top of the silo, the grain ran out and the kids slid wearily down off the slippery stack of greens.

Lionel boarded up the entrance to the silo, and left the fresh oats and timothy to ferment for a few months. When he reopened it for Bossy's dining pleasure, it seemed like a completely different product. Now called silage, it still smelled good, but had a distinctly tangy fragrance that enveloped the yard.

Bossy loved this new form of nourishment. The older boys were in charge of giving her a daily portion that satisfied her hunger. She would have gladly kept on eating past that amount, which could have led to another case of bloating. Esther, not wanting a repeat of Bossy's earlier misadventure, made sure Jim, who took care of Bossy during the day while his siblings were in school, understood that he wasn't doing Bossy any favors by giving her unlimited access to this tasty treat.

The fragrant silage attracted at least one other local ruminant, as well. One winter evening as the family sat around the supper table, they heard a clunking sound on the front porch. Everyone's first thought was that a visitor had arrived, but no one knocked on the door. Lionel got up and opened the door. There stood Bossy, wild-eyed and huffing loudly through her nose. Something had scared her. She attempted to push her way into the house.

"Don't you let that cow in here," Esther warned even as Lionel blocked Bossy's entrance.

"What's wrong with her?" Lionel wondered. All the kids gathered around to comfort the trembling, nearly-hyperventilating animal while Lionel got a flashlight and headed out to see what had thrown her into such a dither. Out in the barnyard, calmly pulling out and munching clumps of silage, stood a large moose. Apparently, Bossy felt safer with her two-legged companions than with this wild relative. Lionel chased the moose away and Bossy, reassured her domain was once again safe, returned to her calm and docile self.

A year or so after Bossy joined the family Lionel took her back to the Muths' farm for a short visit. She returned home in a family way, and in time gave birth to a bull calf. The family named him Buster, and enjoyed the novelty of having a baby animal around the place, though everyone was aware that Buster's eventual fate was as packages of meat in the freezer.

As a newly-freshened cow, Bossy produced more milk than Buster and the family could use, so Esther put out the word that she had milk for sale. In those days before tightened regulations, she sold fresh, raw, unpasteurized milk to many of her neighbors. At a dollar a gallon the family never got rich, but the money did help with the expenses of feeding a cow through the long months of winter.

The New House

Sometimes Esther felt her kids must lie awake nights thinking up ways to make things difficult for her. One ongoing issue revolved around the light in the upstairs bedroom, where all of the kids now slept. In the middle of the room, one side of the slanted ceiling held a bare 100-watt bulb. Its position made it convenient for the first person up the stairs to pull the dangling string and turn on the light. That same accessibility also put it in harm's way when the boys decided to play catch or felt it necessary to throw objects at each other. The shattering of the bulb plunged the room into darkness, causing temporary consternation amongst the kids, as they knew they'd earned another scolding from their mother. One evening Esther heard the tinkle from upstairs, heralding what seemed like the hundredth broken bulb. "Who did it?" she yelled from the kitchen. After a short silence John's voice answered, "I did, but it was an accident."

"It always is," she thought. Aloud she called to John, "Come and get the broom and dustpan and clean it up. The rest of you come down here. Watch out so you don't step in the glass." Grabbing a flashlight and pliers, she climbed the stairs, pulled the string to cut the electricity to the socket and removed the remnants of the bulb.

"This has to stop," she decided. The next day she rounded up some thick wire and fashioned a cage for the light bulb. Once nailed in place, it deflected any balls or other projectiles Esther's offspring tossed to or at one another. It may have been a small victory, but it saved a lot on light bulbs.

The upstairs over the living and store rooms sufficed as bedroom space for a time, but in a couple of years Lionel and Esther agreed on the need to expand. By this time, the charm of an all-log house had worn a bit thin, and with his limited time at home, Lionel knew he didn't have the time to fell, limb and skin logs, let alone fit them together into another room on the house. Thanks to Modern Builders Supply's convenient location, lumber was readily available. Lionel gathered up the boards needed and attached an 8 x 12-foot room to the back of the cabin. Into this new space went two sets of bunk beds and chests of drawers enough to accommodate Jim and the three youngest children. Esther took the opportunity to move her and Lionel's bed out of the living room, as well. Tim, Robert and John remained upstairs. Their mother fervently hoped that the extra elbow room would help maintain some semblance of peace between those three.

Homestead cabin after several additions.

Despite this addition, as the fifties gave way to the sixties, Esther struggled once again with space that seemed to shrink as her children grew. With Lionel working away much of the time and the kids picking at each other, Esther's patience was tried on a daily basis. She tried to keep things positive in her letters to Lionel, but when he got home she decided they needed to have a serious talk.

"I think it's time for a bigger house," she began. "And now that the electricity is more dependable, I want an electric pump and a hot water heater. I've got enough to do without pumping water and heating it on the stove."

Lionel agreed. Thanks to his fairly steady work and their combined frugality, they had some money saved up. And between their own strong backs and several teenage sons, they could supply much of the needed labor on the project. They decided to build just across the yard from the cabin. This way they wouldn't need to extend the driveway, and the construction site would be easily accessible at all times.

Esther, Lionel and the older boys spent hours that winter drawing up various house plans. They finally settled on a plan to make the house 32 x 40 feet, with a full basement. As soon as the worst of spring break-up was past, Lionel started by inviting his offspring to join him in his favorite game—Pick-up Sticks. The older boys knew what this meant, but the younger set had to learn through experience that this game was not as fun as it sounded. Still, the lot for the new house got cleared of sticks and roots, and Lionel hired Don Ledger—a friend from church—who had a Cat, to scoop out the hole for the basement.

Lionel had recently begun a steady job in Kenai, a town about eighty miles from Anchor Point. Since the commute over the rough gravel roads took nearly two hours, he stayed in a small apartment near the jobsite during the week and only came home on weekends. When he was home, he made the most of those long hours of summer daylight, and kept the older boys busy. It took several weekends to complete the pouring of cement for the basement. After that he installed the floor joists. During the week Esther pushed forward with what she and the boys could accomplish without Lionel's direct supervision.

Over the course of the summer and fall the house slowly grew. This would be Esther's dream house. To heat it,

323

Lionel installed an oil furnace. This beast occupied more than half of the east wall of the basement. No longer would Esther be required to stoke a barrel stove at bedtime—and often again during the night—to keep the house at a tolerable temperature. As an added measure of insurance against times of no electricity, Lionel built a fireplace out of concrete along the wall next to the furnace. He hooked it into the ductwork for the furnace so that, while it wouldn't have the fan to force air during power outages, it would at least waft warm air throughout the house.

Fluorescent tubes lighted nearly all of the main floor and upstairs rooms. Being frugal types, Lionel and Esther considered the money saved by using fluorescent lights far more important than any ambience created by incandescent bulbs.

Lionel and the boys hand dug a well in the north corner of the basement and installed an electric pump. Esther would have all the water—hot or cold— she desired at the twist of a faucet handle. Her wood cook stove was left behind in the cabin. The new house contained a modern range that ran on propane. No longer would she have to struggle to keep an even oven temperature with sticks of wood of varying degrees of dryness.

Finally, on Thanksgiving Day of 1960, the new house stood ready for occupation. Esther started the turkey in the new propane stove in the morning, and spent the day directing traffic as her children carried load after load of belongings from the cabin. She cringed to see the amount of snow tracked into both houses as the kids worked, but she knew it was a temporary condition. She could clean the new floor any time, and after today she'd no longer concern herself about the looks of the floor in the old cabin.

What a blessing this new house would be. She looked forward to having a real bedroom. For several years she and Lionel had slept in the living room, and for the past year they'd shared the last cabin addition with four of the kids.

She also eagerly anticipated having a real bathroom. The 2-foot-square cubby that housed a toilet in the cabin had been better than an outhouse, but not much. Bath times in the cabin had been an ongoing pain. The galvanized tub had to be dragged into the house and set next to the barrel stove. Everyone bathed — one after another — in the same water. Not exactly a private, spa-like experience.

The new bathroom, by contrast, was a complete, separate room with a door that locked. In addition to a flush toilet it contained a sink and a bathtub with shower. Since the house used a cesspool, there was still a need to conserve water. The first night in the house Lionel told the kids, "You can run this much water for your bath." He held up his hand, his thumb and forefinger about two inches apart. Baths were for getting clean, not for luxuriating in water up to one's neck. Still not a spa, but at least everyone got his or her own bath water.

Even with its amenities, having one bathroom for a family of nine people led to frequent friction among Esther's offspring. If anyone spent more than a couple of minutes behind the closed door, the likelihood was great that a sibling would be pounding on the door yelling, "What're you doin' in there — homesteading?"

But those conflicts belonged to the future. As that first afternoon in the new house wore on, the smell of the turkey emanating from the oven let everyone know that dinner was near at hand. Esther had made her apple, mince and pumpkin pies the day before, and they were carefully carried across the yard and set on the new kitchen counter. She wanted the rolls to be fresh so, once the flour and other ingredients were brought in, she mixed the dough and set it aside to rise. In the early afternoon she started her daughter peeling several pounds of potatoes that would be needed for the meal.

The small square table that had held the family's meals in the cabin was another item not making the migration to the new house. As he'd not yet had time to buy a larger dining table, Lionel came up with a temporary solution. The large piece of siding he'd cut out of the front of the house for the door, when laid flat, was a perfectly-sized table for the family. While the house was being built, the boys had fastened a net across the middle of this table and played ping pong on it. Now, with the net removed and Esther's good lacy tablecloth spread on it, it was transformed into a fitting foundation for a Thanksgiving feast.

Esther directed the kids as everyone helped get the food on the table for this first meal in the new house. She slipped into her chair at one end of the table and Lionel took his place at the other end. The kids each found places along the sides—the biggest boys, Tim, Robert and John on one side; Jim, Kenny, Mary and Ronny on the other. Tim and Kenny, as the two left-handers, each claimed the corners which would give their left arms room without jabbing a sibling who might object. Esther gazed around. Seven healthy children—at present all behaving and getting along, though she knew that probably wouldn't last. A bountiful feast from which no one would leave hungry. "We sure have a lot to be thankful for," she mused. Looking at Lionel, she knew he had the same thought. Usually the various family members took turns saying a prayer before meals, but on

this day Lionel suggested something different. "Let's sing *The Doxology*," he said. The family sang the prayer

New house, 1960.

326

of thankfulness together:

> Praise God from whom all blessings flow.
> Praise Him all creatures here below.
> Praise Him above, ye heavenly hosts.
> Praise Father, Son and Holy Ghost.

Set Net Fishing at Correia Bend

By the fall of 1961, all of Esther's kids except Jim were in school. Though Lionel had a steady job in Kenai, the rough gravel roads still made a daily commute impractical. He arrived home on Friday evenings, giving Esther more support than she'd had during the past few years. However, she felt the ongoing strain of being the only parent around for the majority of the time. She found it becoming more of an issue as the kids got older.

While there was no secondary school in Anchor Point, the towns on either side of Anchor Point both had high schools. Students who lived north of Anchor Point were bused to Ninilchik, while those to the south went to Homer. Because the bus that ran the North Fork Road route met up with both the Homer and Ninilchik buses at the Anchor Point school, kids — like the Haakensons — who lived on the North Fork Road were given the choice of going to either Homer or Ninilchik. At the time, Ninilchik, the smaller school, had a reputation for emphasizing academics, while Homer was rumored to be more focused on sports.

The previous year when he'd started high school, Tim, strongly supported by his parents, opted for Ninilchik. This meant an hour-long, twenty-mile bus ride each way. He left the house an hour before the other kids, and got home an hour later. "You would think," ruminated Esther, "that he'd be so tired from riding the bus, spending all day at school, and doing homework that he wouldn't have the energy to fight with his brothers." Unfortunately, it seemed like the older boys couldn't keep from aggravating each other. In the days of living in the cabin, she would have sent them outside to split wood when they got belligerent; now, with an oil furnace heating the house and propane fueling the cook stove, the need for all that wood was past. The boys had too much energy and not enough to do to work it off.

Esther brought up her concerns to Lionel one evening in the privacy of their bedroom. "The boys just don't have enough to do. It's bad enough that the younger kids squabble and pick at each other all the time. With the older ones it's turning into fistfights. Some days I feel like all I do is break up fights."

Lionel nodded, but said little. In typical fashion, he and Esther didn't look to their community for solutions. In their minds the problem was not a lack of entertainment; these kids needed more work. Lionel found jobs for Tim, Robert and John to do around the yard. He also stressed the fact that if he heard from their mother that they'd been fighting, they'd have even more work once he got home. Of course, Bossy still needed to be milked both morning and evening, but that only took an hour or so of their time, and Jim was slowly but surely elbowing his brothers out of that particular job. These measures provided a slight reprieve in the fraternal battles, but both parents knew they were simply stop-gaps. They needed a long-term solution.

A potential answer to the problem appeared seemingly by accident. On his weekly drives home on Friday nights, Lionel had fallen into the habit of stopping at a small gas station in the Kasilof area, some forty miles from Anchor Point. He'd become friendly with the owner, and often shared a cup of coffee and a few minutes of conversation before tackling the rest of the rough road home. One evening in the early spring of 1962, as the men talked, Lionel noticed a piece of paper tacked to the wall. "Fishing Site for Sale" it read.

"Say," said Lionel, pulling down the paper, "what do you know about this fishing site?"

"That's Vern Savage's site," the man replied. "It's down the road a ways, a little bit this side of Ninilchik, right next to Correia Creek."

"How can I get ahold of this guy?" Lionel asked.

"Oh, he lives just down the road."

"Maybe I'll think on it for a while." Lionel headed home, but the idea of a fishing site, having been planted, took root and grew like Jack's beanstalk.

He broached the subject to Esther when he got home. "We don't know anything about commercial fishing," Esther pointed out.

"Yeah, well, Ted Rozak does," replied Lionel. "I'll get the scoop from him." Ted Rozak and his wife Ruth had moved to Anchor Point several years previously, and the two families had become friendly, as many of their children were similar in ages and interests.

The next Friday evening, Lionel showed up with the back end of the station wagon stuffed with all manner of gear needed for a commercial fishing operation. "These are the nets they use on the fishing site," he said. "They're called 'gill nets' because they catch the fish by the gills as they swim into 'em." Tim reached into the car and grabbed a clump of netting. As he pulled it out, he saw it was neatly bound with rope in several places, making it into a sort of long tube of netting. He stretched it out on the ground as Robert brought another one and laid it next to Tim's. Back and forth, Lionel and the older boys carefully extracted each net and laid it out on the ground. Further up inside the car sat a cluster of orange-painted barrels with white ends. As the boys started pulling them out Lionel informed them, "These are the buoy kegs. They'll mark the ends of the nets."

Lionel surveyed the various pieces of fishing paraphernalia now littering his yard. He knew he couldn't waste a single moment if he was to be ready when fishing started in mid-June. He spent as much time as he could with his fisherman friend Ted, learning the rudiments of this new business. Then he came home and passed on his knowledge to the boys. Gunny sacks were opened to reveal large ovoid objects, each with a hole running lengthwise through its middle. Lionel explained that these were corks, though most of them were made of Styrofoam. More gunny sacks contained 3-inch-long lead cylinders. When attached to a net, the corks would keep the top afloat while the leads would weigh down the bottom. Ted helped initiate the boys into the mysteries of attaching the corks and leads to new nets, in a process called "hanging." Lionel prepared for this procedure by laying two logs parallel about 12 feet apart in the yard in front of the old cabin. He mounted the logs on short, stout posts and stretched a net between the two logs, with the cork line hanging over one log and the lead line hanging over the other. With one son busy threading and sewing on corks and another doing the same with leads, the job called for a level of teamwork that made fighting difficult. The job was tedious in the extreme, but the boys knew that Lionel expected them to complete the amount of work he assigned them for the week.

Once the new nets were hung, the mending of the old but salvageable ones began. The fishing process was hard on the web of net. Individual strings in the net often broke when they caught on floating logs or other debris that found its way into the net, or even from fish that were too large for the size of webbing. Mending these holes called for a finer twine than was used for hanging the nets. The boys learned the special knot used for this process, and spent hours repairing the nets in preparation for the fishing season. While Tim and Robert mended nets, John, Kenny and Ronny worked on the buoy kegs. The bright orange kegs with their white ends, when anchored securely in place, would be easy to spot even when the water was rough. Each fisherman was assigned a number when he received his license, and each net had to be identified by these numbers. The boys sanded and painted all the kegs, and stenciled the correct numbers on the ends in large, black print.

Another article included in the sale of the fishing site was an old dory, which also needed attention. Its paint had to be scraped and sanded off, and a new coat applied. With all this work to be done, Esther found she enjoyed a little more peace around the house. The boys went straight to their jobs when they got home from school. The excitement of looking forward to the fishing season also distracted them from picking on each other.

The final two large acquisitions for the fishing site were a WWII-era truck, and a small house trailer that would serve as home to the fishermen during the season. The truck, which was simply called "the four-by," wasn't much to look at and was barely street-legal, but served well as a workhorse for the beach. The trailer never came to Anchor Point. It squatted, summer and winter, on the shore against the bottom of the cliff near the Haakensons' fishing location.

House, four-by and car.

By June, Lionel could barely contain his excitement. This experience promised to take his fishing fever to a level he'd only dreamed of. He'd told his boss all about the fishing site, and now advised him not to expect him back at work until sometime in August, after the season was over. While he and the boys gathered fishing materials and ferried them 30 miles up the bumpy gravel highway to the beach, Esther packed kitchen supplies. She knew cooking was going to be almost an afterthought for her men, so she looked for foods that could be prepared quickly. Dried macaroni, cans of beans and beef stew would serve as the main courses. A box of Bisquik®, loaves of bread, margarine, peanut butter and jelly, and canned fruits and vegetables would suffice as side dishes. Esther pulled her daughter from her regular household chores and set her to baking. Several dozen each of chocolate chip, oatmeal raisin and peanut butter cookies would round off meals for the guys. The trailer they'd be living in contained an oil heater and a small propane cooktop with two burners. Some pots and pans that normally went along on camping trips were pressed into service, as well as the oldest, least-breakable plates and cups. And, of course, Esther included that most indispensable of camp supplies — a can opener. There was no electric service to the beach, and the only method of keeping things cold was Correia Creek, which tumbled down the bluff and entered the inlet just yards from the trailer. Bossy's contribution — a gallon of fresh milk — would be kept cool by stashing it in a shady spot a short way up the creek, just above the outhouse.

The season started off with Lionel, 16-year-old Tim and 14-year-old Robert manning the site. Lionel purchased gear licenses for himself and Tim, in addition to their regular commercial fishing licenses. The gear license allowed its holder to fish three nets, giving the Haakenson group 6 nets total. Along the stretch of beach where Lionel's camp was located, the best fishing often happened on the beach nets — those nets that floated during high tide but went dry when the tide went out. Lionel discovered that all the beach net locations were already spoken for, so his nets had to be set further out in the water.

Fishing site.

The allowed fishing periods ran for 24 hours each, starting at 6 a.m. on Mondays and Fridays. Typically, the fishermen along the beach caught mostly sockeye salmon (commonly called reds) for the first weeks of the fishing season. A relatively small number of Chinook, or king, salmon were caught. Because the webbing of the nets was sized for the smaller species of salmon, most kings tore through the net and continued on their merry way. If they were captured, it was usually not by getting caught by the gills but by becoming wrapped in the net in their frantic thrashing attempts to escape. In mid-July the pinks arrived. Most fishermen referred to pinks as "humpies," because of the obvious hump on the backs of the males. The pinks would be followed by the coho, or silver, salmon in August.

On Sunday afternoon before the first opening, Lionel supervised the loading of the 4-by, then said, "Well, boys, are you ready to go slaughter some salmon?"

With an enthusiastic, "Yeah, let's go!" Tim and Robert jumped into the 4-by, and the old truck chugged out the driveway. Esther and the rest of the kids watched it disappear, then turned to their everyday activities. Since there was no phone, they knew they'd have to wait till the guys showed up before they'd know how well they'd done.

Ted had warned Lionel that the season usually started off slowly, and it did — disappointingly so. There were few fish, and not even much debris to tear up the nets. The guys mended the nets, cleaned up around the trailer, and still got home by Tuesday afternoon. On Thursday, they headed back down to the beach, ready to do it all again. Once more, their catch for the Friday period was only about a half-dozen reds.

This pattern continued over several weeks, and Esther and Lionel began to wonder if the venture was going to be successful only in that it kept their teenage boys busy through the summer months. It certainly didn't appear to be a financial success. The money they'd borrowed to buy the operation would need to be paid back. Of course, Lionel would be heading back to his sheet metal job in the fall so the bills would get paid, but not as quickly as they'd hoped. The family would just have to tighten their belts a little.

Esther wasn't worried about that; she'd lived with money shortages for most of her life, and she could do it again. But it was disappointing to have such a poor return for the amount of work invested in this new endeavor.

By mid-July the red run had petered out, though the guys on the Haakenson site saw little difference. They heard reports that many of the fish sites down the beach from them had done much better. Lionel knew he couldn't compete with those guys. Most were long-established sites run by men and women with years — even generations — of experience behind them.

As the season wore on, the fish they caught began to be mostly pinks. Slowly the numbers increased, until in late July there were enough pinks to justify an extra day of fishing. Tuesday, when Lionel heard they would be adding a Wednesday fishing period, he left the boys at the site with a list of chores to get accomplished, and headed home.

Esther wasn't too surprised to see him walk into the house alone. "I heard the emergency announcement on *Fisherman's Corner* that you're getting an extra fishing day." *Fisherman's Corner* was a daily broadcast on several local stations that kept fishermen updated as to total catch, escapement, and other information of interest to the fishing community. "Emergency announcements" were of special importance, because they let the fishermen know when they would be given more time to fish, or when time would be cut back. Transistor radios in every cabin along the beach stayed tuned to catch the latest reports. Esther had gotten into the habit of listening to the report, since, with no CB or telephone, it was the only way she had of knowing what was going on with her men on the beach.

Esther knew Lionel needed to return to the beach as soon as possible. She gathered what canned goods and leftovers she felt they'd use and promised, "I'll run into Homer and get more supplies and bring 'em up to you." She

and the younger kids had made several visits to the site
during the early days when fishing was slow.

The trek down to the beach was an adventure in itself.
First, she drove over 30 miles of gravel road to a spot almost
directly above the fish camp. Here she parked the car, and
hiked with the kids through a field filled with grass and cow
parsnip (commonly called by its Russian name, pushki) until
they reached the bluff that overlooked the inlet. Steep mud
paths zigzagged down the bluff. The earlier trips had been
made with very little extra baggage. This time, each of the
kids wore a pack sack with supplies for the fishermen.
Esther reminded them, when they got rambunctious, to be
careful so they didn't topple over and take an unexpected
slide to the bottom of the bluff.

The last section dropped nearly straight down to the
beach. To navigate this short but perilous path, one end of a
sturdy rope was tied firmly to a tree trunk, and the other
end dangled down almost to the sand below. Each person
took his or her turn to climb down the rope. The kids tackled
the rope with alacrity and scaled the slope in seconds.

Jim had stayed home on this day. Esther remembered
their first trip, when she discovered Jim's fear of the rope.
Her younger kids had scrambled down the rope just as they
did this time. Jim had crouched at the top of the cliff. Esther
could see he wasn't sure he wanted to do this. "Come on,
Jim," she said. "Grab the rope like this and just back down
this path." She demonstrated, then climbed up and handed
him the rope. He took it, but made no attempt to swing
himself into position.

"I can't do it. I fall." he said, trying to give the rope back
to her.

"Yes, you can," she told him. "You turn around and walk
backwards just like I did. Hold onto the rope tight, and you
won't fall."

For several more minutes Esther encouraged, cajoled
and finally commanded him to climb down the rope. She

could see he was terrified of this new experience, but she couldn't leave him sitting at the top of the bluff. She helped him wrap his hands around the rope, then she took hold of it directly below his hands, and together they inched down the bluff. She knew, from the look in his eyes, that he would gladly live the rest of his days without a repeat of this experience. She had decided then that any trip to the beach which included a climb down the rope would not include Jim. He would be safer and happier at home.

Lionel and the boys greeted the sight of fresh provisions with relief. Esther could see that, already, the 24-hour-long fishing periods with one short day in between were tiring them. They'd caught several hundred pink salmon during the Wednesday opening. "I think the run is here," said Lionel. "I'm hearing rumors that if it picks up any more Fish and Game might give us even more time to fish, and possibly even have us fishing non-stop. We aren't gonna have a chance to come home."

"I'll keep listening to *Fisherman's Corner* and bring stuff down when I know you can't make it home."

Lionel had a different plan. "You'd better buy fishing licenses for you and John. I think we're gonna need you down here to help."

"I can't do that! I've got four more kids at home! There's no place for everyone to sleep here. And the cow..."

Lionel shook his head. "Well, we need more hands here. The kids are old enough to take care of things at home by themselves."

Esther reluctantly agreed. She knew Jim would take care of the cow. She had less faith in the work ethic of her other youngsters, but with a clear enough to-do list and strong enough threats, it just might work. Besides, she wouldn't be gone any longer than she needed to be.

In the end, she worked out a compromise. All of the kids, with the exception of Jim, were dying to get down onto the beach. When she returned home for supplies, she chose

Mary, Kenny or Ronny to accompany her to the fish site. A few days later, on her next supply run, someone else got to go. With much prayer and a heads-up to the milk customers to check on the kids when they came for milk, she joined the fishermen.

As July blended into August the run of pinks grew stronger. Fishing was eventually thrown wide open. During a normal fishing period, the men checked the nets every six hours, at each turn of the tide. But this was not a normal time. A historic run of pink salmon flooded the inlet, and the fishermen had no time to do anything but run their boats out to the nets, remove the fish, bring them in to shore, empty them into a truck bed, hastily-constructed boxes, and even unused boats, and dash back out to pick more fish. If Lionel and Esther had wanted a job that would leave their boys too tired to fight, they'd certainly found it that summer.

Under normal conditions, the cannery sent out a truck each day to collect the fish from their customers along the beach. At the peak of the run, the Haakensons waited in vain for several days for the arrival of the cannery truck. With no way to refrigerate the fish, Lionel became concerned about their condition. He directed the kids, "We've gotta keep these fish as cold as we can. Every hour or so you need to dump water on them." He scooped a bucket of water out of the creek that ran beside the cabin and demonstrated. Taking gunny sacks, he soaked them in the creek and spread them over the fish. He stuck his finger under a fish's gill cover and lifted it, exposing the inner gill. "See how bright red the gills are? We need to keep 'em like that. If they lose color it means they're getting old and won't be fit to eat." Until the cannery truck showed up, everyone pitched in as they struggled to keep the fish cool enough to be in a saleable condition.

When the truck finally arrived, Lionel greeted the driver a trifle testily. "Where've you been?"

338

"I'm really sorry," the driver apologized. "The guys down the beach had so many fish, they were fillin' the truck before I could get to you."

"Well, I've had an awful time trying to keep 'em from going bad."

The driver walked over to the burlap-covered crates. He pulled back the gunny sacks and surveyed the fish. "You've done a good job," he said. "A lot of guys just threw their fish in boxes and didn't even try to keep 'em cool. We had to throw 'em all away. I'll be able to salvage at least some of yours."

Unfortunately, despite Lionel's best efforts, much of the fish that had sat for several days had to be destroyed. He and the kids dug a hole in the loose shale that lay at the bottom of the bluff several hundred yards away from the cabin, and pitched in the rejected fish. Later he told Esther, "I sure hate to see all that good salmon going to waste. If this happens again, I think I'll run the fish to the cannery myself in the 4-by." Esther agreed, sharing her husband's aversion to unnecessary wastefulness.

Several weeks later the run of humpies slowed, and Esther was able to return home for good. Between the sheer physical labor of beach fishing, the long tiring hours of gravel road driving, and making sure everyone on the fishing site and back home had everything they needed, she felt completely worn out. She knew she and Lionel were going to have to figure out a better plan for the next fishing season.

In late August ,Lionel and the boys wrapped up the season and brought home all the nets, buoys, the four-by—everything except the camp trailer. Lionel made a trip to the cannery to settle up and receive his pay for the summer. He arrived home with an odd, half-stunned look on his face. He handed Esther the check. When she saw the total, she nearly dropped it. "It's more money than I've ever held in my hand at one time in my whole life," said Lionel.

Esther stared at the check. Over $12,000! It seemed almost sinful to receive such a payday. "What will we do with that much money?" she wondered. Scarcely had that thought formed when her practical mind began supplying answers. "The first thing we'll do is pay off that loan," she told Lionel. "And we need to save enough for taxes."

"Yes, and I want to build a new dory," said Lionel. "The old one leaks and isn't gonna last much longer. A lot of the nets got really ripped up from all the fish this year. They're not worth mending so I'll need to buy new ones, and a new outboard motor. I think I'll tack a lean-to onto the trailer so our living area won't be so cramped. And the boys worked hard. They deserve a paycheck."

Suddenly that $12,000 didn't seem like such a huge amount, but at least it would put a comfortable cushion into their bank account. "We sure have a lot to be thankful for," she told Lionel.

He nodded. "Yes, we do."

When Lionel handed Tim a check for $550 and Robert one for $450, Esther knew the stunned looks on their faces mimicked hers when she first saw the cannery check. She got tickled when John came to her on the sly. "Dad told me to decide how much I think I should get for fishing. What I should tell him?"

"What do you want the money for?" asked Esther.

"I want a bike, but the one I want costs $50. That's a lotta money."

"Well, I think you should ask for what you want. Maybe you'll get it and maybe you won't."

She watched John approach Lionel. "I think I want $50," he said, trying to sound bold.

Lionel wrote out a check and handed it to his son. "Think that'll be enough?" he asked.

John's mouth hung open. "Four hundred dollars? Wow—thank you!" he managed.

A glow spread through Esther. The boys had worked hard all summer; she was glad they were getting paid for it. The kids who kept the homestead running also received some money.

Over the next few years Lionel and the boys continued fishing the beach sites. Some seasons were pretty good, sometimes they were poor, but none came close to rivaling the pink run of 1962.

Rockin' and Rollin' Through the Sixties

After the excitement of that first fishing season, Lionel returned to work in Kenai, and Tim and Robert rode the bus to high school in Ninilchik. John, Mary, Kenny and Ronny continued to attend Anchor Point School. Esther tried to keep Jim busy with chores around the house and taking care of the cow, but she knew he longed for something more. Several years earlier she had talked the first-grade teacher into giving her some *Dick and Jane* primers that were no longer used in the school. She and Lionel had taught Jim how to turn on the reel-to-reel tape recorder and follow along as he listened to their taped voices. Jim enjoyed this for a time, but she saw him spending more time in fantasy play, as he was forced to be alone for hours each day.

The reel-to-reel tape recorder came in handy for another use. Without a telephone, Esther had no way of talking to Gladys except for brief and infrequent visits. Letters were fine, but she longed to hear her sister's voice. When the Dixson family also acquired a tape recorder, the two families began exchanging tapes instead of letters. Everyone eagerly anticipated the arrival of a tape, and would gather around the tape recorder to catch up on the latest news from their city cousins. Sometimes Gladys and her daughter Alice would sing duets for the Haakensons' listening pleasure. Another bit of news imparted by Gladys that was music to Esther's ears was that her sister Alice had moved to Alaska with her two daughters, Travis and Trudy, and her son, Curt. Esther didn't know Alice's reasons for the move, but she welcomed the arrival. Though their opportunities for interaction would still be infrequent, at least she'd have the chance to reconnect with her big sister and get to know her nieces and nephew.

Shortly after school started in 1962, a neighbor showed up with an unusual proposition. "How would you like to keep a piano for a lady? She needs a place to house it for the winter. She gives piano lessons, and will give a special deal to whoever keeps the piano."

Esther was immediately interested. Though she still occasionally played her guitar and harmonica, she missed all the music-making with her parents and siblings. She'd always wished she could play the piano, and hoped some of her kids would enjoy it, too.

She talked to Lionel, who agreed to the idea. The lady, Mary Epperson, came by and visited. She asked if Esther would allow her to give lessons to others at the house, as well. Esther, whose social interactions were limited to church, an occasional visitor and Homemakers' Club, gladly offered to open her home for lessons. The piano was moved in, and every Tuesday Mary Epperson came down from her home in the hills that flanked Anchor Point to the east and spent the day teaching adults from the community. When the school bus dropped off the students in the afternoon, John and Mary and Mary's friend Carol each had a lesson. It was a busy, hectic day, but Esther welcomed the break in routine and the chance to visit with the ladies who came for lessons. On the other days she took advantage of the quiet house during the daytime to do her practicing, because each evening Carol (who didn't have a piano at home) came straight from school and did her practicing, then John and Mary each spent an hour at the keyboard. When Mrs. Epperson was ready to reclaim her piano, Esther ordered a new one through a music store in Homer. That piano suffered years of abuse as Esther's four youngest children practiced, performed and occasionally pounded on it.

Esther enjoyed her own lessons, though she knew her skill level would never wow anyone. Mrs. Epperson held a recital at the school in May of 1963, at which all her students from the Homer and Anchor Point areas were expected to perform. When her turn came, Esther walked to the front of the room with trepidation. Her palms were sweaty and her legs shook. She sat down on the piano bench, knowing she had practiced her pieces to the point that they should come automatically. They didn't. A few measures into the first song, her mind went blank. She started again. Another blank. "Come on, Esther, you've practiced these things till you can play them in your sleep," she scolded herself.

"No," said her brain, and that ended it. All her practice had been for naught. With a shrug, she stood up and walked back to her seat. Taking lessons and playing for her own enjoyment was one thing; performing before this crowd was something else. She talked with Mrs. Epperson after the performance, and the two agreed that Esther could keep taking lessons, but wouldn't be required to perform in recitals.

One summer evening in 1963, Bossy was oddly restless. Usually at milking time she went willingly into the barn, stuck her head into the stanchion, and munched happily on the generous scoop of oats poured out for her by Jim. On this day, she fought all attempts to get her into the barn. Jim went to his mom. "Bossy won't come."

"Mary, Kenny, help Jim get Bossy into the barn," ordered Esther.

With the extra assistance, the cow finally stood in the barn, her head in the stanchion, but she wasn't happy. She tossed her head up and down in protest, ignoring the tasty oats laid out for her. Jim positioned the milking stool and slid onto it. He braced the white enamel milk bucket between his knees, reached for Bossy's teats and began milking. She submitted for a few minutes, then without warning lifted her hoof and planted it—dirt, manure and all—into the bucket.

"Bossy!" yelled Jim, bringing his siblings running back to the barn. The bruised bucket, the spilled milk and Bossy's still-flailing hoof bore witness to the debacle. Kenny grabbed the hobbles, which were rarely needed, and clamped them around Bossy's back legs just above her knees. With those in place, and the bucket rinsed out, the milking got done, but the cow's unusual behavior still puzzled her owners.

About an hour later, as Esther and the kids went about their household chores, a sudden jolt brought everyone to attention. "Earthquake," said Esther. Earthquakes were nothing new to Alaskans, but this one felt a little stronger than the average, almost as if a giant hand had grabbed the corner of the house and given it a sharp jerk.

"There goes Bossy," exclaimed Jim. Rushing to the window, the family saw their milk source hightailing it out the driveway. Further inspection revealed a broken electric fence—more evidence of Bossy's state of mind. She had great respect for the fence and never touched it on purpose.

The kids pursued and captured the runaway bovine, then Esther commented, "Bossy's really been acting strange this evening. I've read about animals that can sense things like earthquakes and storms before they happen. I wonder if she knew that earthquake was coming." Still thinking about earthquakes, Esther's mind turned to another angle. "It seems like we're always inside when an earthquake hits. Some time, I'm gonna try to remember to go outside and see what it feels like."

She got the chance to follow through on this plan on the evening of March 27, 1964. Though the calendar assured her that spring had arrived the week before, outside the window she saw snow still covering everything to a depth of several feet. She checked the thermometer tacked to the windowsill; the temperature was hovering in the high 20s. Pretty standard, she thought, for this time of year. She turned back to the stove, opened the oven door and checked the moose meat roast. It would be done to perfection by suppertime. She went to the pantry and brought out eggs, sugar, corn syrup and the electric mixer to whip up a batch of her special boiled frosting. As she stood at the stove beating the ingredients in a double boiler, she felt something against her legs. Kitty, the family's tabby cat, belly distended from her advanced pregnancy, purred and rubbed against Esther's shins. "You already had your treat when I trimmed the roast," Esther told her. The cat always showed up when Esther sharpened her butcher knife. That sound meant any freezer-burned bits of meat would be coming her way. Realizing that another hand-out wouldn't be forthcoming, Kitty retreated to the blanket-filled box Esther had set in the corner of the bedroom. Kitty knew this was her special spot, and Esther hoped she'd remember it when she went into labor.

When the frosting was done, Esther stacked the two round chocolate cakes she'd baked earlier and coated them with the white fluff. She colored three toothpicks — one yellow, one blue and one red — and inserted them into the cake. These were not to hold the cake together, though they may have served that purpose, as well. They were actually prizes. Whoever found a toothpick received a coin — nickel, dime or quarter, depending on the color of the toothpick. Esther swirled on a little more frosting to camouflage the toothpicks' locations, then made a second small batch of frosting from powdered sugar and butter, tinted it with food coloring, and decorated the cake with yellow flowers, green leaves and the words, "Happy Birthday Tim." As the final touch, she inserted 18 candles.

By the time the kids arrived home from school, supper was nearly ready. Esther assigned Mary to make a salad of lettuce and canned fruit cocktail while she mashed the potatoes and Jim and Kenny set the table.

"Mama," said Ronny, "I don't feel good." He'd been battling a cold for several days.

"Go lie down on the couch till supper," she told him. In a few minutes she realized he'd fallen asleep. "He'll feel better after a nap," thought Esther, and decided not to disturb him. "He'll probably get up when he hears us singing to Tim."

The rest of the family gathered around the table. Because it was Good Friday, Lionel had been able to come home the previous evening, so supper was a little earlier than usual.

Once the meal was eaten, Esther carried in the cake. While Tim lit the candles, Jim, Mary and Kenny ran from window to window pulling the curtains closed. (Half the fun of having candles is darkening the room enough to really appreciate them.)

Lionel led them in singing "Happy Birthday." As they finished the last phrase Tim was smiling. "Did you feel the earthquake?" he asked.

At that, everyone realized the earth was still moving, and the intensity was increasing. "I'm gonna go outside," declared Esther, remembering her resolve of the previous summer. That sounded like fun, so everyone hopped up and headed for the doors, even as the house continued to rock. Ronny woke up as he nearly rolled off the couch from the force of the quake's motion. Not caring to be left alone, he joined the exodus. By the time everyone was outside, the earth was pitching like a boat in stormy seas. Tim noticed Ronny was wearing only socks on his feet, so he picked him up and set him on the hood of the car. Esther took a quick glance around, making sure everyone was safe. She knew this was no ordinary quake. An eerie roar filled the air. The 75-foot spruce trees surrounding the yard resembled blades of grass in a windstorm as they lashed from side to side. The house rocked back and forth on its foundation, space showing between concrete and dirt.

"Mary, quit pushing me!" Esther heard Jim exclaim. She looked over to see her daughter clutching Jim's arm as the two struggled to stay upright.

Kitty dashed out the door and raced frantically toward the barn, nearly high-centering as her huge stomach dragged through the snow banks. Bossy galloped clumsily over the shifting ground up to the electric fence, then stood staring at her humans as if demanding that they make this craziness stop. But it didn't; for over five minutes the rolling, roaring and shaking continued.

The earth finally quit moving and everyone stood braced for a moment, waiting to see if it was truly over. Lionel and Esther took a quick inventory. "Is everyone okay?"

Upon being assured that they'd all survived, Esther shivered and said, "Well, I sure found out what it's like to be outside in an earthquake. Now I'm going in."

As Robert entered the house he flipped a light switch. "The power's off," he said.

"That's not surprising," Lionel replied. "I've never felt a quake like that. Let's see if we can get some reports from Anchorage."

Because of the frequency of power outages, the family kept a battery-powered radio ready at all times. Lionel fiddled with the knobs while the kids fanned out through the house to see what damage had been sustained.

From the pantry came John's voice. "The waffle iron fell down. Looks like it's broke."

"If that's the worst of it, we're in good shape," Esther replied. No other damage was found; even the dinner plates and cake still sat on the table.

As daylight faded everyone wolfed down birthday cake and listened to the radio. At first, all they heard was static. Finally a fuzzy voice came through. "We've just experienced a major earthquake," the voice said. "Please don't panic. Everyone should remain coo-ool, ca-a-a-lm and collected." The announcer dragged out these final words as if by slowing down his speech he could soothe the fears of his listeners.

"Well, it won't be hard to remain cool," commented Esther. "It's still winter and with the power out, the furnace won't run."

"I'll get the fireplace going," replied Lionel. The fireplace standing in the basement beside the furnace—that prior to this had been used mainly as a way to get rid of flammable trash—was about to prove its worth. The older boys brought in enough wood to keep it going, and, while the house didn't stay as warm as it did with the furnace, at least nobody froze.

Over the next days, reports streamed in regarding the damage that had occurred around the state. Seward, on the eastern side of the Kenai Peninsula, was burning after a tidal wave had hit the city and exploded the oil tanks that sat there. Tidal waves had also flooded the island of Kodiak and many towns around Prince William Sound. The city of Valdez had been almost completely destroyed. Two women had died when the entire front of the new JC Penney building in Anchorage toppled onto the sidewalk. Huge cracks had opened in the earth, swallowing homes and people in Anchorage. The control tower at the Anchorage airport had collapsed, killing one man. Nearer to home, word came that the Homer Spit had sunk several feet. Now with each high tide waves washed over it, eroding the road and beach.

Numerous aftershocks rattled the house over the next days. Each one brought activity to a halt as people paused and braced themselves in case it turned out to be a repeat of the big one. Fortunately, all the follow-up temblors were relatively small. That Sunday at church, everyone was bursting to tell of their earthquake experiences. Prayers were offered up—thanksgiving for the safety and lack of damage in Anchor Point, and petitions for God's help for those across the state who had been hit harder, especially those who were mourning their loved ones who were dead or still missing. When Esther went into the bedroom to change her clothes after church, she was greeted by a purring mama cat lying in her special box, her tongue lovingly caressing four newborn kittens. Had the earthquake hastened their arrival? Esther wasn't sure about that, but one thing she did know: if Bossy had a sixth sense for predicting earthquakes, it had certainly failed this time.

Thanks to the heroic efforts of the crews at Homer Electric Association, power was restored in a matter of days. Word arrived that the road to Anchorage would be impassable for the immediate future. The Portage area, near the end of Turnagain Arm, had sunk several feet. Like the Homer Spit, now each time the tide came in, sea water washed across the road. Homes in the area had to be abandoned, since being filled with salt water every 12 hours made for unpleasant living conditions. In addition to the sunken areas, many bridges along the highway had collapsed during the quake.

Esther wondered how her parents and siblings in the Anchorage area had fared, but with disrupted mail service and no phone, she had no way to contact them. She relied on the saying that had become their standard farewell: "No news is good news." If any of them had been injured or killed, she was sure someone would have gotten word to her. Ham radio operators throughout the state were working around the clock helping to put worried people, both inside and outside Alaska, in touch with their loved ones.

When word finally arrived from Gladys, Esther discovered some of the family had had a close call. Several of Gladys's children had attended a Good Friday matinee at the Denali Theater on Fourth Avenue. Her husband, Maurice, went to pick the kids up, but hadn't returned when the quake struck. Gladys was a nervous wreck by the time they arrived home, shaken but unhurt. They found out later that Anchorage's Fourth Avenue sustained some of the most severe damage in the city. If the moviegoers had still been in the building, many of them probably would have been injured or killed.

On Esther's next visit to the Homestead Supply, a strong smell of pickles assailed her nostrils. Dick Rutt, the postmaster and store owner, tried to smile as he greeted her. "Just about every can and jar fell off the shelves," he told her.

"Fortunately, not all the jars broke, but it's gonna take a long time to clean up this mess."

Esther shook her head in sympathy. She knew a small business owner like Mr. Rutt barely stayed afloat at the best of times. And to think that businesses all over Southcentral Alaska had suffered as much damage or more. She knew it was going to take a long time for Alaskans to recover from this disaster.

But recover they did. Within a month, road crews constructed temporary bridges and shored up road beds so Anchorage was once again accessible to the folks living on the Kenai Peninsula. Businesses slowly rebuilt, aided by money spent as Alaskans repaired their homes and other structures, and bought cars, appliances and other materials to replace those destroyed in the quake or the tidal waves that followed it.

Two months later, in May of 1964, Tim graduated from Ninilchik High School. Esther was thrilled with his accomplishment, and even happier that his future plans included college. After fishing with his dad for the summer, Tim headed to Fairbanks to attend the University of Alaska. Unfortunately, the fishing season had been mediocre, leaving funds short for the school year. After one semester, he was forced to drop out and work a series of odd jobs around the Fairbanks area.

In the fall, Lionel's job took him to Juneau to work on the Federal building. Esther once again took on the role of single parent for most of the winter. Several breaks allowed Lionel to come home for a week once in a while, which helped her cope.

On one such visit in the early months of 1965, Lionel commented, "This Juneau job is gonna last through the summer, so I won't be here for the fishing season this year. I'm thinking of letting Tim run the site."

Esther thought it sounded like a good idea. "I know he'd like to go back to college this fall, and what he earns from fishing will help him with tuition and living expenses."

Lionel continued, "Since Robert will be fishing over on Kalgin Island, John can work with Tim. The other kids can help out if he needs more crew."

Tim was thrilled in his quiet way, to be entrusted with the fish site. After three years as deckhand, he looked forward to taking on the responsibility of head man. Having helped Lionel prepare for each of the prior seasons, he knew what he needed to do. He arrived home from Fairbanks in the early spring and immediately went to work hanging and mending nets, painting buoys and making sure the skiffs and motors were in good repair.

As spring approached, Lionel's letters indicated that he was missing his wife and family. Finally he wrote suggesting that Esther bring the younger kids down to Juneau for a visit. John, Mary, Kenny and Ronny had seen very little of the world outside of Anchor Point, and he presented this trip as a way to broaden their horizons, and see a little of their state's capital city at the same time. Esther had inherited her mother's love for travel and willingly agreed to the scheme. This was the first real road trip she had taken since the drive to the States in 1951. Though this trip was shorter, she would be doing all of the driving, and didn't have Lionel to depend on if something went wrong. The music teacher, Mary Epperson, planned to ride with the family to Juneau, where she would meet up with some friends.

Esther knew she couldn't stay away long. Jim would stay home to take care of the livestock, which now included seven Rhode Island Red hens (which were normally the responsibility of Mary, Kenny and Ronny) in addition to the cow. Tim and Robert were around to keep things running on the homestead, but Robert would soon be heading to a summer fishing job on Kalgin — an island some 40 miles from

352

Anchor Point out in the middle of Cook Inlet—and Tim needed to get down to the fish site.

Just days after school ended in May, Esther, John, Mary, Kenny, Ronny and Mrs. Epperson piled into the station wagon and headed to Anchorage. Although Juneau lay to the southeast, the route that would take them there ran to the northeast for the first several hundred miles. The travelers stopped the first night at the Dixsons' home in Birchwood, some twenty miles past Anchorage. They wanted to be well rested when the trip started in earnest.

Early the next morning they started off. Esther enjoyed pointing out familiar landmarks as the car neared Palmer. Her kids had been up this way a few times to visit Laurence's family on the farm, but they didn't know the area well. She entertained her passengers with stories of her youth in the Palmer area, continuing to reminisce as the road led them through the mountains north of Palmer and on into the more remote sections of the Glenn Highway. She heard the older kids trying to scare 10-year-old Ronny with threats of what the Canadians might do to them when they crossed the border. "Oh, Canadians are just like us," she reassured her nervous youngest son.

Many times she questioned the wisdom of enclosing four rambunctious youngsters in the confines of a car for so many hours. Mary Epperson tried to help, suggesting word association games or composing an acrostic poem from the word "Alaska" to pass the time. Unfortunately, the contributions from the younger set quickly deteriorated. Starting off with "A is for altitude" seemed like a hopeful beginning. At "k" John came up with, "K is for Kenny, so square and so pink," which made no sense, but tickled the funny bones of all the kids, and caused a complete collapse of the game.

A few miles past the Canadian border, Esther pulled into the town of Beaver Creek in the Yukon Territory. Here they went through Canadian customs, then found a hotel. After a night's rest they were back on the road, and soon turned south toward the town of Haines Junction. Beyond the junction they reentered U.S. territory, driving on to the Alaska town of Haines. Here the next phase of the adventure began, as they left the road behind and boarded a ferry which was part of the Alaska Marine Highway system. Juneau, Alaska's capital city was accessible only by air or sea. The ferry *Malaspina* was by far the largest vessel any of Esther's children had ever seen. To Esther, it seemed quite similar in size to the *St. Mihiel*, on which she had sailed 30 years ago when she first came to Alaska with her fellow colonists. Esther drove the car onto the lower level of the ferry, then the family and Mary Epperson took what possessions they felt they'd need for a night onboard, and climbed the stairs to the upper decks. To save money, Esther hadn't reserved a stateroom, so the family draped their belongings over chairs in one of the public areas. The kids soon disappeared, anxious to explore this monstrous ship, which seemed to them like a floating town. Though the restaurant was only a small snack bar and the store sold mostly souvenirs, the novelty kept them occupied. Esther relaxed and visited with Mrs. Epperson. This voyage was scheduled to last all night, so eventually the kids returned and curled up in chairs. It wasn't the most comfortable sleep, but Esther figured everyone could stand it for one night.

Early the next morning the *Malaspina* docked in Juneau, where Lionel stood anxiously waiting to be reunited with his family. Esther was glad to turn over the driving to him, as navigating through strange cities made her nervous. Lionel dropped Mrs. Epperson off at her friends' home, then took his wife and offspring to the apartment house where he lived. He and a co-worker rented adjacent rooms, and this friend had volunteered to turn his room over to Lionel while the family was in town. Lionel and Esther stayed in Lionel's room, while the four kids shared the co-worker's apartment.

Esther soon was thankful that this visit was only going to last for a few days. Not that she wasn't glad to see Lionel and didn't want to spend more time with him. No—the problem turned out to be her kids, who for the past 10 years had had 100 acres on which to roam, play and blow off steam without getting in anyone else's way. She'd made sure they packed things like an "Authors" card game, books and comics to keep them entertained—and quiet—during times when Lionel was working and not available to take them around to the local sights. How those kids turned a simple game of Authors into a rowdy giggle-fest she couldn't understand, but they managed. One morning she sat at the table reading the newspaper, sipping coffee and enjoying a few quiet moments after Lionel left for work. Suddenly a racket erupted outside the door. Some sort of wheeled conveyance rattled past the room, accompanied by whoops that sounded suspiciously like Kenny and Ronny. As she headed for the door to investigate, a third voice joined the commotion.

"You boys leave those buggies alone," the voice barked.

Esther jerked the door open in time to see Kenny and Ronny each pushing a baby carriage toward an angry, red-faced woman.

"Boys, get in here!" Esther ordered, once the buggies had been restored to their owner. "What were you doing out there?" she demanded when she had them corralled in the room.

"We were playing with those baby buggies," explained Kenny. "We weren't hurtin' them."

"We just wanted to race 'em," Ronny clarified. "Then we saw they had brakes and we wanted to see if they'd lay rubber. We didn't know the lady'd get mad."

Esther sighed. This is what happened when you took high-spirited boys out of the woods and tried to conform them to city life. "You can't go around taking other people's things without asking."

"We weren't stealing," Kenny defended himself. "We weren't gonna keep 'em. We were just playin' around."

"Stick to your own stuff and you'll stay out of trouble," recommended Esther.

A few days later Esther and her kids said good-by to Lionel, boarded the ferry and sailed back to Haines. The subsequent car trip home seemed easier now that she had traveled the road once before. A stop in Anchorage at her parents' place brought her up-to-date with their exciting news. They had just paid off the 30-year loan that had been hanging over their heads since they moved to Alaska. In celebration, Fred and Laura were taking a vacation to Norway and Sweden. Though Laura had never lived abroad and didn't know her Swedish relatives, Fred had cousins and other loved ones in Norway he hadn't seen for many years. Esther was delighted to see her parents getting a chance to relax and enjoy themselves after a life of hard work.

Arriving home, Esther noticed Jim seemed a little miffed at the travelers. With Tim busy getting ready for fishing and Robert now gone across the inlet to Kalgin Island, all the home chores had fallen on him. She couldn't really allay Jim's hurt at being left behind, but she complimented him on how well he'd taken care of everything in her absence.

Someone else had missed Esther, making her glad she'd returned home quickly. Her friend Ruth Rozak needed her support. Ruth had undergone cancer surgery several years earlier, and that, combined with a number of other health problems, left her in constant pain. Though Esther couldn't help her friend with the physical ailments, she could do the one thing that Ruth needed most — listen. Ruth knew she could drop by at any time of the day or night and always find a sympathetic ear. When nothing else helped to soothe her friend's nerves, Esther would suggest, "Let's pray." After a period of fervent prayer, she could tell that Ruth had relaxed, and she was able to send her home in a more serene frame of mind.

Tim and John headed down to the fish site almost immediately, as the start of the season was only a week or so away. Esther and the rest of the kids hurried to get the garden planted with potatoes, broccoli, carrots, radishes and turnips. In a small greenhouse on the back lawn she planted tomatoes and cucumbers. Those types of plants wouldn't survive outside even in the best Alaskan summer. Every evening Esther stoked the small wood stove Lionel had made and installed in the greenhouse. This kept the interior sufficiently warm to preserve the lives of the delicate plants. On sunny days she opened the small windows on each end of the greenhouse to keep her leafy charges from roasting in the heat. By fall she would harvest a few dozen tomatoes and several small cucumbers. Not much return for her daily vigilance, but she liked to serve her family fresh homegrown produce when she could. Someone gave Esther a small lilac bush, which she planted on the back lawn over the septic tank and tended faithfully for years. Every year it grew green leaves and appeared healthy, but it never got any taller, and never produced any lilacs.

As the summer of 1965 progressed, Esther felt increasingly sorry for Tim. The fishing season was the poorest in many years, and the Haakenson site did worse than most. Tim had hoped to earn enough money to return to college, but at this rate he would be lucky to cover the season's expenses. He hung on, hoping against hope that a late run of pink salmon would hit, but it didn't. Esther knew he felt that he'd let his dad down, that perhaps Lionel could have done better. She also knew fishing was a gamble — if there were no fish there was nothing the fishermen could do about it. When Tim finally closed up the site for the season, he joined the Rozaks at their site for a short time, where he fished silvers.

It was during this late summer interval, when the older guys were still away from home, that young Ronny saw Esther's courage in action. Ronny was 10 years old, small, but already close to overtaking his petite mother in size. At this time of year, Alaska was past the point of continual daylight, and residents again experienced a few hours of darkness. Late one evening Jim, Ken and Mary had all gone to bed; Esther sat up reading while Ronny dawdled around, in no particular hurry to retire. Suddenly Esther looked up. "Did you hear that?" she asked.

"I didn't hear anything," Ronny replied.

"I thought there was a noise outside. Y'know we've been hearing about those teenagers going around siphoning gas out of cars..." Esther jumped up and headed to the porch. Ronny hung back, ready to dive behind the couch if his mother told him to hide.

Instead, Esther flipped on the porch light and stuck her head out the door. "Who's there?" she demanded in her toughest, gruffest voice.

Silence. Then came a quiet click, as if someone was trying to close a car door without being heard. Esther glanced back at Ronny. From his expression, she knew he'd heard it, too. She turned her face back toward the darkness, making sure whoever was out there could hear: "Ronny, get the gun!"

A .22 rifle always stood in one corner of the porch. Its purpose was to scare the occasional moose out of the garden, or chase off dogs, weasels or other critters that might come after the chickens. Not sure he'd heard correctly, Ronny responded, "What?"

Esther wasn't used to having her orders questioned by her children. "Get me that gun! Now!"

On legs of jelly Ronny trod over to the .22, picked it up and carried it to Esther. "You're not gonna shoot 'em, are you?" he quavered.

"You're d--n right I'll shoot 'em," Esther declared. That kind of language let Ronny know his mom was more mad than scared, and determined to protect her property and, more importantly, her kids. She stood there under the porch light, rifle in hand, scanning the darkness for several minutes, and finally said, "They must be gone."

Whether the intruders managed to steal noiselessly away or merely hugged the ground, eating dirt in frightened silence until Esther went into the house was never determined. No gasoline was missing from her car in the morning, though, and nothing more was ever seen or heard of nocturnal prowlers around the Haakenson house.

Shortly after that incident, Tim came home from fishing the Rozaks' site with a few dollars to augment his paltry summer's earnings, but not enough to return to college. Instead, he headed down to Juneau where he worked as a surveyor. Robert was now a senior at Ninilchik, John was a junior, and Mary a freshman. Kenny and Ronny still attended the elementary school in Anchor Point. The younger kids took care of the chickens before and after school, but Jim looked in on the poultry during the day, and had full charge of the cow. Esther called on him for chores around the house, as well, but she knew he still pined for the opportunity to go to school. Aside from going to church and attending the weekly movie at the Anchor Point community building, Jim had few opportunities to get out and socialize.

Lionel finally finished his Juneau job in January and went to work in Soldotna. He decided to commute, tackling the sixty miles of still-gravel road every day. Since he spent an hour and a half driving in each direction, Esther felt like she saw just slightly more of him than she had when he'd only come home on weekends.

Tim, having saved his money during his time in Juneau, returned to college in Fairbanks for the second semester. Letters arrived from him

(L-R) Back row: Jim, Lionel, John, Robert; front row: Ronny, Esther, Mary, Ken. (ca 1966)

359

regularly. In mid-winter he sent the word that Esther had been dreading — he'd received his orders from the Selective Service. He could enlist in the military branch of his choice or be drafted. Esther didn't have a television, so didn't see the same coverage of the war in Viet Nam that much of the nation did, but she followed it in the newspaper and by radio news. She'd known, with so many sons nearing draft age, the chances were good that they'd be called. Still the reality struck a chill through her.

Prayer had always been part of Esther's daily life, but now those prayers took on added fervor. Tim wrote to say he'd gotten a deferral until the end of the school year, at which time he had decided he'd join the Navy. Even knowing she had several months before her son would be in harm's way, Esther began her petitions to the Almighty to keep him safe.

When Tim entered the service he was sent to the Navy's training center in Port Hueneme, California . Soon his letters told of a family who had adopted him and one of his buddies, inviting them over for dinner whenever their schedules allowed. One member of this family was a young lady named Melody. She began to figure more prominently in Tim's letters, and Esther could tell he was more than a little interested in her. Esther added this relationship to her prayer list. Because of the isolation of life on the homestead, her kids hadn't done much dating. Now Esther hoped that Tim would showthe same good sense he'd shown in other aspects of his life. By the time Tim went to Viet Nam in 1967 he and Melody were engaged.

In the fall of 1966, Robert headed to Fairbanks for college. Before long, he received his draft notice. With the same options Tim had been given, he chose to join the Air Force, and by March of 1967 he was in basic training at Homestead Air Force Base in Florida. Shortly after completing basic training he, too, was sent to Viet Nam.

Amid all this upheaval, Gladys sent word that Laurence's wife, Pat, had died. Anticipating that her brother would need help caring for his ten children, Esther offered to take in some of his kids. Unfortunately, Laurence dealt with his grief by drawing away from all relatives. He tried for a while to keep his family intact, but eventually found it necessary to find temporary homes for several of the younger kids. He never did approach Gladys or Esther about keeping any of them. It was nearly a decade before Esther heard from him again.

Back at home, life carried on. John graduated in the spring of 1967 and fished the beach site with Lionel and Kenny. Mary and Ron also spent part of the summer on the fish site. That summer marked a red-letter event in the lives of the inhabitants of the lower Kenai Peninsula, as the last portion of the road to Anchorage—the stretch between Anchor Point and Ninilchik—finally got paved. In the fall John went to work at the sheet metal shop where Lionel worked, commuting with him each day. The commute time

John, in his Army dress uniform.

dropped to about an hour each way, thanks to the new pavement.

In January of 1969, John received his draft notice. Unlike his brothers who chose other branches of the service and ended up with 3-year hitches, John opted to be drafted into the Army, since that meant he would only serve 2 years. By July of '69 he, too, was in Viet Nam.

Esther's daily perusal of the Anchorage newspaper did little to calm her concerns for her boys, as most of the reports dealt with battles fought and the number of deaths. Esther's heart ached for the mothers who received that dreaded visit from a military official saying their loved one was dead or missing in action. She remembered the agony her parents and siblings had endured while Laurence was a prisoner of war in Germany. She knew she had no earthly power to help her sons, but she could pray. Gladys's son, Don, was also sent to Viet Nam, so he was added to Esther's daily prayers.

Over the years Esther had grown close to the ladies from the church, and during this time of fear and uncertainty, she reached out to them. Every Thursday morning they met for a time of Bible study and fellowship. Edna, Phyllis, Ruth, Ramona, Libby…she gazed around at their faces, feeling love for each one. She had always been shy about praying aloud in a group, but with these ladies she felt safe, accepted. She could pour out her heart to God and be sure they would surround her with comfort and love. And they rejoiced with her when, early in 1969, Tim returned from Viet Nam.

Broadening Horizons - 1969

That spring Mary graduated from high school and made plans to attend a small Christian junior college in Nebraska in the fall. Lionel and Esther decided to use the occasion for a trip Outside — their first substantial road trip together since 1951, when Mary had been an infant.

In late July, Lionel, Esther, Jim, Mary, Ken and Ron set out for the Lower 48. Aside from the short jaunt across Canada during the Juneau trip in 1965, Ken and Ron had never been out of Alaska. Obviously, Mary didn't remember the 1951 trip, so the parents felt that this would be a worthwhile excursion just for its educational value, aside from the opportunity to meet Lionel's side of the family, most of whom had never visited Alaska. The cow and chickens had been farmed out to friends who could be trusted to take good care of them, and Esther eagerly looked forward to the change of scenery.

Mile after mile of gravel road greeted them once they were on the Alaska Highway (as the Alcan Highway had been renamed). Some areas along the highway experienced extremes in temperature ranging from the 90s in the summer to -50 or lower in the winter. These wide swings in temperature wreaked havoc on all human endeavors, including roads. Every summer brought construction crews out to repair the previous winter's damage. Sometimes travelers were allowed to creep by the work zones with very little delay; at other times cars lined up for as long as an hour. Even where there was no work underway, the state of the roads didn't encourage haste. The best stretches of road were surfaced with a rough composite called chip-and-tar that was only slightly less bumpy than gravel. Lionel was a careful driver, and Esther was aware that her carload of teenagers chafed at the long, slow drive. Jim was always a model passenger, as he usually counted cars for an hour or so, then dozed for the rest of the day.

Occasionally Lionel, after fighting drowsiness for a time, would turn the steering wheel over to Esther. As soon as their dad fell asleep in the passenger's seat, her sons implored her from the back seat, "Mama, see if you can go a little faster or we're *never* gonna get off this road."

The city of Dawson Creek, British Columbia, marked the end of the Alaska Highway. From this point the road was paved, and Lionel pointed the car east—bound for his family farm in North Dakota. The trans-Canada highway was a welcome change from the road so recently traveled. The car buzzed along quickly and smoothly, passing from the mountains of British Columbia into the plains of Alberta and Saskatchewan. As the travelers passed through a series of towns of varying sizes, each surrounded by miles and miles of grain fields, Esther knew Lionel felt a sense of coming home. This was the kind of land he had grown up with.

As they drove into yet another prairie town, Mary spoke up. "What's that tall skinny building over by the railroad tracks? I've seen one in every town we've gone through."

Lionel looked over at Esther, who chuckled. Only half in jest he asked, "Where have we failed? Our daughter doesn't know what a grain elevator is."

"I wondered about those, too," said Ken.

Lionel spent the next several miles trying to explain to his Alaska-bred children the structure and use of grain elevators. As they drove, the sky darkened. Finally, glancing up through the windshield, Lionel commented, "Looks like we're gonna get some rain."

About that time a flash of lightning pierced the black clouds and rain washed down in quantities never seen by the younger Haakensons. "It's a thunderstorm!" exclaimed Ken. Lionel, unable to see out the windshield, pulled off the road to wait out the storm.

"I wanna hear some thunder!" Ronny cranked down his window. Mary opened the window on her side of the car, and in a moment Esther's three youngest were hanging out the windows, practically drowning in the downpour, but thrilled to be witnessing their first thunderstorm.

"Shut the windows—I'm gettin' wet," complained Jim.

"Yes, shut the windows," Esther seconded.

The kids reluctantly pulled their soaked heads into the car. They waited in a line-up of cars until the rain eased and Lionel was again able to drive. Though her damp youngsters caused the windows to fog up, Esther was glad they'd gotten a chance to see a thunderstorm. Ronny and Ken had complained almost nonstop since they'd left Alaska, convinced that anything the rest of the world had that Alaska didn't probably didn't amount to much, anyway. She hoped these experiences would give them a slightly broader view of the world.

At Portal, North Dakota, they reentered the United States. By the time they cleared customs the sun had set. Lionel drove slowly through the darkened streets, searching for a motel where they could spend the night. The evening was warm, and the kids rolled down the car windows. "Here's something you don't see in Alaska," commented Esther. "It's dark out, and it's warm." The kids had to agree. During Alaska's summer months nights might grow dusky, but never completely dark, and even in midsummer, nighttime temperatures could dip into the 40s or lower.

As the car continued to creep through the town, Ken asked, "What's that sound?"

"What sound?" Lionel, whose hearing wasn't as sharp as it once was, couldn't hear the mysterious noise.

"It sounds kind of like a whirring," Ronny tried to explain.

Lionel shook his head. Esther spoke up. "It's crickets."

"It can't be crickets," Mary said. "It never stops. The sound keeps going."

"That's what crickets do." Lionel and Esther shared another amused glance. What a lot of simple things their kids had missed out on, growing up in Alaska. Thunderstorms, grain elevators, crickets…all things she and Lionel had taken for granted when they'd lived Outside.

When they reached Barton, the youngsters enjoyed several days with their uncles, aunts and cousins, sampling North Dakota farm life. Jim, confused about the whole idea of geography, got out of the car in North Dakota, and wondered if he'd be back home in Alaska tomorrow.

Leaving North Dakota, the family drove down to Nebraska, where they dropped off Mary's trunk and other belongings she'd packed for college. From there they took a southwestern route, cutting across the desert states till they reached California. There they spent a few days with Lionel's sisters Lil and Hulda near Los Angeles.

Tim's fiancé, Melody, lived in Oxnard with her family, and Lionel and Esther, knowing they wouldn't be able to make it back down to California for the wedding, planned to stop and meet her.

Lil did her best to prepare Lionel for freeway driving before the family left her home, but it was a little like explaining a thunderstorm to kids who knew only the less-violent rains in Alaska. Melody's mother, Rita, had sent directions telling them which exit to take off the freeway and how many red lights they'd encounter before they got to the house. Lionel, unfamiliar with roads having more than one lane in each direction, found himself in the middle of about a zillion lanes of California traffic, in which every driver seemed to know where he or she was going and was in a huge hurry to get there. At one point, as Esther and the kids argued over the map, a car in the far right lane honked. Esther turned her harassed look on the driver, who motioned to her to move into his lane. Maybe having Alaska license plates saved the family from a nasty confrontation, though in all probability a number of other drivers on the road that day had a good bit of pithy advice for that poky car in the wrong lane.

Arriving safely—if with lacerated nerves—at Melody's home, the Haakensons spent a couple of days getting acquainted with Tim's future wife and in-laws. Ken and Ron pulled Melody aside and pleaded with her to ride back to Alaska with them. "At least come along so you can drive on the freeway," they begged. "Dad's gonna get us all killed." Melody regretfully declined, explaining that she had a job and college—and a wedding to prepare for.

From Oxnard, Lionel headed the car north to Seattle, where his brothers Herman and Earl lived. There they left Mary, who spent a few days with her newly-met cousins before flying to Nebraska for school. Lionel, Esther and the boys headed back up the Alaska Highway. Another 1,500 miles of gravel road extinguished—temporarily at least—any wanderlust that may have smoldered within the car's passengers.

Thankful to be back in Alaska, Ken and Ron returned to school and Lionel resumed working in Soldotna. Tim, who had spent his final year in the Navy on the Aleutian Island of Adak, was discharged in October and went to California to work until his wedding the following June.

Esther's days continued to be filled with chores, church, Bible study and supporting her friend Ruth through her health struggles. She also developed an interest in natural foods and vitamins which led her to read extensively about the topic and order many more vitamins than she could ever use. And always in her heart and prayers were the boys in Viet Nam—Robert, John and her nephew Don.

Sharing Sorrows and Joys

May of 1970 brought Ken's graduation from Ninilchik
High School and Mary's return from Nebraska. In June, Tim
and Melody married at her parents' home in California.
Esther wished she could be there for the wedding, but
finances and the impending fishing season didn't allow it.
The newlyweds set out immediately for Alaska and, after a
week-long "honeymoon" traveling the Alaska Highway,
settled in Anchorage.

Ken, Ron and Mary joined Lionel that summer working
on the fish site, while Esther and Jim kept things humming
along on the homestead, caring for the cow, chickens and
garden, and providing milk to customers.

In September, Esther drove Mary to Anchorage to fly
back out to Nebraska for school. They had a couple of hours
of free time before Mary's flight, so they dropped by the
restaurant where Gladys worked as a waitress. As soon as
Esther saw Gladys's pale face she knew something was
wrong. Gladys slipped into a chair across the table from her
sister.

"What's wrong?" Esther asked, hoping it was not what
she feared.

"Maurice called," Gladys replied. "He said a couple of
officers came out to the house. They wouldn't say what they
wanted. I'm afraid it's Don. Since he's Maurice's stepson
they probably won't tell him anything till they talk to me."
She reached out to pick up her coffee cup and Esther could
see her hand shaking.

Esther felt the same dread she'd experienced when
word came of Laurence's capture by the Germans. She knew

that officers didn't show up at a person's door with good news. She hated to leave, but Mary had to get to her plane.

After dropping Mary at the airport Esther returned to the restaurant and remained until Gladys got off duty. The two drove out to Gladys's home where they waited until the officers came back with the official word—Don had been killed. Esther wished she could take away the grief she saw on her sister's face but she knew there was nothing she could do or say. Only time would dull the pain. She remained with Gladys, praying with her, letting her talk, cry or whatever she needed to do to get through each painful minute. Don's body was brought home and buried in the cemetery on Fort Richardson. When Esther's responsibilities demanded that she return to Anchor Point, she did so reluctantly, her heart still with Gladys and her loss.

Through the next months, Esther felt as never before the miles that separated her from Gladys. Turning once again to prayer, she asked God to comfort Gladys at the same time as she continued to plead for her own sons' safety in the war zone. The two families had continued exchanging reel-to-reel tapes instead of letters. As the months went by, Esther was relieved to hear Gladys's taped messages begin to sound more like her old self.

By December, Robert had returned to the States. Though he wasn't able to make it home himself, as his present to the family, he paid Mary's airfare so she could come home for Christmas. All of Esther's offspring except Robert and John gathered in Anchor Point for the holiday. Tim and Melody used the occasion to share their big news—Lionel and Esther were going to be grandparents.

Mary graduated from junior college in the spring of 1971 and came home to look for work. Bob Williams, longtime church-family friend and owner of Anchor Point's Modern Builders Supply, soon offered her a job at his new business location in Homer. Several of his other employees lived on the North Fork Road too, so Mary was able to ride into

369

Homer with them each day, saving her the expense of buying a car. Ron was now Lionel's only deckhand, as Ken had begun an apprenticeship training program with the electricians' union in Anchorage.

As Jim saw his siblings leaving the nest and returning to talk about their new lives and jobs, Esther knew he felt left out. Several times he asked her point-blank, "Can I get a job?" How could she explain to him—this responsible, hardworking young man—that in a town like Anchor Point there weren't jobs for someone with his challenges? In fact, any kind of job was scarce in Anchor Point. All her children had to travel at least as far as Homer—16 miles away—to find work. Jim didn't drive, his reading ability was limited to a few sight words, his speech was difficult for outsiders to understand—she didn't know of any employer who would consider hiring him. She often saw him in the yard acting out fantasy jobs. One day he might stand on the driveway, flashlights in his hands, directing airplanes down a runway only he could see. Another day he climbed in and around an abandoned skiff, straining to pull in non-existent nets that his imagination had filled with fish. Jim had always walked his siblings out the quarter-mile-long driveway to meet the bus, even though he was never allowed to ride. Ron—the only one still in school—accepted Jim's presence as a matter of course. What did surprise him was Jim's insistence that he was going to get a job. The family's neighbor and friend, Uncle Bert, had moved away for several years, but had recently returned, moved back into his cabin and now worked at the Anchor Point School as custodian. Whenever Jim glimpsed Bert's house through the trees separating Bert's property from the Haakenson property, he'd say, "I'm gonna get a job. Uncle Bert's gonna get me a job."

On a Saturday in early June, Jim walked into the house where Lionel sat reading the newspaper and Esther worked on some mending. "Bert got me a job," he said.

370

Having been down this path before and knowing they had no good answers, his parents continued with their activities. Minutes later came a knock on the door. There stood Bert, trembling with excitement. "Jim came down and visited with me a little while ago," he began. "He asked if I could get him a job at the school."

Lionel started to shake his head regretfully, but Bert continued. "I think I can do it. I'm gonna talk to the guy up at the Borough office in Soldotna. There are lots of little jobs he could handle. I could probably keep him busy all day."

Jim sat quietly, a grin on his face, as his parents stared at him in amazement. This son of theirs had depths they'd never imagined. While they were thinking of all the obstacles that would keep him from getting a job, he'd gone to the one man in town who could find work for him. Excitement raced through Esther. A job for Jim would be a dream come true.

"I don't suppose the borough would pay him very much," Bert cautioned.

"That doesn't matter," Lionel responded, catching Bert's enthusiasm. "Just working would be pay enough for him."

"I won't let 'em get away with that," Bert declared.

Over the next months, Esther, Lionel and Bert contacted anyone at the school headquarters who might be able to help. No one had ever considered hiring someone with Down syndrome for a job with the school district, so they were sailing into uncharted waters. By fall they had gotten permission for Jim to work under Bert's direction. Bert scored another coup as he convinced the powers that be to allow Jim, as a school district employee, to ride the bus to school and back each day.

The summer of 1971 was also a time of anticipation for the loved ones of Tim and Melody. Their baby would be the first grandchild for both sides of the family. The bundle of joy was due in mid-August, and Melody's mother, Rita, arrived from California near the beginning of the month to be sure she was in time for the birth. Esther, with Jim's job starting near the same time, waited anxiously at home for word that the baby had arrived. At first Rita admonished her daughter—an avid walker—to take it easy for fear she'd go into labor at an inopportune time. "I came up here to be a grandmother, not a midwife," she said.

Anticipation turned to puzzlement as Melody's due date came and went with the baby showing no signs of being eager to enter the world. Esther, no longer able to stand the suspense, caught a ride to Anchorage, planning to stay for several days with Gladys while awaiting the baby's birth. The days became weeks, and as mid-September neared the doctor questioned Melody.

"Maybe we got it wrong. Maybe you weren't as far along as you thought."

"No," Melody insisted, "I was pregnant at Christmas. This baby is 'way past due."

"That can be dangerous," her doctor replied. "It'll start losing weight and could even die if we wait too long. We'd better induce labor."

Melody returned home and informed the grandmas-in-waiting, "They're going to induce labor in the morning."

That night Esther and Rita shared the sofa bed in Tim and Melody's living room. The two women had found they had many common interests besides their offspring, including religion, politics and vitamins. Now Esther, blankets pulled up to her chin, giggled as Rita, who sat with her arms wrapped around her knees, related a confrontation she'd had with a man who'd disparaged her favorite natural-foods author. "I told him, 'Maybe you should read one of her books before you start shooting your mouth off like that.'"

The bedroom door opened and an extremely perturbed Melody stomped out. "You two are going to have to quit visiting and go to sleep! I need to get some rest before I go into the hospital tomorrow."

Esther tittered again at the irony of the situation. She and Rita were acting like junior high girls at a sleepover, while Melody played the role of parent, demanding that they be quiet.

"Isn't she cute?" Rita crooned, sending them both into more giggles.

"Just pipe down and go to sleep," Melody advised as she turned back to the bedroom.

"I guess we'd better be quiet," Esther whispered.

"You're right," answered Rita. "Let's say a prayer that all goes well tomorrow."

After the prayer the two finally slept.

The next morning Tim dropped the three women at the hospital and went on to work. In those days fathers weren't allowed into the delivery room, so he didn't see any advantage to hanging around. Esther sat in the waiting room with Rita, both of them chattering to release their nervous energy.

Throughout the day the baby continued to dillydally. Melody's labor would start, then cease. Another dose of medication would start the contractions, then they'd stop again. Finally, in the late afternoon, labor began in earnest and in a matter of minutes Keith Michael Haakenson made his long-awaited appearance.

The two grandmothers hurried to the viewing window. Through it they watched the nurse as she weighed and measured the most beautiful baby ever born in Anchorage, if not on the entire planet. As the nurse stretched the measuring tape from his feet to his head, the baby craned his neck from side to side trying to keep his eyes on her.

"Look at him," Esther nudged Rita. "He's already alert and watching what she's doing."

"He's a smart one, for sure," Rita agreed.

Moments later, the nurse brought young Keith out to his waiting grandmas. As Esther held him, she thought back over her life, a life that had nearly ended at birth. Through years of sickness and hardships she'd persevered. When told she shouldn't have any more children after Jim, she responded by having another half-dozen, all of whom were strong and healthy, with the promise of full lives ahead of them. Jim had a job. Her three boys who served in Viet Nam were all safely back in the U.S. And now, with this sweet little one, a new generation was beginning—a generation she had helped bring about. "Yes, Esther," she murmured, "you've got a lot to be thankful for."

Epilogue

Esther continued to live in her home in Anchor Point for the next forty-one years. She and Lionel welcomed more daughters-in-law, grandchildren and finally — after Lionel had despaired of Mary ever getting married — a son-in-law.

Once Lionel retired, he and Esther started taking an annual drive out the Alaska Highway, making up for all the years when children, finances and farm animals prevented them from traveling.

Esther saw Jim complete a successful career as a custodian; he spent more than 25 years cleaning the school, cheering on his team at sporting events and bossing teachers as well as students. He was as excited about his job on his last day of work as he'd been on the first day.

As the years passed, Esther found herself slowed by failing vision and brittle bones. She outlived all four of her siblings, losing the last one, Gladys, in 2006.

Jim and Esther, 1983

Jim died in 2001 due to complications from Alzheimer's — a common problem for people with Down syndrome. Lionel succumbed to failing health and a series of strokes in 2008. Despite these losses, Esther demonstrated an immense capacity for finding joy in the small moments of everyday life — a visit from a friend, the antics of her cat, or munching on a handful of jelly beans.

Left: Lionel and Esther, 60th anniversary party, 2003.

Bottom Left: Esther, Lionel and great-grandbaby, about 2007.

Esther's fiery spirit gradually faded to a gentle glow that continued to warm all who encountered her. Her greatest delight was spending time with family; she loved it when grandchildren brought their children to visit Great-Grandma Esther.

When it became necessary to move into an assisted living facility in Homer, she charmed caregivers and fellow residents alike with her kindness and courtesy, never failing to show appreciation for any service rendered to her. She continued to look forward to attending church services, where she sang every word of the old songs by and from the heart. Those who spoke to her, thinking they might cheer her, came away feeling blessed by her loving spirit.

Esther passed away on March 12, 2013. At her memorial service, as friends and family shared their thoughts and memories, one theme emerged again and again. Regardless of circumstances, Esther's attitude remained positive and her conviction of God's goodness was reflected in the words she so often repeated: "I have a lot to be thankful for."